A Guide to the Works of Eugen Rosenstock-Huessy

A Guide to the Works of Eugen Rosenstock-Huessy

Chronological Bibliography

by
LISE VAN DER MOLEN

with a

Key to the Collected Works on Microfilm

Argo Books • Essex, Vermont

Wipf and Stock Publishers
199 W 8th Ave, Suite 3
Eugene, OR 97401

A Guide to the Works of
Eugen Rosenstock-Huessy
By van der Molen, Lise

ISBN 13: 978-1-62032-446-2
Publication date 1/28/2013
Previously published by Argo
Books, 1997

Distributed and managed by
Wipf and Stock Publishers.
For all orders and inquiries
please contact us at:

http://www.wipfandstock.com
info@wipfandstock.com
orders@wipfandstock.com

Contents

Preface

A Guide to the Works of Eugen Rosenstock-Huessy is the product of the dedication and collaboration of many people who have committed themselves over the years to preserving, and to making more generally available, the legacy of this original thinker. This guide is now the most comprehensive, up-to-date, and convenient key to Rosenstock-Huessy's writings.

The *Guide* has integrated two major efforts: first, the compilation of a definitive bibliography of Rosenstock-Huessy's books and essays; and second, the preparation of a microfilm edition of those writings, some 35,000 pages in all, including transcriptions of surviving recordings of lectures.

The *Guide* is designed to serve as a finding-aid to the microfilm edition, indicating the reel number for all of the works. At the same time, by cross-referencing the bibliography and the microfilm locator numbers, and by including an alphabetical list of titles, this volume makes it possible to approach Rosenstock-Huessy's writings from various access points.

Lise van der Molen's Chronological Bibliography is the fruit of many years of indefatigable and painstaking research. Earlier, less complete, and differently organized versions of Mr. van der Molen's bibliography—published as a book by the Edwin Mellen Press in 1989, and as a supplement to George Allen Morgan's *Speech and Society* (University of Florida Press, 1987)—are entirely superseded by the present publication. We wish to express gratitude to the University of Florida for supporting the fundamental work of entirely reorganizing the bibliography after the publication of the earlier versions. That task was completed under the supervision of Professor Harold Stahmer, with the aid of three student assistants: Brian Carson, Jeffrey Stone, and Christoph Geissler.

The microfilming of the collected works of Rosenstock-Huessy, completed in 1994, was made possible by a grant in 1991 from Dr. Cynthia O. Harris and Leo O. Harris. Aside from printed works and manuscripts, the film includes transcriptions of Professor Rosenstock-Huessy's lectures, many of which were first recorded in the 1940s and 1950s by students at Dartmouth College. Two of those students, C. Russell Keep, Jr., and Clinton C. Gardner, took responsibility for preserving these invaluable tapes, which later were copied and distributed. Harold Stahmer initiated the project that resulted in their full transcription by Mark and Frances Huessy. Frances Huessy must also be credited for the difficult task of assembling and editing the present *Guide*.

The publication of the *Guide* was made possible by a bequest to the Eugen Rosenstock-Huessy Fund from the estate of Dr. David Glasser, a student of Professor Huessy's in the 1950s.

In 1994, the Eugen Rosenstock-Huessy Fund formally donated to the Baker Library at Dartmouth College a set of the microfilms, copies of the tapes and transcriptions, and all of the original materials from which the microfilm edition was made. It should be noted, too, that the eighteen-reel microfilm of Rosenstock-Huessy's works, tapes of lectures with transcriptions, and many of Professor Rosenstock's books and essays continue to be available for purchase from Argo Books.

We trust that this guide will be an effective and reliable tool for all explorers of Rosenstock-Huessy's eternal horizons.

As this *Guide* went to press, word came of the death of George Allen Morgan, on June 24, 1997. Dr. Morgan devoted years of his life to Rosenstock-Huessy's work. He provided crucial assistance in the preparation of the original English-language edition of *The Christian Future* (1946) and, following an outstanding academic and diplomatic career, he wrote *Speech and Society: The Christian Linguistic Social Philosophy of Eugen Rosenstock-Huessy* (1987) and compiled a detailed index to Rosenstock-Huessy's work. The Board of Directors wishes particularly to honor George Morgan's life-long achievement and his dedication to our common purposes.

— Board of Directors
Eugen Rosenstock-Huessy Fund

How to Use this Guide

The *Guide* is organized into three parts, of which Part II, the Chronological Bibliography, is the heart. Each entry therein is a full citation, arranged first by year of publication—from 1903 to 1996—and then listed alphabetically within each year. At the end of each entry, information is provided on the location of the item in the microfilm series, by reel number.

The entries in the Chronological Bibliography, in addition to all the relevant publication data for every printed item, include also Lise van der Molen's notes on re-issues, reprints, and re-uses of original pieces of writing and provide cross-references to unpublished works, translations, and transcriptions.

Part I is an alphabetical list of titles, in some cases using shortened citations. These are cross-referenced to the year of publication, leading the reader to the chronological list, where the full citation may be found and the location of the work in the microfilm edition.

Finally, Part III is simply an inventory of the works microfilmed, organized by reel number. Thus, this section, which is also roughly chronological, indicates the contents of each reel of the eighteen in the series.

A Note on the Bibliography

by
Lise van der Molen

The *Chronological Bibliography* includes references to all of Eugen Rosenstock-Huessy's books and articles published through 1996, as well as his sermons, his recorded lectures, and his unpublished writings. The materials in the latter group are at Four Wells (Norwich, Vermont), Baker Library at Dartmouth College (Hanover, New Hampshire), Argo Books (Essex, Vermont), the Archiv der Eugen Rosenstock-Huessy Gesellschaft (Bethel/Bielefeld) and the Bäuerle Archiv (Stuttgart). Not included are the manuscripts of the published books, a large number of Rosenstock-Huessy's letters and poems, notes to articles and lectures, excerpts from other works, and what can only be described as "many random pages." I have entered such items as, for example, "Strafrecht" (ca. 1919) and "Schiffahrtrecht" (ca. 1926). It should be noted that I was uncertain about dates for some of the unpublished writings and have indicated them with "ca."

The cross references apply to both published and unpublished items and are my own attempt to help the reader track the full breadth of Rosenstock-Huessy's output. This enhancement over previous versions of the bibliography provides the reader with more complete information. The arrangement of entries chronologically also makes this edition easier to use. Other innovations include the addition of nearly 100 items and the alphabetic reorganization of each year's entries. I am very grateful for the opportunity, with this edition, to present a more comprehensive and accurate bibliography of Rosenstock-Huessy's works.

A Guide to the Works of Eugen Rosenstock-Huessy

Part I

Alphabetical List of Titles

Part I

Alphabetical List of Titles

The typographic conventions appearing throughout the *Chronological Bibliography* apply to this title index, as follows:

- books are listed in *italics;*
- magazine articles and chapter titles are listed in quotation marks (as are a few unpublished articles or monographs that were originally untitled and have since been assigned titles); and
- unpublished works are listed without special typography.

A

"A magánjog néhány új alapfogalmáról" **1929**
Abbau der politischen Lüge **1924**
"Abélard, Pierre" **1962**
"ABC in Politik" **1923**
"'Abschlag,' 'Abschlagen,' 'abschlägig,' 'abschläglich,' 'Abschlagung'" **1932**
"Abseitige" Gedanken zur Soziologie nach Schelskys "Ortsbestimmung der Soziologie" (unpublished) **1959**
Abstammen und Zustammen **1963**
The achievements of the various persons **1945**
Address delivered before Parent Teacher Association of Shady Hill School **1934**
(6) Die ältesten amtlichen Berichte über die Evangelien. (7) Das Wort selbst. (8) Offenbarung **1955**
Afterglow **1959**
"Akademik oder Argonautik" **1981**
"Die Akademie der Arbeit in der Universität Frankfurt a.M." **1921** (two entries), **1922**
"Die Akademie der Arbeit 1920" **1968**
"Alphons Maria Ratisbonne" **1927**
Das Alter der Kirche. Kapitel und Akten **1928**
American Social History – 1959 (lectures) **1959**
America's Contribution to Philosophy (lecture notes) **1949**
Das Amt der Jugend **1933**

"An die Mitarbeiter der Akademie der Arbeit" **1922**
"An die Russen. Naturforschung oder Gesellschaftslehre?" **1959**
An eine hohe Juristen-Fakultät Juli 1914 zu Leipzig **1914**
"Andragogik" **1924**
"Anfänge meines Friedensdienstes" **1969**
Das Angebliche Danteepigramm in Leipzig **1908**
"Angewandte Seelenkunde. Anlässlich Karl Haase, *Angewandte Seelenkunde* (Gotha, 1921)" **1923**
Angewandte Seelenkunde: Eine programmatische Übersetzung **1924**
Ansprache an Gäste aus England in der Akademie der Arbeit **1921**
"Ansprache bei der Beerdigung des Vaters Theodor Rosenstock" **1928**
The Antidote to Teaching **1940**
Antwort oder Anruf an den Verfasser der Rede: "Warum ich gerne ein Nihilist sein möchte" **1947**
"Aphorismen über den Aphorismus" **1982**
"Aphorismus und Kurztitel" **1929**
Apologia pro vita mea **1933**
Applied Science of the Soul **1984**
"Arbeiterbildung" **1924** (two entries)
"Arbeiterfreizeiten" **1924**
"Der Arbeitsdienst als Erzieher" **1932**
Arbeitsdienst—Heeresdienst? **1932**
Arbeitsdienstpflicht in Bulgarien **1928**
"Arbeitsgemeinschaft" **1920**
"Die Arbeitsgemeinschaft der Astronomen" **1920**
"Arbeitskraft ohne gestern und morgen. Die falsche Sozialpolitik und die falsche Betriebspolitik kulminieren in die Unmoral der Arbeitslosigkeitsversicherung" (unpublished) **1933**
Das Arbeitslager **1931**
"Arbeitslager" **1933**
"Arbeitslager als Sonntag" **1931**
"Das Arbeitslager für Jungarbeiter, Jungbauern und Jungakademiker in Löwenberg vom 14. – 31. März 1928" **1928**
Die Arbeitslager innerhalb der Erwachsenenbildung **1930**
"Die Arbeitslager innerhalb der Erwachsenenbildung," *Jahrbuch der Erwachsenenbildung* **1930**
"Arbeitslosenversicherung" (unpublished) **1932**
"Die Arbeitslosenversicherung vermehrt das Übel der Arbeitslosigkeit" (unpublished) **1932**
Arbeitsrecht (lectures, unpublished) **1928**
"Arbeitsrecht und Arbeiterbildung. Die Voraussetzungen der Frankfurter Akademie der Arbeit" **1920**

Arbeitstagung mit Prof. Eugen Rosenstock-Huessy in der Evangelischen Akademie Arnoldshain **1957**

Arbeitswissenschaft **1928**

"Armistice Day. Zachariah 1:11c, 13, 15, 2:12c" **1951**

"The Army Enlisted against Nature" **1934**

Articulated Speech **1937**

Articulated Speech (a follow-up to 1937 item?) **1938**

The Artist and His Community **1940**

"Ascent of Taurus" **1947**

Der Atem des Geistes **1951, 1991**

The Atlantic Revolution **1940**

Attack on My Generation. For Granville Clark in the dark days of 1940 **1940**

Au risque du langage **1997**

Aufbau und Verwaltung der Justiz **1921**

Die Auferstehung der Wahrheit **1919**

"Augstinus und Thomas in ihrer Bedeutung für das Denken unserer Zeit" **1927**

"Aus der Geschichte des Arbeitsdienstes" **1932**

"Die Ausbildung des Volksbildners. Vortrag in Braunau am Inn, 1920," *Die Arbeitsgemeinschaft* **1922**

"Die Ausbildung des Volksbildners (1920–1921)," *Die Neue Richtung in der Weimarer Zeit* **1960**

"Aussprachen zu dem Vortrag: Ökonomen" (tape) **1960**

Autobiographic note on his youth **1947**

Autobiographic statement (August 12–13, 1965) **1965**

Autobiographical Statement for Harold Stahmer **Undated**

Autobiography by Eugen Rosenstock-Huessy **1947**

B

"Baptism the entry to a new corporality"(unpublished) **1952**

"A Balance Sheet. Confidential Report on Camp William James" **1941**

"Der barmherzige Samariter des Denkens (über Ernst Michel)" **1948**

The Battle Against Segregation **1940**

Die Bedingung des Friedens **1918**

Before and after Karl Marx, Prophesies Fulfilled and Unfulfilled: The Four Disangelists—Marx, Nietzsche, Darwin, Freud – 1954 (lectures) **1954**

"Der Begriff des Lebensraumes und die Methode der Soziologie" **1926**

"Die Bemannung der Hochschule" **1959**

Bemerkungen zu Emil Brunner **1931**

Bericht über das dritte schlesische Arbeitslager für Arbeiter, Bauern und Studenten **1930**

Bericht über die beiden Referate am 9. und 10. Dezember 1925 auf der Berufsschulwoche Frankfurt a.M. **1925**
"Der Beruf aus neuer ökumenischer Sicht" (tape) **1965**
Der Beruf in neuer ökumenischer Sicht (transcript of tape) **1986**
"Beruf und Job" (tape) **1965**
Der beschränkte Untertanenverstand **1929**
"Bestimmung der Wirtschaft in einer revolutionierten Welt," *Offene Welt* **1958**
Bestimmung der Wirtschaft in einer revolutionierten Welt (Diskussionsbeitrag, unpublished) **1958**
"Betriebsverfassung des Hochkapitalismus" **1924**
Bible Study Peter-Paul-John **1955**
Bibliography–Biography **1959**
"Die Biologie der modernen Fabrik"(tape) **1965**
Biology and the Life of Life **1946**
"Bolschewismus und Christentum" **1919**
"Der Bourgeois. Redaktioneller Kommentar zu der Anzeige Dr. Bruno Altmanns 'W. Sombart'" **1919**
The Brattle Street Lectures **1939**
"Brief an ***, Magdeburg 18.2.20 (über Karl Barths Römerbrief)" **1995**
"Brief an Rudolf Ehrenberg, 26 March 1947" **1987**
"Briefe" **1973**
Briefe, B.G. und Amalie Niebuhrs an Dore Hensler und an Karsten Niebuhr (1806–1814) **1911**
"Briefe Eugen Rosenstock-Huessys aus der Frühzeit unserer Arbeitsgemeinschaft" **1975**
"Briefliche Äusserungen über Ursprung und Eigenart des sprachsoziologischen Denkens" **1977**
"Briefliche Äusserungen zu zeitgenössischen Gedankengängen" **1976**
"Bruchstücke eines verkürzten Sachsenspiegels" **1913**
"Buch und Funk" **1966**

C

"Charge to Rev. Roy Chamberlain" (unpublished) **1942**
Christ Moses Pharao **1947**
Des Christen Zukunft oder Wir überholen die Moderne **1955, 1985**
"Das Christentum inkognito" **1956**
The Christian Future, or The Modern Mind Outrun **1946**
Christmas 1939, First Advent. Introduction to a planned new edition of *Out of Revolution* **1939**

The Circulation of Thought – 1949 (lectures) **1949**
Circulation of Thought: Mental Biology (lecture notes) **1949**
The Circulation of Thought – 1954 (lectures) **1954**
The Circulation of Thought – 1956 (lectures) **1956**
A Classic and a Founder **1937**
The Co-creators **1954**
Comments on the Document by Emil Brunner, "The Ethical Reality and Function of the Church" **1942**
"A Common Vocabulary for Teachers and Students" **1940**
Comparative Religion – 1954 (lectures) **1954**
"Conceptualism" **1962**
"Concordance" **1962**
"Confessions of Saint Augustine" **1962**
"Correction on Paying the Price" **1940**
Correspondence and Existence **1968**
The Credentials of Teaching **1940**
Creed; The Power of the Pentecostal Sects; Jehovah's Witnesses; Armageddon **1952**
The Creed **1940**
The Cross of Reality, Draft preface to **1941**
The Cross of Reality – 1953 (lectures) **1953**
The Cross of Reality – 1965 (lecture) **1965**
Cruciform Character of History – 1967 (lectures) **1967**
The Crusade of the Star-spangled Banner (unpublished) **1953**

D

Daimler Werkzeitung 1919/20 **1991**
"Dante Alighieri" **1962**
Darmstädter Vorträge Wissen und Reden von Staat und Gesellschaft **1923**
"David" **1962**
Death by Abstractions **1952**
Demons of Peace or The Soul at War **1944**
Denkschrift der Deutschen Schule für Volksforschung und Erwachsenenbildung über die Bedeutung sozialpädagogischer Gesichtspunkte und die Führerbildung beim Freiwilligen Arbeitsdienst **1932**
Denkschrift des 30. Juli **1914**
Denkschrift: Über die geistige Sanierung des Daimlerwerks Krankheitsdiagnose; Untaugliche Heilmittel **1919**
Denkschrift über die Möglichkeit der Abwendung einer Militärdiktatur **1917**

Denkschrift zur Schliessung der Akademie für Kunst und Kunstgewerbe zu Breslau **1932**

"Descartes, René" **1962**

Deutsche Aufsätze O. I. (Ober Prima) **1905**

Deutsche Aufsätze U.I. (Unter Prima) **1904**

"Deutsche Nation und deutsche Universität. Zur intensiven Seite der Hochschulreform" **1930**

Deutsche Schule für Volksforschung und Erwachsenenbildung sucht zehn Ingenieure (unpublished) **1927**

Die Deutsche Schule für Volksforschung und Erwachsenenbildung **1927**

Die Deutschen im Gespräch **1954**

"Deutscher Stamm, deutsches Volk, deutsches Reich, deutsche Nation" **1927**

Deutschland in der öffentlichen Meinung des Auslandes **1920**

"Deutschlands Kommunisten und Faschisten" **1923**

"Dialectic" **1962**

"Dialogue" **1962**

Dich ruft dein Stern. Das ägyptische Ka und der mythische Mensch **1954**

"Dich und Ich. Was folgt aus der empirischen Grammatik?" **1954**

"Dich und mich. Lehre oder Mode?" **1954**

Dienen op de planeet. Korte en lange adem in het derde millennium **1988**

Dienst auf dem Planeten—Kurzweil und Langeweile im dritten Jahrtausend **1965**

"Dienstpflicht?" **1929**

"Dionysius the Areopagite" **1962**

"Divine Comedy, The" **1962**

"Dr. Johnson's Cat and the Assimilation of Reality" **1936**

"The Domestic Parallel to War. As told to George F. Havell" **1942**

Dominic, Saint, de Guzman 24.6.1170 – 6.8.1221 **1962**

A Draft of a Petition to His Excellency The President of the United States **1940**

"Drei Gaben des Heiligen Geistes" **1955**

"Das Dreigestirn der Bildung" **1921**

"Das Dreigestirn der Bildung 1920" **1960**

"Dringe ein Dringe ein Zion dringe ein in Gott" **1930**

"Das Dritte Reich und die Sturmvögel des Nationalsozialismus" **1931**, **1995**

"Das dritte Tor noch offen!" **1927**

"Der dritte Weltkrieg" **1951**

The Driving Power of Western Civilization: The Christian Revolution of the Middle Ages **1950**

"Duns Scotus" **1962**

E

Eastern and Western Christendom **1941**
Ebenbild **1917**
Economy of Times – 1965 (lectures) **1965**
Education in the Third Phase of the Industrial Era. Applied Science versus Representative Education **1939**
"Edwards, Jonathan" **1962**
The Egyptian Ka and Mythical Man **1947**
"Ehe auf Vertrag" **1955**
Die Einheit des menschlichen Schicksals in Kriegsheer und Friedenswirtschaft **1956**
"Einladung zur Zeitbuchreihe 'Epoche'" **1977**
"Einleitung zu: Adolf Wagenmann, *Wie schnell bewegen sich die Himmelskörper?* **1920**
"Einleitung zu 'Die Heimkehr' von Hans Heinrich Ehrler" **1920**
Elsass-Lothringen und der Militarismus **1917**
"Emerson, Ralph Waldo" **1962**
The End of the World or When Theology Slept **1941**
"Das Ende der Dialektik Ketzer-Papst, oder: das Jahrtausend des Samariters" **1968**
Ends and Beginnings of Philosophy. Crux of Philosophy versus Cross of Reality. The Soil of Thought and The Country of the Thinker. Father Henson or the University of Adversity **1936**
Englandreise Tagebuch **1925**
Das englische Budget **1929**
Enttäuschte Wirtschaft **1929**
Entwurf Europäisches Völkerkonzert **1917**
Entwurf Vorwort zur 2. Auflage der Vollzahl der Zeiten **1958**
Epilogue to The Spirit of the Alphabet **1947**
"Epilog zu: Furor Teutonicus oder Furor Classicus?" **1959**
Episcopatus regni Siciliae tempore Suevico **Undated**
"Die Epochen des Kirchenrechts" **1919**
Epochenteilung-Epochenbildung **1956**
"Das Ereignis der Relativitätstheorie. Die Einschaltung der Wissenschaft ins Leben" **1920**
Die Erschaffung aus dem Nichts? **1962**
Die Erschütterung der Wissenschaft (und das Evangelium) **1923**
Erwachsenenbildung in den deutschen Landen **1930**

Erwachsenenbildung und Betriebspolitik **1929**
"Erwachsenenbildung und Betriebspolitik" **1930**
Erwachsenenbildung und Schlesisches Arbeitslager (unpublished) **1929**
"Erwachsenenbildung und Schlesisches Arbeitslager" **1929**
"Erwiderung (auf Dr. Karl Helmanns Erwiderung S. 625–659)" **1930**
Erwiderung. Zu Dr. Adolf Scheffbuch über die Preissenkung in: *Volksdienst* **1931**
Establishing Relations **1945**
"Les Étudiants et l'université au service de la société. Rôle social de l'université **1932**
"Etwas vom Innenleben fürs Innenleben" **1919**
Eugen Friedrich Moritz Rosenstock **1923**
"Eugen Rosenstock an Paul Tillich" **1983, 1993**
Eugen Rosenstock-Huessy (On *Out of Revolution*) **1938**
"Eugen Rosenstock-Huessy über die Akzente seiner geschichtlichen Erfahrung," *Mitteilungen der Eugen Rosenstock-Huessy Gesellschaft* **1973**
"Eugen Rosenstock-Huessy über die Akzente seiner geschichtlichen Erfahrung," *Alma Mater Joachimica* **1974**
"Eugen Rosenstock-Huessy über Universalgeschichte" **1975**
"Europa ist nicht mehr die nette Mitte der Welt" **1957**
Europa und die Christenheit **1919**
Die europäische Krise in England **1926**
Das europäische Sechstagewerk **1928**
"Die Europäische Wandlung oder Die Lebensalter müssen ihr angenehmes Mass wiederbekommen" (unpublished) **1957**
Die europäischen Parteien **1917**
Die Europäischen Revolutionen und der Charakter der Nationen **1951, 1961, 1987**
Die Europäischen Revolutionen. Volkscharaktere und Staatenbildung **1931**
"Europas Amerika und Amerikas Europa" **1963**
"Eva und die Folgen der Arbeitsteilung" **1987**
Evozieren und Revozieren oder Die Auflockerung der sozialen Fronten als christliche Aufgabe **1956**
"Der ewige Prozess des Rechts gegen den Staat" **1919**
"Exil. Translation of *Hugo von St. Victor. 12. Jh.*" **1968**
"Existentialism" **1962**

F

Faculty Address on The Future of Christianity **1941**
Faculty address on "The Potential Christians of the Future" **1941**
Faculty Seminar with Dr. Rosenstock-Huessy **1940**
"Eine Fahrt ins 'Neuwerk'" **1923**
"Faraday, Michael" **1962**
Fashions of Atheism – 1968 (lecture) **1968**
"Fehlerquellen der praktischen Prüfung" **1920**
Ferien 1921 **1921**
Festspiel anlässlich Karls Physikum und Clairs Geburtstag und Burschung **1908**
The First Cycle of Letters to Cynthia (Harris) **1943**
First part of a letter to Ulrich Jung or Hans Peter Veraguth, June 6, 1964 **1972**
For Prof. John U. Nef (on the method of sociology) **1942**
Forerunner of *The Christian Future* (1946) **1940**
"Die Fortschritte der Gesellschaft und die Soziologie. Universität oder Schule?" **1959**
Frage und Antwort **1957**
Frankfurt in der Staufferzeit 1152–1250 **1919**
Frankreich-Deutschland. Mythos oder Anrede? **1957**
"Franz Rosenzweig und Eugen Rosenstock. Judentum und Christentum" **1935**
Freiheit der Meere **1917**
"Die Freizeit des Akademikers" **1929**
"Freizeiten her!" **1925**
"Friedensbedingungen einer Weltwirtschaft" **1959**
Friedensbedingungen einer Weltwirtschaft. Zur Ökonomie der Zeit **1988**
"Eine Friedenswoche" **1961**
Friedrich Nietzsche's Function in the Church and the Crisis of Theology and Philosophy **1942**
The Fruit of Lips, or, Why Four Gospels? **1978**
Führer und Funktionär oder die radikale Wendung der Soziologie **1932**
Für Lehrer. Eine Fussnote zur *Sprache des Menschengeschlechts* **1964**
Für Ursprung der Sprache **1925**
Funeral Prayer **1952**
"Funeral Service for Margrit Rosenstock-Huessy" **1959**
Die Funktion des Apostel Paulus und die Sendung der Deutschen **1932**
"Furor Teutonicus oder Furor Classicus?" **1959**
The Future of Natural Law **1938**
The Future Way of Life **1942**

G

"Der Gang des Arbeitstages" **1919**
"Der Gast" **1953**
"Gast und Geist oder Stammeszunge und Geisteszunge" **1957**
Gedanken eines Kriegers **1919**
"Gedanken über das Weltgeschehen" **1919**
"Gedanken von Eugen Rosenstock-Huessy. Tageslosungen für den Monat November" **1968**
"Die Gefangenschaft des Volkes" **1930**
"Das Geheimnis der Universität" **1950**
Das Geheimnis der Universität **1958**
"Das Gehirn kann nicht bereuen" (tape) **1964**
"Das Gehirn kann nicht bereuens" (excerpts from tape) **1984**
"Der Geist des Menschen ist der heilige Geist" **1926**
Geist und Zeitgeist **1919**
"Die geistige Struktur des deutschen Ostens" **1927**
"Die geistigen Bewegungen der Gegenwart" **1926**
"Eine Generation allein ist nicht geschichtsmächtig. Zum Generationsproblem (Zitate ausgewählt von Fritz Vilmar)" **1957**
"The Generations of the Faith" **1961**
The German Plan of War for 1940 **1940**
Geschichte muss erzählt werden **1967**
"Die Geschichtsnot und die Gefahr der Barbarei" **1932, 1995**
"Das Gesetz der Technik" **1952**
Gesetz oder Sakrament? **1925**
"Gesetz oder Sakrament? Zur Ehedikussion" **1927**
"Die Gesetze der christlichen Zeitrechnung" (tape) **1958**
Die Gesetze der christlichen Zeitrechnung (transcript) **1982**
Die Gesetze unserer Zeitrechnung **1924**
Das Gespräch vor Zeugen **1919**
"Das Gespräch vor Zeugen," *Mittelungsblatt der Eugen Rosenstock-Huessy Gesellschaft* **1985**
Die Gestalten unserer Zeitrechnung **1924**
"Gesunde oder zweckmässige Arbeitshaltung" **1920**
Das Gewissen der europäischen Parteien **1917**
"Der Glaube der Ökonomen" **1963**
"Der Glaube der Ökonomen" (tape) **1963**
Der Glaube der Ökonomen und die Ökonomie des Glaubens **1960**
"Glaube und Hoffnung. Ein Nachwort zu Evanston. Korrespondenz mit Gerhardt Bartning und Eugen Rosenstock-Huessy" **1955**

"Glückhafte Schuld" **1954**
God in America or Survival Values for Americans **1940**
"God is Free" **1945**, **1990**
God's Peace. Christmas Greetings, 1941 **1941**
Goethe und Bismarck **1917**
"Die Götter des Landes und der Götze Raum" **1959**
Grammar as Dogma or as Social Science? **1945**
Grammatical Method – 1962 (lectures) **1962**
Greek Philosophy – 1956 (lectures) **1956**
Die Grenzen des Sozialpolitikers **1929**
"Der Grund der inneren Krise" **1917**
"Grundsätze über eine Bildungsstätte für erwachsene Arbeiter. Denkschrift, September 1920" **1931**

H

The Happy Guilt **1939**
"Hegel und unser Geschlecht" **1924**
Der heilige Karl und der eiserne Karl **1932**
"Heiliges Römisches Reich Deutscher Nation" **1915**
Heilkraft und Wahrheit. Konkordanz der politischen und der kosmischen Zeit **1952**, **1991**
Die Heimkehr der Europäer **1930**
"Die Heimkehr der Gesellschaft" **1954**
"Henrich Steffens" **1932**
"Herakleitos von Ephesos schreibt an Parmenides von Elea" **1956**
"Heraklit an Parmenides" **1956**
"Heretic and Pope" **1968**
"Das Herz der Welt. Ein Maßstab der Politik" **1923**
Herzogsgewalt und Friedensschutz **1910**
Das Herzogtum in der ersten Hälfte des deutschen Mittelalters **1912**
The Hinge of Generations – 1953 (lectures) **1953**
Historiography – 1959 (lectures) **1959**
History makes sense. (On Nietzsche) **1941**
History Must be Told (LP record jacket) **1955**
History Must Be Told – 1954 Draft (lectures) **1954**
History Must Be Told – 1955 **1955**
"Hitler and Israel, or, On Prayer" **1945**
"Hitler und Israel oder Vom Gebet" (translation, unpublished) **1955**, (revised translation) **1987**

I

Indivisibillimus **1950**
Industrievolk **1924**
"Der Ingenieur im Kampf gegen die Unrentabilität des Betriebes" **1926**
The Inheritors of Industry. Ecodynamics of a Mechanized World **1935**
Die Institution in Recht und Staat **1919**
Instructors' note on "The Speech of Humankind" **1966**
Die Interims des Rechts **1964**
"Die Interims des Rechts" **1990**
Interview in Münster (tape) **1958**
"Interview, Radio Bremen (Irmgard Bach, 1958)" **1962**
Interview, "Rosenstock-Huessy back at Santa Cruz" **1968**
Interview, on *Werkstattaussiedlung* **1929**
An interview with Eugen Rosenstock-Huessy by Kendig Brubaker Cully **1972**
Der Inventar Einleitung zu *Die Frucht der Lippen – Die Strategie der Sprache* **1962**
"Invocatio vom 28.6.1970" **1970**
Invocation **1970**
"Ist der Bundesrat Rat oder Regierung?" **1917**
"Italien und Deutschland" **1919**

J

Ja und Nein **1968**
"Das Jahrtausend des Samariters" **1968**
"Jakob Grimm und unser Erlebnis der deutschen Sprache" **1953**
"Jeder sein eigener Astronom" **1920**
The Jewish and the Christian Trinity **1966**
The Jewish Anti-Semites or the Academic Vocabulary for Judaism **1955**
"Job Corps Interview, by Dick Broderson" (tape) **1966**
Judaism Despite Christianity **1969**
"Judas Ischariot und die preussischen Konservativen. Zum Auftreten der politischen Diabolik" **1932**
"Judas Ischariot und die preussischen Konservativen zum Auftreten der politischen Diabolik" **1995**
"Die Judenemanzipation" **1932**
"Die jüdischen Antisemiten oder die akademische Form der Judenfrage" **1951**
Jugend und Alter (unpublished) **1929**
Jugend und Alter in der modernen Gesellschaft (unpublished) **1929**

"Jugend und Alter in der modernen Gesellschaft" **1929**
Jungfrauengeburt **1946**

K

Der Kampf zwischen Stadt und Land im 17. Jahrhundert **1931**
"Karfreitag, Karsamstag, Ostersonntag" (tape) **1962**
Karl der Grosse und das Schicksal der Kirche **1925**
Karlsruhe Seminar: Die Sprache der Werkstatt **1921**
"Kastengeist und Mandarinentum" **1922**
"Des Kaufmanns Dienst am Volke" **1924**
"Des Kaufmanns Sorgen. Aus den Lebenserinnerungen des Johann Gottlob Nathusius" **1920**
"Die Kirche am Ende der Welt" **1930**
"Die Kirche und die Völker. Abriss und Überblick" **1930**
"Kirche und Arbeit—Eine Rede" **1928**
"Kirche und Beruf" **1929**
Komburghefte **1927**
Königshaus und Stämme in Deutschland zwischen 911 und 1250 **1914**
"'Der Konzil in Permanenz.' Zur Frage der Universität" **1963**
Das Kreuz der Wirklichkeit, Erster Band **1950**
Das Kreuz der Wirklichkeit, Band II **1950**
Das Kreuz der Wirklichkeit **1950**
"Der Kreuzzug des Sternenbanners" **1918**
Kriegsheer und Rechtsgemeinschaft **1932**
"Kriegsheer und Rechtsgemeinschaft" **1995**
Die Krise der Universität **1919**
"Die Krise der Universität" **1919**
Künftige Widersacher der Kirche" **1983**
"Ein Kulturbild aus Norddeutschland" **1920**
Die Kunst der Frage **1957**

L

"Laienbildung oder Volksbildung?" **1921**
Landfriedensgerichte und Provinzialversammlungen vom neunten bis zwölften Jahrhundert **1910**
"Laodizee—Wie rechtfertigt sich ein Volk?" **1954**

M

Myth, Saga, Legend and Necessity **1955**
Mythical Grammar **1938**

N

"Nachträgliche Erwägungen Eugen Rosenstock-Huessys zu *Angewandte Seelenkunde* aus dem Erscheinungsjahr 1924" **1969**
"Nachträgliche Erwägungen zu 'Angewandten Seelenkunde'. Zusätze zum psychosozialen Programm" **1924**
"Die nackte Arbeit," *Literarische Beilage der Augsburger Postzeitung* **1924**
"Die nackte Arbeit," *Rhein-Mainische Volkszeitung* **1924**
Der nächste Homer **1954**
"Name" **1962**
"Die Namen Deutsch und Völkisch" **1928**
"Neu-Deutschland. Geschichte einer Siedlung" **1920**
"Der Neubau der deutschen Rechtsgeschichte" **1920**
Die Neubauverlage **1919**
Das neue Bewusstsein Europas **1917**
"Neue Literatur über die deutschen Königswahlen" **1913**
The New Nature of Christianity **1945**
The Next Homer **1944**, **1947**
"The New Re-production Economy after the World Wars" (unpublished) **1945**
"Newman, John Henry Cardinal" **1962**
Nicolaus von Cues **Undated**
"Nietzsche, Friedrich Wilhelm" **1962**
Nietzscheana **1942**
Nietzsche's Masks **1944**
"Nietzsche's Untimeliness" (unpublished) **1942**
"Nominalism" **1962**
"Not und Wende in der Arbeiterbewegung" **1924**
Notfall **1962**
Notiz über "Die Ökonomisierung einiger Privatrechtsbegriffe grundlegender Art" **1929**
"Notiz über sich selbst" **1927**
Notizen über Missverständnisse im Wissenschaftlichen Vokabular—Zur Ägyptologie **1963**
Notker Teutonicus (Labeo) von Sankt Gallen **1903**

O

"Die 'Objektiven Unwahrheiten des Bischofs Dr. Otto Dibelius'" **1966**
Obozy Integracyjne Naślązku w latach dwudziestych i trzydziestych **1993**
"Ökonomen—Vortrag gehalten in der Heidelberger Universität" (tape) **1960**
Ökonomen. Vortrag in der Aula der Heidelberger Universität" **1960**
Ökonomen. Vortrag in der Aula der Heidelberger Universität **1980**
"Die Ökonomie des Glaubens" **1963**
"Die Ökonomie des Glaubens" (tape) **1963**
"On Natural Law" **1978**
On the *De Magistro* of St. Augustine **1938**
On the Renaissance and Revolution of Medieval Studies **1939**
On the Wings of the Dove Invocation **1963**
The One and the Many. No Theology without Trinity **1937**
De onbetaalbare mens **1966**
"Opvoeding der volwassenen in de Duitsche Gewesten" **1930**
Die Ordnung unseres geistigen Lebens **1950**
Die Ordnung unseres geistigen Lebens von 1100–2000 **1950**
"Orientierung im dritten Jahrtausend, Heft 1" **1983**
"Orientierung des dritten Jahrtausends, Heft 2" **1984**
"Orientierung des dritten Jahrtausends, Heft 3" **1985**
"Orientierung des dritten Jahrtausends, Heft 4/5" **1986**
The Origin of Speech **1981**
"Original Grace. A Sermon on Good Friday" **1952**
"Ostblock oder Siberien?" **1921**
Ostfalens Rechtsliteratur unter Friedrich II. **1912**
Our Faith in Science **1946**
Our Means of Resistance (lectures) **1938**
"Our Raft in Time" and "World History, Church History, History of Society" (unpublished) **1945**
Our Stand Against the Current Fallacies **1940**
Our Urban Goggles **1948**
Out of Revolution: Autobiography of Western Man **1938, 1993**
Out of Revolution, A preface to a planned new edition of **1941**
"Outside the Church" **1948**

P

P. Clodius Pulcher, Abiturarbeit im Joachimsthalschen Gymnasium Berlin **1906**

The Pacification of the New Nationalism **1939**
"Paracelsus" **1962**
"Paracelsus in Basel" **1922**
"Paragraph 218 des Reichsstrafgesetzbuchs" von Dr. Eugen Rosenstock **1921**
Part of a letter to a theologian on the Trinity **1970**
Part of a letter to Wim Leenman at the founding of the Rosenstock-Huessy-Huis in Haarlem, 1970 **1971**
"Partei und Volksbildung" **1921**
"Partner und Stämme der Industrie. Der Marxismus hat seine Zugkraft als Heilswahn eingebüsst" **1953**
Parts of letters to Adele Rosenzweig and to Else Freund **1974**
"Parts of letters to Dr. Georg Müller" **1969**
The Patience for Liberty **1938**
Peace Corps – 1966 (lectures) **1966**
Peace in Deed **1941**
"A Peace Within" **1940**
The Penetration of the Cross. Abraham, Jesus, Lao-tzu, Buddha **1939**
"Pentecost and Mission" **1954**
Perioden der Geschichte **1923**
Perpetual Features of Education **1939**
"Persönliches von Einstein" **1920**
Pfarrer und Laie in der Kirchenpolitik **1928**
"Pfingsten hat schlechte Zeiten" (tape) **1966**
"Die philosophischen Grundlagen des Arbeitsrechts" **1922**
Philosophy and The Social Sciences **1942**
Plan einer Deutschen Schule für Volksbildung und Volksforschung **1926**
"Die Planetarischen Gesetze in Stamm, Staat und Reich" **1915**
Planetary Man **1950**
"Planetary Man. In memoriam Oswald Spengler," *New English Weekly* **1946**
Planetary Man: In Memoriam Oswald Spenger **1946**
Planetary Service **1978**
"Plato" **1962**
"Plezier in het schelden" **1968**
Die Politik als Lehre vom Staat **1922**
Politik der Weltalter. Die Hölle der Politik **1920**
Politische Geschichte als Heilsgeschichte **1932**
Politische Reden — Vierklang aus Volk, Gesellschaft, Staat und Kirche **1929**
"Die Polychronie des Volks" **1927**
Population Trends and Economic Changes" **1942**
Potential Teachers – 1952 (lectures) **1952**
Practical Knowledge of the Soul **1988**

"Praise Him Above, Ye Heavenly Hosts. Ephesians 6:12" **1956**
"The Predicament of History" **1935**
"Predigt eines Laien in Amerika. Zum Unabhängigkeitstag. Das Gesetz der Freiheit" **1948**
A preface to a planned new edition of *Out of Revolution* **1941**
"Die Presse als Träger und Erzieher der öffentlichen Meinung" **1929**
Premises for Thought at Dartmouth about the Future of Dartmouth **1943**
Der preussische Staat **1918**
Primus Sermo Secundus Sermo Tertius Sermo **1955**
"Principium Doctoris" **1914**
Privilege and Future Opportunity of the University (lectures, unpublished) **1938**
Privilege and Future Opportunity of the University (summaries, unpublished) **1938**
Prolegomena for Ursula and Walter Seemann **1949**
"Prolog (und Epilog) zu den Briefen Eugen Rosenstocks und Franz Rosenzweigs—fünfzig Jahre später übersetzt aus *Judaism Despite Christianity*" **1969**
"Protestantismus und Seelenführung" **1929, 1964**
Protestantismus und Volksbildung **1925**
"Protestantismus und Volksbildung" **1926**
Purpose of Camp William James **1940**
"Psychotechnik" **1920**

Q

"The Quadrilateral of Human Thought" **1965**
The "quarters" of speech **1943**
The Question of the Empty Grave **1940**

R

Rathaus und Roland im deutschen Stadtrecht zwischen 1186 und 1280 **1912**
"Raumzeit oder Zeitraum?" **1955**
Reaktionär (J. F. Böhmer) und Revolutionär (Bakunin) **1920**
Das Recht! **1921**
Das Recht und die rechtswissenschaftlichen Methoden **1930**
Recht und Wirtschaft **1929**
Der Rechtsbestand des preussischen Wahlrechts **1917**

Rede des Herrn Prof. Rosenstock-Huessy gehalten in der Protestversammlung gegen die Schliessung der Akademie **1932**
"Reflexionen über das Thema Quatember" **1953**, **1987**
Reichskanzler und Premier **1917**
Religio depopulata **1926**
"Religionsphilosophie der Gesellschaft" **1927**
The Renaissance of Mind and Body **1945**
"Rendering Accounts" **1940**
"Republic" (political unit) **1962**
"Republic" (of Plato) **1962**
"Research" **1962**
"Reverendissime!" **1930**
Review: Nikolaus Berdjajews *Das neue Mittelalter. Betrachtungen über das Schicksal Russlands und Europas* **1927**
Review: Alfred Freunds *Technik, ihre Grundlagen für Alle* (Leipzig, 1920) **1921**
Review: Karl Heldmanns *Das Kaisertum Karls des Grossen* **1929**
Review: H. Hellers *Freie Volksbildung* (Leipzig, 1925) **1925**
Review: Edwin Mayer-Hombergs *Die fränkischen Volksrechte im Mittelalter* **1914**
Review: Ernst Michels *Renovatio*. "Zur Zwiesprache zwischen Kirche und Welt, Stuttgart, 1947" **1948**
Review: Ferdinand Ossendowskis *Tiere, Menschen und Götter* **1924**
Review: Henri Pirenne, *Mohammed and Charlemagne* **1957**
Review: Otto Selzes *Die Gesetze der produktiven und reproduktiven Geistestätigkeiten* (Bonn, 1924) **1924**
Review: Dipl.-Ing. Dr. E. W. Seyferts *Der Arbeiternachwuchs in der deutschen Maschinenindustrie* (Berlin, 1920) **1921**
Review: M. Värtings *Die Macht der Massen* **1928**
Review: Leo Weismantels *Schule der Volkschaft* **1925**
Review: Crane Brinton's *The Anatomy of Revolution* and Roger Bigelow Merriman's *Six Contemporaneous Revolutions* **1939**
Revolution **1947**
"Revolution" **1962**
"Revolution als Dienst" (unpublished) **1964**
Revolution als politischer Begriff in der Neuzeit **1931**
"Revolution als politischer Begriff in der Neuzeit," *Abhandlungen der schlesischen Gesellschaft für vaterländische Kultur* **1931**
Revolution as a political concept **1938**
"Revolution, Soziologie und Universität" **1960**
"Revolutionen oder Revolutionäre?" **1964**

The Rise and Fall of Nationalism and Internationalism **1939**
The Rhythm of Society: Life and Learning Coordinated **1934**
"Robert von Erdberg, 6. Juni 1866 – 6. Juni 1926" **1926**
"The Role of Language" (unpublished) **1935**
The Role of the Apostle Paul in the Papal Revolution of the Eleventh Century **1934**
Dr. Rosenstock's report on his visit to England **1926**
Rosenstock-Huessy Papers, Vol. 1 **1981**
"Rückblick auf die *Kreatur*" **1947, 1965**
"Die rückwärts gelebte Zeit. Unsere Erfahrungen von 1918 bis 1928" **1930**
Rules for the Second World War **1941**

S

St. Augustine – 1962 (lectures on "The Bionomics of Language") **1962**
St. Augustine, *De Magistro* (four chapters) Summary **1938**
"Saint-Simon, Claude Henri de" **1962**
"Saint-Simon—der erste Soziologe" **1958, 1988**
"Salamis und die Thermopylen. Ein Beitrag zur Erneuerung der Universität" **1950**
Die Sankt Georgs Reden **1916**
Saturnalien **1950**
Schiffahrtrecht **1926**
"Die Schranke des Sozialpolitikers" **1929**
"Schulreform und Hochschule" **1924**
Schwäbisch Hall und England **1968**
Schwarzrotgoldene Pflichten der Presse **1917**
Science, Superstition, Education and The Three Storeys of a University **1938**
"Science, Superstition, Education and The Three Storeys of a University" **1996**
The Science of Bodies and The Appeal to Somebody (lectures) **1939**
Scio cui credidi **1919**
Das Sechste Buch von Homers Odyssee **1903**
The Secret of the Temple or Underwriting the Sky **1947**
The Secret of the University **1950**
"Die Seele von William James" **1995**
"Die seelischen Wirkungen der modernen Arbeitsordnung" **1925**
"Selbstgespräch des Verfassers" **1994**
"Der Selbstmord Europas" **1919**
"Sermon on Philippians 3:20, 21, 4:4, 5c" **1957**

"Sermon on Philippians 3:21" **1962**
Sex and Sequence **1942**
Shame, Self-knowledge and Freedom **1956**
"The Singular and the Plural in the Sciences" (unpublished) **1937**
Sieger und Besiegte **1933**
"Sieger und Besiegte. Deutschland zwischen französicher und russischer Revolution" **1994**
"Sklaverei oder Regeneration? Gedanken zur Gefährdung des Arbeitsdienstes" **1932**
"The Social Function of Adult Education" **1930**
"Social Sciences" **1962**
"Socrates. Plato, Socrates, and Athens" **1962**
"Sohn und Vater bei der Berufswahl. Aus den Briefen Anselm von Feuerbachs des Älteren" **1920**
Soldiers in the Larger Sense **1942**
Soldiers of the Impossible **1942**
The Soul of William James **1942**
Sozialaristokratie und Arbeitslosigkeit **1932**
"Sozialer Dienst der Universität und ihrer Studenten" **1932**
"Der Sozialismus als Antithese" **1929**
"Sozialpolitik und Arbeitsrecht" **1925**
Soziologie (notes for lectures) **1929**
Soziologie (unpublished) **1930**
"Soziologie. Auszüge" **1956**
Soziologie. Bd. 1, *Die Übermacht der Räume* **1956**
Soziologie. Bd. 2, *Die Vollzahl der Zeiten* **1958**
Soziologie I. Die Kräfte der Gemeinschaft **1925**
Soziologie, 1. und 4. Stunde (unpublished) **1929**
"The Speech of Humankind," Instructors' note on **1966**
Speech and Reality **1970**
"*Soziologie II,* Letters to Georg Müller on" **1977**
The Spirit of Recognition **1939**
"The Spirit of the Alphabet" **1947**
Spraak en Werkelijkheid **1978**
"Die Sprache der Ereignisse" **1924**
Die Sprache des Menschengeschlechts (Broschüre) **1962**
Die Sprache des Menschengeschlechts. Eine leibhaftige Grammatik in vier Teilen, Bd. 1 **1963**
Die Sprache des Menschengeschlechts. Eine leibhaftige Grammatik in vier Teilen, Bd. 2 **1964**
"Die Sprache des Westens" **1955**

"Sprache und Geschichte" (lecture) **1957**
Staat **1947**
Staat und Grenze **1917**
"Staatsfamilie oder öffentliches Leben?" **1924**
Stadt und Land **1931**
"Stalins Einebnung und die Chronologie der Weltkriegsrevoltuion" **1961**
"Der Stein der Weisen. Ein altes Gespräch" **1920**
"Die Stellung der Akademie unter den übrigen Schulen. Aus einem Brief des ersten Leiters" **1931**
Stomatology **1961**
Strafrecht **1919**
"Student and University Service to the Community" **1932**
"Sudhoff, Karl" **1962**
Sun and Horizon: The Distribution of Cosmic and of Historical Facts in Ancient Egypt **1950**
Supertime, or The Correspondences of Society. Investigations in the Field of Biography, Time, Politics and Education **1942**
Surrender to Whom? (On Germany after the War) **1944**
"Swedenborg, Emmanuel" **1962**
Syllabus, Kuno Francke Lectures 1934–1935 **1935**
"Symblysma oder Überschwang der Jesuiten" **1948**
"Symbol und Sitte als Lebensmacht" **1928**
"Symbol und Sitte als Lebensmächte" **1929**
Symprochoresis or The Jesuits Come Home **1948**
"Synodalis" **1913**

T

Talk by Eugen Rosenstock-Huessy at Four Wells **1958**
"Talk by Rosenstock-Huessy" (tape) **1964**
Talk with Franciscans – 1965 (lectures) **1965**
"Der technische Fortschritt erweitert den Raum, verkürzt die Zeit, zerschlägt menschliche Gruppen" **1962**
Tenses, Times and Trinity, or The Abuse of Education **1966**
The Terms of the Creed **1955**
Theodizee oder Laodizee? **1932**
Theophrast von Hohenheim **1923**
"Theorien von gestern—Praktiken von wann?" **1958**, **1986**
There are no Synonyms **1944**
There is more time than you think **1958**

360 + 5 and The Year as Period **1955**
The Three Sciences **1941**
"Die tiefste Quelle der Arbeit" **1920**
"Timaeus" **1962**
"Time and Historicity of Man" **1964**
Time and Space in Education **1940**
"Time Bettering Days" (unpublished) **1954**
Die Tochter—Das Buch Rut **1988**
Toegepaste Zielkunde **1982**
Toekomst Het Christelijk Levensgeheim **1993**
Der Ton der fehlt **1960**
Der Ton der fehlt **1963**
A Township College (lectures) **1940**
"Tribalism" **1959**
The Tribes of the Spirit **1926**
"Tribute from a 'Post-Goethian'" **1968**
"Tutilo of St. Gallen, and the Origin of Drama" **1957**
Two letters: "An Bürkle" and "An Achim" **1957**
Two Reflections on the Role of Egypt **1954**

U

"Über die Verlegung der Fürstenschulen nach Westdeutschland" **1962**
Über einige neue Grundbegriffe des Privatrechts **1929**
"Über einige neue Grundbegriffe des Privatrechts," *Beiträge zum Wirtschaftsrecht* **1931**
"Über 'Reich,' 'Staat' und 'Stadt' in Deutschland von 1230–1235" **1930**
Die Umkehr in der Ausbildung **1931**
Die Umwandlung **1968**
Der unbezahlbare Mensch **1955**
Und dreimal: Die Nation **1930**
"Die ungeschriebene Verfassung," *Akademische Rundschau* **1929**
Die ungeschriebene Verfassung **1929**
The United States and Communism **1946**
Universal History – 1949 (lectures) **1949**
Universal History – 1951 (lectures) **1951**
Universal History – 1954 (lectures) **1954**
Universal History – 1955 (lectures) **1955**
Universal History – 1956 (lectures) **1956**
Universal History – 1957 (lectures) **1957**

V

"Verrückt gewordene Ökonomie oder mehrsprachiger Friede" **1984**
"Verrückt gewordene Ökonomie oder vielsprachiger Friede" **1993**
"Das Versiegen der Wissenschaft und der Ursprung der Sprache" **1925**
Versuchslehrgang des Instituts der Arbeit, "Arbeit, Arbeiter, Arbeitsgestaltung" **1925**
"Vico, Giovanni Battista" **1962**
Vitamine **1946**
"Vivit Deus" **1951**
Volk. Ein Beitrag zur Vertiefung des Begriffes "Volk" in leiblichem und geistigem Sinne **1933**
"Das Volk Gottes in Gegenwart, Vergangenheit und Zukunft" **1965**
"Das Volk Gottes in Vergangenheit, Gegenwart, Zukunft" **1961**
Volk, Persönlichkeit, Arbeit **1920**
"Das Volk zwischen Himmel und Erde" **1932**
"Volksbildung in der Universität" **1928**
"Volksbildung in der Universität" **1929**
"Volksbildungstag in Braunau a.I." *Donauland* **1921**
"Volksbildungstag in Braunau am Inn" *Hochland* **1920**
Volkskirche und Volkssiedlung **1928**
Der Volksname Deutsch **1970**
Die Volksordnung **1923**
Volksrecht und Hausherrschaft **1913**
"Volksstaat und Reich Gottes. Eine Weihnachtsbetrachtung" **1918**
V. Der Vollständige und der Selbstständige Mensch **1950**
Vom anderen Ende **1929**
Vom Industrierecht. Rechtssystematische Fragen **1926**
"Vom Neuland zwischen Pädagogik und Demagogik" **1926**
"Vom Staat zum Stamm" **1929**
"Vom Staatsbürger zum Flüchtlingsstaat" **1961**
Von einer Grammatik der benannten Menschen **1955**
Vorlesungen Staatstheorien der Gegenwart, 2nd Series **1914**
Vorlesungen Staatstheorien der Gegenwart, 3rd Series **1914**
Vorschlag zur Gründung von Kämpferbünden + Entwurf zum Aufruf nach Gründung eines Kämpferbundes **1919**
"Vorträge in der Sarepta-Schule" (tape) **1963**
Vortrag von Professor Rosenstock: Über "Volk." Ein Beitrag zur Vertiefung des Begriffs "Volk" in leiblichem und geistigem Sinne **1995**
Vorurteile **1917**
"Vorwort" preface to Helmuth von Moltke, *Die beiden Freunde* **1957**
De Vrucht der Lippen—Waarom vier evangelien **1981**

W

Adolf Wagenmann **1920**
"Die wahren Eigenschaften des Politikers" **1924**
Die Wahrhaftigkeit des Hochschullebens **1924**
"Die Wahrheit der Ketzer" **1968**
The Wailers **1962**
"Walton, Izaak" **1962**
Wandlungen im Recht **1930**
"War-Election-Genius" or "The Threefold Inspiration" (unpublished) **1944**
"Was bedeutet die Stadt für das christliche Leben?" **1949**
Was geht die Industrie die Erwachsenenbildung an? **1928**
"Was ist der Mensch? Eine Laienabwehr" **1953**
Was kostet die Geschichte? **1955**
"Was kostet die Geschichte?" **1985**
"Was soll man denn sonst tun?" **1923**
"Webb, Beatrice" **1962**
"Webb, Sidney James, 1st Baron Passfield" **1962**
"Weber, Max" **1962**
"Webster, Daniel" **1962**
Der Weg Europas nach dem Krieg **1927**
Die Weggelaufene Eschatologie **1957**
"Die Weggelaufene Eschatologie," *Mitteilungen der Eugen Rosenstock-Huessy Gesellschaft* **1975**
Die Weigerung des Quintaners **1961**
"Weil der Geist weht, wo er will...Zur Frage Tillichs: Gibt es noch Universität?" **1931**
"Weizsäcker, Freiherr Viktor von" **1962**
"Die Welt vor dem Blick der Kirche" **1923** (two entries)
"Weltfriedensdienst statt Weltbürgerkrieg" (tape) **1963**
Die Weltteile **1917**
"Die Weltzeituhr" **1952**
"Wer hat Recht?" **1920**
"Wer ist Gottes Volk?" (tape) **1961**
Wer kann heut das Deutsche Reich regieren? **1918**
"Wer sind die Götter?" **1959**
Werkstattaussiedlung **1922**
"Werkstatthygiene" **1925**
"Werkstattkommandite" **1925**
"Das Wesen des Fascismus" **1923**

"Weshalb heissen wir Deutsche?" **1932**
"Wesley, John" **1962**
What Future for the Professions? – 1960 (lectures) **1960**
What is new about sociology? **1950**
"What Is the City Doing to Christian Life? An Analysis of the Future Relation between the City of Man and the City of God" **1948**
"What They Should Make Us Think" and "What We Should Make Them Do" **1940**
"Whitehead, Alfred North" **1962**
"Whitman, Walt" **1962**
Whom Money Cannot Buy, Ecodynamics of a Mechanized World and The Fractions of Man in Industry **1966**
"Why do good people suffer? The Bible asks and answers" **1955**
"Die Wiederaufbau des Einzelnen," *Daimler Werkzeitung 1919/20* **1919**
"Der Wiederaufbau des Einzelnen," *Frankfurter Zeitung und Handelsblatt* **1919**
Die Wiedergeburt des Reichstags **1917**
Die Wiedergeburt der Wissenschaft aus der Vollmacht der Sprache **1960**
"Wieland, Christopher Martin" **1962**
"William James. Der Philosoph des amerikanischen Lebens," *Thema* **1950**
William James der Philosoph des modernen Amerikanischen Lebens **1947**
"William Ockham" **1962**
"William of Champeaux" **1962**
William Stanley, the Sixth Earl of Derby's Sonnets for Elizabeth de Vere 1591–1598 **1954**
William Stanleys—des sechsten Grafen von Derby—Sonette für Elisabeth de Vere 1591–1598" **1980**
"Winckelmann, Johann Joachim" **1962**
Wirkungen der europäischen Krise auf England **1926**
"Wissenschaft, Aberglaube, Erziehung und Die Drei Stockwerke einer Universität" **1996**
Witchcraft **1962**
"Wittgenstein, Ludwig Joseph Johann" **1962**
"Wittig, Joseph" **1962**
"Wolf, Friedrich August" **1962**
"Wolfram von Eschenbach" **1962**
Die Wollust, Die Syphilis, Die Eifersucht **1947**
"Workproject." Incomplete notes on Camp William James (unpublished) **1941**
The Wooer's Fate **1945**
"Ein Wort von Augustin und eins von Goethe" **1928**

"Würzburg, das erste geistliche Herzogtum in Deutschland" **1913**
"Wundt, Wilhelm Max" **1962**
"Wycliffe, John" **1962**

X

"X" **1962**
"Xenophon" **1962**

Y

"Y" **1962**
"Youth and Authority" **1940**

Z

"Z" **1962**
"Zarathustra" **1962**
Der Zauber des Menschen **1931**
"Zeitbessernde Tage? Eine Frage an die akademische Welt wegen 'ihrer' Zeit" **1959**
Zeitgeist, Mythos, Krieg **1956**, **1980**
Die Zeitliche Ordnung. Arbeitszeit **1925**
"Zen" **1962**
"Zeno of Citium" **1962**
"Zeno of Elea" **1962**
Zerfall und Ordnung des Industrievolks **1923**
"Zeus" **1962**
"Zoroastrianism" **1962**
"Zukunftsglaube. Ein Brevier für Futurologen" **1970**
Zum Patmos Datum, Phaenomeno-nomie oder Epiphanio-nomie **1947**
"Zur Ausbildung des mittelalterlichen Festkalenders" **1912**
Zur Germanisierung der Kirche aus dem Mittelalterlichen Festkalender **1911**
"Zur Problematik des religiösen Sozialismus. Über Tillichs *Masse und Geist*" **1976**
Zur Quellenfrage des Sachsenspiegels von Dr. iur. et phil. Eugen Rosenstock **1923**

Part II

Chronological Bibliography with a Key to the Collected Works on Microfilm

Part II

Chronological Bibliography with a Key to the Collected Works on Microfilm

1903

Notker Teutonicus (Labeo) von Sankt Gallen. Seinen lieben Eltern, 24. Dezember 1903, von Eugen Rosenstock. Manuscript on parchment, 45 pp.; typescript by L. van der Molen, 12 pp. Archiv der Eugen Rosenstock-Huessy Gesellschaft. Unpublished.
REEL 1, ITEM 1.

Das Sechste Buch von Homers Odyssee, übersetzt von Eugen Rosenstock. Seiner lieben Mutter zum 14. Februar 1903. Manuscript, 31 pp.; typescript by L. van der Molen, 7 pp. Archiv der Eugen Rosenstock-Huessy Gesellschaft; Abschrift at Four Wells. Unpublished.
REEL 1, ITEM 2.

1904

Deutsche Aufsätze U. I. (Unter Prima). 1. [I. Hegeso, Proxenas Tochter, Beschreibung und Deutung des Grabreliefs; II. Schillers Hero und Leander und die Beiden Königskinder; III. Was lässt sich gegen Luthers Übersetzungsprinzipien einwenden? IV. Religion und Kinderlehre bei Hans Sachs; V. Menschenleben in Gefahr! VI. Inwiefern bedeutet die (moralische) Besserung im Charakter des Fürsten in Lessings "Emilia Galotti" dramatisch eine Verschlechterung? VII. Lessing über Shakespeare.] 68 pp; typescript by L. van der Molen, 16 pp. Four Wells. Unpublished.
REEL 1, ITEM 3.

1905

Deutsche Aufsätze O. I. (Ober Prima). [I. Welche homerische Gestalt hat das stärkste Innenleben? II. Morgen und Abend (ein Wettstreit); III. "Und wer sich vermisst, es klüglich zu wenden, Der muss es selber bauend vollenden," nachgewiesen an dem Schicksal der Fürstin von Messina; IV. Genug ist nicht genug; V. Schiller und Körner; VI. Goethe und das Thüringer Land; VII. Wie kommt die Versöhnung zwischen Tasso und Antonio zu stande?] 60 pp.; typescript by L. van der Molen, 15 pp. Four Wells. Unpublished.
REEL 1, ITEM 4.

1906

P. Clodius Pulcher, Abiturarbeit im Joachimsthalschen Gymnasium Berlin. 1906. 75 pp. Archiv der Eugen Rosenstock-Huessy Gesellschaft. Unpublished.
REEL 1, ITEM 5.

1908

Das Angebliche Danteepigramm in Leipzig. Seminararbeit bei Prof. Karl Hampe. 1908, Anfang. Manuscript, 39 pp.; typescript by L. van der Molen, 20 pp. Archiv der Eugen Rosenstock-Huessy Gesellschaft. Unpublished.
REEL 1, ITEM 6.

Festspiel anlässlich Karls Physikum und Clairs Geburtstag und Burschung, verfasst von Eugen Rosenstock, veranstaltet von der Bande. Uraufführung zu Heidelberg Stiftsmühle. Copied by Else Götz. July 28, 1908. 10 pp. Archiv der Eugen Rosenstock-Huessy Gesellschaft. Unpublished.
REEL 1, ITEM 7.

1910

Herzogsgewalt und Friedensschutz (Breslau: M. & H. Marcus, 1910; reprint, Aalen: Scientia Verlag, 1969). 205 pp. Deutsche Provinzialversammlungen des 9. – 12. Jahrhunderts Untersuchen zur deutschen Staats- und Rechtsgeschichte begründet von Otto von Gierke im Jahre 1878. Alte Folge, Heft 104. {Includes *Landfriedensgerichte und Provinzialversammlungen vom neunten bis zwölften Jahrhundert* (1910) as Part 1.}
REEL 1, ITEM 9.

Landfriedensgerichte und Provinzialversammlungen vom neunten bis zwölften Jahrhundert. Inaugural-Dissertation zur Erlangung der Doktorwürde einer Hohen Juristischen Fakultät der Ruprecht-Karls-Universität zu Heidelberg (Breslau: M. & H. Marcus, 1910), 52 pp. {First part of *Herzogsgewalt und Friedensschutz* (1910).}
REEL 1, ITEM 8.

1911

Briefe, B. G. und Amalie Niebuhrs an Dore Hensler und an Karsten Niebuhr (1806–1814), eds. Heinrich Meisner, Eugen Rosenstock, and Erich Schmidt (Berlin: Litteraturarchiv-Gesellschaft, 1911), 88 pp. Mitteilungen aus dem Litteraturarchive in Berlin, Neue Folge 4.
REEL 1, ITEM 10.

Zur Germanisierung der Kirche aus dem Mittelalterlichen Festkalender. Weihnacht 1911. Seinen Eltern überreicht von Eugen Rosenstock. On parchment, 25 pp.; typescript by L. van der Molen, 8 pp. Forerunner of "Zur Ausbildung des mittelalterlichen Festkalenders" (1912). Four Wells. Unpublished.
REEL 1, ITEM 11.

1912

Das Herzogtum in der ersten Hälfte des deutschen Mittelalters. Probevorlesung gehalten zu Leipzig. July 18, 1912. 10 pp. Archiv der Eugen Rosenstock-Huessy Gesellschaft. Unpublished.
REEL 1, ITEM 15.

Ostfalens Rechtsliteratur unter Friedrich II. (Weimar: Verlag Hermann Böhlaus Nachfolger, 1912), vi + 147 pp. Texte und Untersuchungen.
REEL 1, ITEM 12.

Rathaus und Roland im deutschen Stadtrecht zwischen 1186 und 1280, Weihnachtsangebinde für Karl Zeumer, 24 Dez. 1912 (Leipzig: Handschrift der Spamerschen Buchdruckerei, 1912), 47 pp.
REEL 1, ITEM 13.

"Zur Ausbildung des mittelalterlichen Festkalenders," *Archiv für Kulturgeschichte,* Bd. 10 (Leipzig and Berlin: 1912): 272–282.
REEL 1, ITEM 14.

1913

"Bruchstücke eines verkürzten Sachsenspiegels," *Zeitschrift der Savigny Stiftung für Rechtsgeschichte* 34, Germanistische Abteilung (Weimar: Verlag Hermann Böhlaus Nachfolger, 1913): 408–410.
REEL 1, ITEM 16.

"Neue Literatur über die deutschen Königswahlen," *Zeitschrift der Savigny Stiftung für Rechtsgeschichte* 34, Germanistische Abteilung (Weimar: Verlag Hermann Böhlaus Nachfolger, 1913): 487–541. Also appeared as a reprint. {Reviews of: Herman Bloch, *Die stauffischen Kaiserwahlen und die Entstehung des Kurfürstentums,* Forschungen, 1911; Johannes Krüger, *Grundsätze und Anschauungen bei den Erhebungen der deutschen Könige in der Zeit von 911 bis 1056,* 1911; Max Buchner, *Die Entstehungsgeschichte der Erzämter und ihre Beziehung zum Werden des Kurkollegs mit Beiträgen zur Entstehungsgeschichte des Pairkollegs in Frankreich,* 1911; Max Buchner, *Die Entstehung und Ausbildung der Kurfürstenfabel,* 1912; Mario Krammer, *Das Kurfürstenkolleg von seinen Anfängen bis zum Zusammenschluss im Renser Kurverein des Jahres 1338,* 1913.}
REEL 1, ITEM 17.

"Synodalis," *Neues Archiv,* Bd. 38, Gesellschaft für ältere deutsche Geschichtskunde (Hannover and Leipzig: 1913): 307–309.
REEL 1, ITEM 18.

Volksrecht und Hausherrschaft. June 22, 1913. 21 pp. First 6 pages and pp. 12–14 missing. Manuscript; typescript by L. van der Molen, 4 pp. {Related in content to *Königshaus und Stämme* (1914). Taken verbatim from pp. 385f. The title comes from the final of 5 chapters.} Four Wells and Archiv der Eugen Rosenstock-Huessy Gesellschaft. Unpublished.
REEL 1, ITEM 21.

"Würzburg, das erste geistliche Herzogtum in Deutschland," *Historische Vierteljahresschrift* 24. Jg., der ganzen Reihe, 16, Jg. (Leipzig: 1913): 68–77.
REEL 1, ITEM 19.

"Die Zuverlässigkeit der 'Lebensnachrichten über B. G. Niebuhr'," *Historische Zeitschrift* 110, 3. Folge, Bd. 14 (Munich and Berlin: 1913): 566–573.
REEL 1, ITEM 20, WITH PP. 572–573 REVERSED.

1914

An eine hohe Juristen-Fakultät Juli 1914 zu Leipzig. Zur Organisation der Aufarbeitung der "sächsischen" Rechtsgeschichte. Letter of 3 pp. + sketch (both incomplete): Die Aktenbestände in Leipzig, 1 p. Archiv der Eugen Rosenstock-Huessy Gesellschaft. Unpublished.
REEL 1, ITEM 27.

Denkschrift des 30. Juli. Vorschlag an Prof. Dr. Richard Schmidt zur Staatenbildung unter den slavischen Nationalitäten nach dem Krieg. July 30, 1914. 4 pp. Typescript by L. van der Molen, 1 p. Archiv der Eugen Rosenstock-Huessy Gesellschaft and Four Wells. {See *Judaism Despite Christianity* (1969), p. 74.} Unpublished.
REEL 1, ITEM 25.

Königshaus und Stämme in Deutschland zwischen 911 und 1250 (Leipzig: Felix Meiner, 1914; reprint, Aalen: Scientia Verlag, 1965), xii + 416 pp.
REEL 1, ITEM 22.

"Principium Doctoris," *Festgabe für Rudolf Sohm zum goldenen Doktorjubiläum* (Duncker und Humblot, 1914): 87–101.
REEL 1, ITEM 23.

Review: Edwin Mayer-Hombergs *Die fränkischen Volksrechte im Mittelalter*, Bd. 1, Die fränkischen Volksrechte und das Reichsrecht (Weimar, 1912), *Historische Zeitschrift* 113 der ganzen Reihe, Folge 3, Bd. 17 (Munich and Berlin: 1914): 340–345.
REEL 1, ITEM 24.

Vorlesungen Staatstheorien der Gegenwart. 2nd Series, 6 lectures. May and June, 1914. pp. 17–178. First lecture (incomplete). Typescript by L. van der Molen, 28 pp. Archiv der Eugen Rosenstock-Huessy Gesellschaft; Abschrift at Four Wells. Unpublished.
REEL 1, ITEM 26.

Vorlesungen Staatstheorien der Gegenwart. 3rd Series, 9 lectures. June and July, 1914. 239 pp. Typescript beginning with 15th page, L. van der Molen, 60 pp. Archiv der Eugen Rosenstock-Huessy Gesellschaft; Abschrift at Four Wells. Unpublished.
REEL 1, ITEM 26.

1915

"Heiliges Römisches Reich Deutscher Nation," *Die Hilfe* 48, Gotteshilfe, Selbsthilfe, Staatshilfe, Bruderhilfe. Wochenschrift für Politik, Literatur und Kunst, ed. Friedrich Naumann (1915): 773–774.
REEL 1, ITEM 28.

"Die Planetarischen Gesetze in Stamm, Staat und Reich." Autumn 1915. 7 pp.; typescript by L. van der Molen, 3 pp. Archiv der Eugen Rosenstock-Huessy Gesellschaft and Four Wells. {Title by L. van der Molen. This is an article, in a manuscript written by Margrit Rosenstock-Huessy, that begins with "Der Gang der Staatenwelt ist ein gesetzmässiger durch die Zeiten."} Unpublished.
REEL 1, ITEM 30.

Ursprung des Rechts. Die übliche Einteilung des Rechts. Vom Befehl. Adel, Raum, Boden, Gewalt. August 18 and 19, 1915. 9 pp. Four Wells. Compiled by Eckart Wilkens. {In: Eugen Rosenstock-Huessy, *Weg von der Skizze Ursprung des Rechts* 18./19. August 1915 *Zum Industrierecht* 1926, *Zu den Interims des Rechts*, 1964; presented at a conference on Rosenstock-Huessy, Waterloo, Ontario, Canada, 1982, pp. 4–7.} Unpublished.
REEL 1, ITEM 31.

"Die Verfassung Giolitti," *Die Hilfe* 28, Gotteshilfe, Selbsthilfe, Staatshilfe, Bruderhilfe. Wochenschrift für Politik, Literatur und Kunst, ed. Friedrich Naumann (1915): 448–450.
REEL 1, ITEM 29.

1916

Die Sankt Georgs Reden. Der Jahrgang. 1916. 102 pp. Four Wells. {Sixteen of the planned 49 speeches ("Reden"). Cf. *Judaism despite Christianity* (1969), pp. 89f. and 151f. = Franz Rosenzweig, *Briefe und Tagebücher* (1979), pp. 219f. and pp. 311f.} Unpublished.
REEL 1, ITEM 33, WITH SOME PAGES REVERSED OR MISSING.

"Die Verdeutschung des Sachsenspiegels," *Zeitschrift der Savigny Stiftung für Rechtsgeschichte* 37, Germanistische Abteilung (Weimar: Verlag Hermann Böhlaus Nachfolger, 1916): 498–504.
REEL 1, ITEM 32.

1917

Denkschrift über die Möglichkeit der Abwendung einer Militärdiktatur, von Dr. iur. Rosenstock Privatdozent des Staatsrechts an der Universität Leipzig. 1917 (after July 19). 9 pp. (incomplete) Part III. 4 pp. Archiv der Eugen Rosenstock-Huessy Gesellschaft and Four Wells. Unpublished.
REEL 1, ITEM 37.

Ebenbild. 1917. Typescript by Eugen Rosenstock-Huessy, 3 pp.; handwritten, 10 pp; typescript by L. van der Molen, 6 pp. Archiv der Eugen Rosenstock-Huessy Gesellschaft and Four Wells. Unpublished.
REEL 1, ITEM 39.

Elsass-Lothringen und der Militarismus. December 18, 1917. 7 pp. (p. vi missing); typescript by L. van der Molen, 2 pp. Archiv der Eugen Rosenstock-Huessy Gesellschaft and Four Wells. Unpublished.
REEL 1, ITEM 40.

Entwurf Europäisches Völkerkonzert. 6 Kapitel "Urzelle" der Europäischen Revolutionen [1. Behauptung; 2. Probe; 3. Anwendung; 4. Durchführung; 5. Beweis (pp. 2 and 3 missing); 6. Darstellungen.]. 1917. 29 pp. Four Wells. Unpublished.
REEL 1, ITEM 41.

Die europäischen Parteien. 1917. 7 pp. {Fragment without page numbers up to last two: pp. 12 and 13; continuation of unpublished item, "Das Gewissen der europäischen Parteien" (1917)}. Typescript by L. van der Molen, 3 pp. Archiv der Eugen Rosenstock-Huessy Gesellschaft. Unpublished.
REEL 1, ITEM 38.

Freiheit der Meere. End of 1917 / beginning of 1918. 8 pp., typescript by L. van der Molen, 3 pp. Archiv der Eugen Rosenstock-Huessy Gesellschaft and Four Wells. Unpublished.
REEL 1, ITEM 42.

Das Gewissen der europäischen Parteien. August 1917. 12 pp. Archiv der Eugen Rosenstock-Huessy Gesellschaft and Four Wells. {Outline of *Die Hochzeit des Kriegs* (1920), pp. 31–46 ("Das Geschichtsbild der europäischen Parteien.").} Unpublished.
REEL 1, ITEM 43.

Goethe und Bismarck. July 1917. 9 pp. Archiv der Eugen Rosenstock-Huessy Gesellschaft. {= *Die Hochzeit des Kriegs* (1920), pp. 17–30, with revisions at the beginning and end.} Unpublished.
REEL 1, ITEM 44.

"Der Grund der inneren Krise," *Das Neue Deutschland* 6 (November 1917): 87–89.
REEL 1, ITEM 34.

"Ich und die Stunde sind eins. Zur Bestattung von Reinhold Wurzmann." April 15, 1917. 8 pp. Archiv der Eugen Rosenstock-Huessy Gesellschaft. {With a letter to the family, 3 pp.} Unpublished.
REEL 1, ITEM 35.

"Ist der Bundesrat Rat oder Regierung? Zum Streit über Artikel 9 der Reichsverfassung," *Die Hilfe* 51, Bd. 20, Gotteshilfe, Selbsthilfe, Staatshilfe, Bruderhilfe. Wochenschrift für Politik, Literatur und Kunst, ed. Friedrich Naumann (December 1917): 735–736.
REEL 1, ITEM 36.

Luther und die Paulskirche. 1917. 17 pp. {pp. i–vii, pp. 8–12 are not numbered + pp. ii–vi; p. i of the 2nd part is missing. Substituting for the missing page is one page from the Darmstädter Vorträge (1923), included in the typescript). Typescript by L. van der Molen, 6 pp. Archiv der Eugen Rosenstock-Huessy Gesellschaft and Four Wells. Unpublished.
REEL 1, ITEM 45.

Das neue Bewusstsein Europas. 1917. 6 pp. + 1/2 p. handwritten. Archiv der Eugen Rosenstock-Huessy Gesellschaft. Unpublished.
REEL 1, ITEM 46.

Der Rechtsbestand des preussischen Wahlrechts. August / September 1917. 17 pp. (pp. 15–17 handwritten.) Archiv der Eugen Rosenstock-Huessy Gesellschaft. Unpublished.
REEL 1, ITEM 47.

Reichskanzler und Premier. End of 1917 / beginning of 1918. 6 pp. (incomplete); typescript by L. van der Molen, 2 pp. Archiv der Eugen Rosenstock-Huessy Gesellschaft and Four Wells. Unpublished.
REEL 1, ITEM 48.

Schwarzrotgoldene Pflichten der Presse. 1917. 2 versions, 5 and 2 pp.; typescript by L. van der Molen, 3 pp. (includes both versions). Archiv der Eugen Rosenstock-Huessy Gesellschaft and Four Wells. Unpublished.
REEL 1, ITEM 49.

Staat und Grenze. 1917. 12 pp. (not numbered); typescript by L. van der Molen, 6 pp. Archiv der Eugen Rosenstock-Huessy Gesellschaft and Four Wells. Unpublished.
REEL 1, ITEM 50.

Der Verfassungsausgleich Europas. 1917. 8 pp.; typescript by L. van der Molen, 4 pp. Archiv der Eugen Rosenstock-Huessy Gesellschaft. Unpublished. {Written during WWI, Verdun.}
REEL 1, ITEM 51.

Vorurteile. 1917. 7 pp.; typescript by L. van der Molen, 2 pp. Archiv der Eugen Rosenstock-Huessy Gesellschaft and Four Wells. Unpublished.
REEL 1, ITEM 52.

Die Weltteile. 1917. 7 pp.; typescript by L. van der Molen, 6 pp. Archiv der Eugen Rosenstock-Huessy Gesellschaft. Unpublished.
REEL 1, ITEM 53.

Die Wiedergeburt des Reichstags. [a. Bismarck und die Paulskirche; b. Die drei Gewalten; c. Forderungen; d. Die neue Mehrheit; e. Die neue Minderheit.] 1917. 38 pp. Archiv der Eugen Rosenstock-Huessy Gesellschaft. Unpublished.
REEL 1, ITEM 55.

1918

Die Bedingung des Friedens. January 15, 1918. 13 pp.; typescript by L. van der Molen, 4 pp. Archiv der Eugen Rosenstock-Huessy Gesellschaft. Unpublished.
REEL 1, ITEM 58.

"Der Kreuzzug des Sternenbanners," *Hochland* 16, Bd. 1, Monatsschrift für alle Gebiete des Wissens, der Literatur und Kunst, ed. Karl Muth (November 1918): 113–122. {Also in *Europa und die Christenheit* (1919), pp. 11–20.}
REEL 1, ITEM 56.

Der preussische Staat. After November 9, 1918 / perhaps in 1919. 7 pp. Archiv der Eugen Rosenstock-Huessy Gesellschaft. Unpublished.
REEL 1, ITEM 59.

"Volksstaat und Reich Gottes. Eine Weihnachtsbetrachtung," *Hochland* 16, Bd. 1, Monatsschrift für alle Gebiete des Wissens, der Literatur und Kunst, ed. Karl Muth (December 1918): 229–239. {Also in *Europa und die Christenheit* (1919), pp. 21–31.}
REEL 1, ITEM 57, WITH PAGES 234–235, 236–237, AND 238–239 REVERSED.

Wer kann heut das Deutsche Reich regieren? Dr. iur. Eugen Rosenstock Privatdozent an der Universität Leipzig. 1918. 11 pp.; typescript by L. van der Molen, 3 pp. Archiv der Eugen Rosenstock-Huessy Gesellschaft. Unpublished.
REEL 1, ITEM 54.

1919

Die Auferstehung der Wahrheit. 1919. 49 pp.; typescript by L. van der Molen, 20 pp. Archiv der Eugen Rosenstock-Huessy Gesellschaft. {First draft of "Der Selbstmord Europas," *Hochland* (1919). = *Die Hochzeit des Krieges*, (1920), pp. 160–203; *Die Sprache des Menschengeschlechts*, Bd. 2 (1964), pp. 45–84.} Unpublished.
REEL 1, ITEM 71.

"Bolschewismus und Christentum," *Hochland* 16, Bd. 2, Monatsschrift für alle Gebiete des Wissens, der Literatur und Kunst, ed. Karl Muth (June 1919): 225–228. {= *Die Hochzeit des Krieges* (1920), pp. 150–155, expanded.}
REEL 1, ITEM 62.

"Der Bourgeois. Redaktioneller Kommentar zu der Anzeige Dr. Bruno Altmanns 'W. Sombart: *Der Bourgeois*. Zur Geistesgeschichte des modernen Wirtschaftmenschen' (Berlin, 1914)," *Hochland* 16, Bd. 2, Monatsschrift für alle Gebiete des Wissens, der Literatur und Kunst, ed. Karl Muth (May 1919): 117–132. {See *Werkstattaussiedlung* (1922), p. 251.}
REEL 1, ITEM 63.

Denkschrift: Über die geistige Sanierung des Daimlerwerks Krankheitsdiagnose; Untaugliche Heilmittel; Vorschlag: A. Richtung; B. Gestalt. 1919. 6 pp. Archiv der Eugen Rosenstock-Huessy Gesellschaft. Unpublished. {Reprint, *Daimler Werkzeitung 1919/20* (Moers: Joh. Brendow & Sohn, 1991): XXXVIIf.}
REEL 1, ITEM 72.

"Die Epochen des Kirchenrechts," *Hochland* 16, Bd. 2, Monatsschrift für alle Gebiete des Wissens, der Literatur und Kunst, ed. Karl Muth (April 1919): 64–78. {= *Die Hochzeit des Krieges* (1920), pp. 123–149, and *Das Alter der Kirche* (1928), pp. 587–617.}
SEE (1920) DIE HOCHZEIT DES KRIEGES; (1928) DAS ALTER DER KIRCHE.

"Etwas vom Innenleben fürs Innenleben," *Daimler Werkzeitung 1919/20* 2, ed. P. Riebensahm and Eugen Rosenstock (Stuttgart-Untertürkheim: Daimler-Motoren-Gesellschaft, 1919): 24–25. {Written under the pseudonym "F. Wondratschek."}
REEL 1, ITEM 64.

Europa und die Christenheit (Kempten-Munich: Jos. Köselsche Buchhandlung, 1919). 31 pp.
REEL 1, ITEM 60.

"Der ewige Prozess des Rechts gegen den Staat," *Zeitschrift für Rechtsphilosophie in Lehre und Praxis* 2 (1919): 219–241. {Also appeared as a reprint. Also in *Die Sprache des Menschengeschlechts*, Bd. 1 (1963), pp. 578–602 ("Der Sprachprozess gegen den Staat. Aus den letzten Monaten des Kaiserreichs"). Written under the pseudonym "F. Wondratschek."}
REEL 1, ITEM 65.

Frankfurt in der Staufferzeit 1152–1250. 1919 (ca.). 1 p. (incomplete); typescript by L. van der Molen, 1 p. Archiv der Eugen Rosenstock-Huessy Gesellschaft. Unpublished.
REEL 1, ITEM 73.

"Der Gang des Arbeitstages," *Daimler Werkzeitung* 2, ed. P. Riebensahm and Eugen Rosenstock (Stuttgart-Untertürkheim: Daimler-Motoren-Gesellschaft, 1919): 18–21. {Cf. *Werkstattaussiedlung* (1922), p. 101.}
REEL 1, ITEM 66.

Gedanken eines Kriegers. Aus einem Briefe. 1919 (ca.). In a newspaper, p. 4, no. 50. Archiv der Eugen Rosenstock-Huessy Gesellschaft.
REEL 1, ITEM 74.

"Gedanken über das Weltgeschehen," *Daimler Werkzeitung* 9, ed. P. Riebensahm and Eugen Rosenstock (Stuttgart-Untertürkheim: Daimler-Motoren-Gesellschaft, 1919): 159. {Written under the psuedonym "F. Wondratschek."}
REEL 1, ITEM 67.

Geist und Zeitgeist. End of 1919, 3 attempts of 1, 2, and 3 pp. and two fragments of 1 and 11 pp. (pp. xiv–xxiv); typescript by L. van der Molen, 2 and 6 pp. Archiv der Eugen Rosenstock-Huessy Gesellschaft. Unpublished.
REEL 1, ITEM 67A.

Das Gespräch vor Zeugen (Verlagsdruckerei Würzburg, 1919), 4 pp. Archiv der Eugen Rosenstock-Huessy Gesellschaft. {= "Das Gespräch vor Zeugen," *Mitteilungsblatt der Eugen Rosenstock-Huessy Gesellschaft* (1985): 5–9.}
REEL 1, ITEM 61.

Die Institution in Recht und Staat. Rede zu Heidelberg den 28. Juli 1919. In der selbigen Vortragsreihe als "Der Mensch in Recht und Staat" (II). July 28, 1919. Six fragments prepared for the speech, 13 pp.; typescript by L. van der Molen, 4 pp. Archiv der Eugen Rosenstock-Huessy Gesellschaft. Unpublished.
REEL 1, ITEM 75.

"Italien und Deutschland," *Daimler Werkzeitung* 4, ed. P. Riebensahm and Eugen Rosenstock (Stuttgart-Untertürkheim: Daimler-Motoren-Gesellschaft, 1919): 57–58.
REEL 1, ITEM 68.

Die Krise der Universität. Dokumentation aus Anlass des Vortrags "Scio cui credidi." 1919. 32 pp. Archiv der Eugen Rosenstock-Huessy Gesellschaft. [pp. 30–31, Dr. Wunderle in Fränkisches Volksblatt den 5. Juli; p. 32, Brief Dr. Wunderle an Eugen Rosenstock 5.7.19; pp. 33–35, Weismantel an Rosenstock; pp. 36–40, Rosenstock an Wunderle 7.7.19; pp. 41–43, Rosenstock an Weismantel; pp. 44–46, Hans Ehrenberg an Weismantel 9.7.19; pp. 47–49, Hans Ehrenberg in Fränkisches Volksblatt; pp. 50–59, Die Krise der Universität. Ein offener Brief an meine Freunde von Leo Weismantel; pp. 60–61, Rosenstock an Weismantel 5.8.1919.] {Cf. Scio cui credidi (1919) and "Die Krise der Universität" (1919).} Unpublished.
REEL 1, ITEM 76.

"Die Krise der Universität," *Hochland* Bd. 2, Monatsschrift für alle Gebiete des Wissens, der Literatur und Kunst, ed. Karl Muth (16. Jg., 1919): 192–197 {Written under the pseudonym "Doctor Libertus." Expanded in *Die Hochzeit des Krieges* (1920), pp. 204–215}.
SEE (1920) DIE HOCHZEIT DES KRIEGES.

"Leonardo da Vinci," *Daimler Werkzeitung* 4, ed. P. Riebensahm and Eugen Rosenstock (Stuttgart-Untertürkheim: Daimler-Motoren-Gesellschaft, 1919): 45–49.
REEL 1, ITEM 69.

Der Mensch in Recht und Staat. Rede zu Heidelberg den 23. Juni 1919. In a series of lectures: Neun Vorträge im Saal des Kaufmännischen Vereins unter dem Titel: Vom Individuum zur Gemeinschaft. [I. Die individualistische Seelenform in Religion, Kunst, Dichtung, Staat und Recht; II. Die Überwindung der individualistischen Seelenform in Religion, Kunst, Dichtung, Staat und Recht.] June 23, 1919. Fourteen fragments prepared for the speech, 51 pp.; typescript by L. van der Molen, 16 pp. Archiv der Eugen Rosenstock-Huessy Gesellschaft. Unpublished.
REEL 1, ITEM 77.

Die Neubauverlage (Zur Gründung Patmos, Moriah und Eleusis). 1919. 3 pp. Archiv der Eugen Rosenstock-Huessy Gesellschaft. Unpublished.
REEL 1, ITEM 78.

Scio cui credidi (several fragments for the lecture at Würzburg, June 30, 1919). 25 pp., not numbered; typescript by L. van der Molen, 14 pp. Archiv der Eugen Rosenstock-Huessy Gesellschaft. {Cf. Die Krise der Universität (1919) and "Die Krise der Universität" (1919).} Unpublished.
REEL 1, ITEM 79.

"Der Selbstmord Europas," *Hochland* 16, Bd. 2, Monatsschrift für alle Gebiete des Wissens, der Literatur und Kunst, ed. Karl Muth (September 1919): 529–553. {Also in *Die Hochzeit des Krieges* (1920), pp. 160–203, and *Die Sprache des Menschengeschlechts*, Bd. 2 (1964), pp. 45–84 (expanded).}
SEE (1920) DIE HOCHZEIT DES KRIEGES ; (1964) DIE SPRACHE DES MENSCHENGESCHLECHTS.

Strafrecht. 1919 (ca.). 1 p. (incomplete); typescript by L. van der Molen, 1 p. Archiv der Eugen Rosenstock-Huessy Gesellschaft. Unpublished.
REEL 1, ITEM 80.

Unter der Kanzel. 1919. 2 versions of 13 and 14 pp.; typescript by L. van der Molen, 5 pp. (including textual discrepancies). Archiv der Eugen Rosenstock-Huessy Gesellschaft. Unpublished.
REEL 1, ITEM 81.

Vorschlag zur Gründung von Kämpferbünden + Entwurf zum Aufruf nach Gründung eines Kämpferbundes. 1919. 4 + 2 pp. Four Wells. Unpublished.
REEL 1, ITEM 82.

"Der Wiederaufbau des Einzelnen," *Daimler Werkzeitung* 5, ed. P. Riebensahm and Eugen Rosenstock (Stuttgart-Untertürkheim: Daimler-Motoren-Gesellschaft, 1919): 81–82. {= "Der Wiederaufbau des Einzelnen," *Frankfurter Zeitung* (1919).}
REEL 1, ITEM 70.

"Der Wiederaufbau des Einzelnen," *Frankfurter Zeitung und Handelsblatt* 504 (July 11, 1919). {= "Der Wiederaufbau des Einzelnen," *Daimler Werkzeitung 1919/20* (1919).}
SEE (1919) "DER WIEDERAUFBAU."

1920

"Arbeitsgemeinschaft," *Daimler Werkzeitung* 7, ed. P. Riebensahm and Eugen Rosenstock (Stuttgart-Untertürkheim: Daimler-Motoren-Gesellschaft, 1920): 87–93. {= Shorter version of *Die Hochzeit des Krieges* (1920), pp. 253–269.}
REEL 2, ITEM 84.

"Die Arbeitsgemeinschaft der Astronomen," *Daimler Werkzeitung* 5/6, ed. Paul Riebensahm and Eugen Rosenstock (Stuttgart-Untertürkheim: Daimler-Motoren-Gesellschaft, 1920): 73.
REEL 2, ITEM 85.

"Arbeitsrecht und Arbeiterbildung. Die Voraussetzungen der Frankfurter Akademie der Arbeit," *Frankfurter Zeitung und Handelsblatt* 808 Morgenblatt (October 31, 1920). {Also in *Im Kampf* (1926), pp. 103–113.}
SEE (1926) IM KAMPF.

Deutschland in der öffentlichen Meinung des Auslandes. 1920. 8 pp. Archiv der Eugen Rosenstock-Huessy Gesellschaft. Unpublished.
REEL 2, ITEM 104.

"Einleitung zu: Adolf Wagenmann, *Wie schnell bewegen sich die Himmelskörper?*," *Daimler Werkzeitung* 5/6, ed. P. Riebensahm and Eugen Rosenstock (Stuttgart-Untertürkheim: Daimler-Motoren-Gesellschaft, 1920): 74.
REEL 2, ITEM 86.

"Einleitung zu 'Die Heimkehr' von Hans Heinrich Ehrler," *Daimler Werkzeitung* 5/6, ed. P. Riebensahm and Eugen Rosenstock (Stuttgart-Untertürkheim: Daimler-Motoren-Gesellschaft, 1920): 85.
REEL 2, ITEM 87.

"Das Ereignis der Relativitätstheorie. Die Einschaltung der Wissenschaft ins Leben," *Daimler Werkzeitung* 5/6, ed. P. Riebensahm and Eugen Rosenstock (Stuttgart-Untertürkheim: Daimler-Motoren-Gesellschaft, 1920): 63–64. {Also in *Im Kampf* (1926), pp. 89–90.}
REEL 2, ITEM 88.

"Fehlerquellen der praktischen Prüfung," *Daimler Werkzeitung* 2/4, ed. P. Riebensahm and Eugen Rosenstock (Stuttgart-Untertürkheim: Daimler-Motoren-Gesellschaft, 1920): 53.
REEL 2, ITEM 89.

"Gesunde oder zweckmässige Arbeitshaltung," *Daimler Werkzeitung* 1, ed. P. Riebensahm and Eugen Rosenstock (Stuttgart-Untertürkheim: Daimler-Motoren-Gesellschaft, 1920): 14–15. {Written under the pseudonym "Fritz Wurzmann." Authorship uncertain.}
REEL 2, ITEM 90.

Die Hochzeit des Krieges und der Revolution (Würzburg: Patmos-Verlag, 1920), 306 pp. Die Bücher vom Kreuzweg Erste Folge.
REEL 2, ITEM 83.

"Jeder sein eigener Astronom," *Daimler Werkzeitung* 5/6, ed. P. Riebensahm and Eugen Rosenstock (Stuttgart-Untertürkheim: Daimler-Motoren-Gesellschaft, 1920): 84.
REEL 2, ITEM 91.

"Des Kaufmanns Sorgen. Aus den Lebenserinnerungen des Johann Gottlob Nathusius," *Daimler Werkzeitung* 1, ed. P. Riebensahm and Eugen Rosenstock (Stuttgart-Untertürkheim: Daimler-Motoren-Gesellschaft, 1920): 19–24.
REEL 2, ITEM 92.

"Ein Kulturbild aus Norddeutschland. Aus dem alten Prospekt einer Bremer Firma," *Daimler Werkzeitung* 1, ed. P. Riebensahm and Eugen Rosenstock (Stuttgart-Untertürkheim: Daimler-Motoren-Gesellschaft, 1920): 11–13.
REEL 2, ITEM 93.

"Die Leistung der Psychotechnik," *Daimler Werkzeitung* 2/4, ed. P. Riebensahm and Eugen Rosenstock (Stuttgart-Untertürkheim: Daimler-Motoren-Gesellschaft, 1920): 37–41. {= Shorter version of "Psychotechnik," *Hochland* (1920).}
REEL 2, ITEM 94.

"Neu-Deutschland. Geschichte einer Siedlung," *Daimler Werkzeitung* 15/18, ed. P. Riebensahm and Eugen Rosenstock (Stuttgart-Untertürkheim: Daimler-Motoren-Gesellschaft, 1920): 282–287.
REEL 2, ITEM 96.

"Der Neubau der deutschen Rechtsgeschichte," *Die Arbeitsgemeinschaft,* Monatsschrift für das gesamte Volkshochschulwesen, ed. Werner Picht, with Robert von Erdberg and A. H. Hollemann (Leipzig: 1920): 132–140, 172–181.
REEL 2, ITEM 95.

"Persönliches von Einstein," *Daimler Werkzeitung* 5/6, ed. P. Riebensahm and Eugen Rosenstock (Stuttgart-Untertürkheim: Daimler-Motoren-Gesellschaft, 1920): 73.
REEL 2, ITEM 85 (PART OF "DIE ARBEITSGEMEINSCHAFT DER ASTRONOMEN").

Politik der Weltalter. Die Hölle der Politik. 1920. 22 pp. (Sixteen pages follow the table of contents; 3 unnumbered pages follow p. 1; likewise, two unnumbered pages follow p. 16.) Incomplete. Typescript by L. van der Molen, 6 pp. Archiv der Eugen Rosenstock-Huessy Gesellschaft. {It looks like a preliminary study for an issue, 4 or 5, of the journal *Weltalter*.} Unpublished.
REEL 2, ITEM 105.

"Psychotechnik," *Hochland* 17, Monatsschrift für alle Gebiete des Wissens, der Literatur und Kunst, ed. Karl Muth (February 1920): 510–526. {= "Die Leistung der Psychotechnik," *Daimler Werkzeitung 1919/20* (1920), abridged.}
REEL 2, ITEM 97.

Reaktionär (J. F. Böhmer) und Revolutionär (Bakunin). Zwei Urteile über unser Reich vor seiner Gründung. 1920 (ca.). 3 pp. (very incomplete and damaged); typescript by L. van der Molen, 2 pp. Archiv der Eugen Rosenstock-Huessy Gesellschaft. Unpublished.
REEL 2, ITEM 106.

"Sohn und Vater bei der Berufswahl. Aus den Briefen Anselm von Feuerbachs des Älteren," *Daimler Werkzeitung* 2/4, ed. P. Riebensahm and Eugen Rosenstock (Stuttgart-Untertürkheim: Daimler-Motoren-Gesellschaft, 1920): 55–57.
REEL 2, ITEM 98.

"Der Stein der Weisen. Ein altes Gespräch," *Daimler Werkzeitung* 8, ed. P. Riebensahm and Eugen Rosenstock (Stuttgart-Untertürkheim: Daimler-Motoren-Gesellschaft, 1920): 103–105.
REEL 2, ITEM 99.

"Die tiefste Quelle der Arbeit," *Daimler Werkzeitung* 1, ed. P. Riebensahm and Eugen Rosenstock (Stuttgart-Untertürkheim: Daimler-Motoren-Gesellschaft, 1920): 15–16. {Written under the pseudonym "Kunstgewerbezeichner Friedrich Wondratschek."}
REEL 2, ITEM 100.

Volk, Persönlichkeit, Arbeit. Grundsätzliches zur Frankfurter Akademie der Arbeit. 1920. 2 pp. (fragment). Archiv der Eugen Rosenstock-Huessy Gesellschaft. Unpublished.
REEL 2, ITEM 107.

"Volksbildungstag in Braunau am Inn," *Hochland* 18, Monatsschrift für alle Gebiete des Wissens, der Literatur und Kunst, ed. Karl Muth (1920): 237–240. {= "Volksbildungstag in Braunau a.I," *Donauland* (1921).}
REEL 2, ITEM 101.

Adolf Wagenmann. 1920. 7 pp. not numbered; typescript by L. van der Molen, 2 pp. Archiv der Eugen Rosenstock-Huessy Gesellschaft. {Outline of an obituary?} Unpublished.
REEL 2, ITEM 103.

"Wer hat Recht?" *Daimler Werkzeitung* 5/6, ed. P. Riebensahm and Eugen Rosenstock (Stuttgart-Untertürkheim: Daimler-Motoren-Gesellschaft, 1920): 84–85. {Written under the pseudonym "Fritz Eitel."}
REEL 2, ITEM 102.

1921

"Die Akademie der Arbeit in der Universität Frankfurt a.M.," *Freiheit* [Graz] (November 1921). {= "Die Akademie der Arbeit," *Die Arbeitsgemeinschaft* (1922); = "Die Akademie der Arbeit," *Der Grundstein* (1921).}
SEE (1922) "DIE AKADEMIE DER ARBEIT."

"Die Akademie der Arbeit in der Universität Frankfurt a.M.," *Der Grundstein* 43 (1921): 288–289. {= "Die Akademie der Arbeit," *Die Arbeitsgemeinschaft* (1922); = "Die Akademie der Arbeit," *Freiheit* (1921).}
SEE (1922) "DIE AKADEMIE DER ARBEIT."

Ansprache an Gäste aus England in der Akademie der Arbeit. 1920/21. 5 pp. (incomplete); typescript by L. van der Molen, 3 pp. Archiv der Eugen Rosenstock-Huessy Gesellschaft and Four Wells. {= *Im Kampf* (1926), pp. 129–131 ("Englische und deutsche Volksbildung," pp. 129–133).} Unpublished.
REEL 2, ITEM 112.

Aufbau und Verwaltung der Justiz. Einführungsvortrag zu einer Kurs von 10 Stunden (wohl an der Akademie der Arbeit). 1921. 17 pp.; typescript by L. van der Molen, 3 pp. Archiv der Eugen Rosenstock-Huessy Gesellschaft. Unpublished.
REEL 2, ITEM 113.

"Das Dreigestirn der Bildung," *Die Arbeitsgemeinschaft* 2, Monatsschrift für das gesamte Volkshochschulwesen, ed. Werner Picht, with Robert von Erdberg and A. H. Hollemann (Leipzig, 1921, written in 1920): 177–199. {Also in *Im Kampf* (1926), pp. 20–42; = "Das Dreigestirn der Bildung," *Die Neue Richtung* (1969), pp. 61–87.}
SEE (1926) IM KAMPF OR (1960) "DAS DREIGESTIRN."

Ferien 1921. Zur Heimkehr am 25. Oktober 1921 in die Riviera di Francoforde. 1921. 31 pp. (23 pp. in Harold M. Stahmer's transcription). Archiv der Eugen Rosenstock-Huessy Gesellschaft. Unpublished.
REEL 2, ITEM 114.

Karlsruhe Seminar: Die Sprache der Werkstatt. 1921/1922. 9 pp.(incomplete). Numbered for 5 classes. Typescript by L. van der Molen, 5 pp. Archiv der Eugen Rosentock-Huessy Gesellschaft. Unpublished.
REEL 2, ITEM 115.

"Laienbildung oder Volksbildung?" *Volksbildungsarchiv* 8, Heft 12 (1921): 381–388.
REEL 2, ITEM 108A.

"Ostblock oder Siberien?" *Osteuropa und Wir*. Das Problem Russland, erörtert von Dr. Eberhard Sauer, Dr. Eugen Rosenstock, Prof. Dr. Hans Ehrenberg (Schlüchtern: Neuwerk-Verlag, 1921): 71–78.
REEL 2, ITEM 108.

"Paragraph 218 des Reichsstrafgesetzbuchs" von Dr. Eugen Rosenstock, Leiter der Arbeitsakademie zu Frankfurt (Gegen einen Zeitungsaufsatz von Pfarrer Wünsch zur Aufrechterhaltung des staatlichen Verbots der Abtreibung). 1921. 10 pp. (pp. 1–8, 8a, 9); typescript by L. van der Molen, 3 pp. Archiv der Eugen Rosenstock-Huessy Gesellschaft. Unpublished.
REEL 2, ITEM 116.

"Partei und Volksbildung," Jubiläums-Nummer der *Frankfurter Volkszeitung* Blatt 3, Nr. 226 (October 1, 1921): 17. {Also in *Im Kampf* (1926), pp. 160–175.}
SEE (1926) IM KAMPF.

Das Recht! 1921, Frankfurt. 7 pp. Archiv der Eugen Rosenstock-Huessy Gesellschaft. Unpublished.
REEL 2, ITEM 117.

Review: Alfred Freunds *Technik, ihre Grundlagen für Alle* (Leipzig, 1920), *Die Arbeitsgemeinschaft* 2, Monatsschrift für das gesamte Volkshochschulwesen, ed. Werner Picht, with Robert von Erdberg and A. H. Hollemann (Leipzig: 1921): 318–319.
REEL 2, ITEM 109.

Review: Dipl.-Ing. Dr. E. W. Seyferts *Der Arbeiternachwuchs in der deutschen Maschinenindustrie* (Berlin, 1920), *Werkstattstechnik* 3 (1921): 76–77.
REEL 2, ITEM 110.

"Die Unterrichtsmethode der Akademie der Arbeit in Frankfurt a.M.," *Zentralblatt für die gesamte Unterrichtsverwaltung in Preussen* 63, Nr. 397 (1921): 302–304. {= "Die Unterrichtsmethode," *Zentralblatt der christlichen Gewerkschaften Deutschlands* (1921); = "Die Unterrichtsmethode," *G.A.D.* (1923). Also in *Im Kampf* (1926), pp. 122–128.}
SEE (1926) IM KAMPF.

"Die Unterrichtsmethode der Akademie der Arbeit in Frankfurt a.M.," *Zentralblatt der christlichen Gewerkschaften Deutschlands* 21, Nr. 10 (1921): 244–246. {= "Die Unterrichtsmethode," *Zentralblatt für die gesamte Unterrichtsverwaltung in Preussen* (1921); = "Die Unterrichtsmethode," *G.A.D.* (1923). Also in *Im Kampf* (1926), pp. 122–128.}
SEE (1926) IM KAMPF.

"Volksbildungstag in Braunau a.I.," *Donauland* 4, Bd. 2, Monatsschrift für alle Gebiete des Wissens, der Literatur und Kunst (Kempten, 1921): 237–240. {= "Volksbildungstag in Braunau a.I.," *Hochland* (1920).}
SEE (1920) "VOLKSBILDUNGSTAG."

"Zwölf Bücher," *Die Zwölf Wegbereiter*. Ein Almanach persönlicher Beratung für das Jahr 1921, ed. Leo Weismantel (Munich/Frankfurt: Verlag der Arbeitsgemeinschaft, 1921), pp. 43–45.
REEL 2, ITEM 111.

1922

"Die Akademie der Arbeit in der Universität Frankfurt a.M.," *Die Arbeitsgemeinschaft* 3, Monatsschrift für das gesamte Volkshochschulwesen, ed. Werner Picht, with Robert von Erdberg and A. H. Hollemann (Leipzig: 1922): 147–152. {= "Die Akademie der Arbeit," *Der Grundstein* (1921); = "Die Akademie der Arbeit," *Freiheit* (1921).}
REEL 2, ITEM 119.

"An die Mitarbeiter der Akademie der Arbeit," (Frankfurt a.M.: Werner und Winter GmbH, March 13, 1922), 4 pp. Archiv der Eugen Rosenstock-Huessy Gesellschaft.
REEL 2, ITEM 120.

"Die Ausbildung des Volksbildners. Vortrag in Braunau am Inn, 1920," *Die Arbeitsgemeinschaft* 3, Monatsschrift für das gesamte Volkshochschulwesen, ed. Werner Picht, with Robert von Erdberg and A. H. Hollemann (Leipzig: 1922): 73–90. {Also in *Im Kampf* (1926), pp. 150–167; "Die Ausbildung des Volksbildners," *Die Neue Richtung* (1960), pp. 88–102, abridged.}
SEE (1926) IM KAMPF.

"Kastengeist und Mandarinentum," *Beamtenjahrbuch* (April 1922): 166–168.
REEL 2, ITEM 121.

"Paracelsus in Basel," *Neuwerk* 4, Ein Dienst am Werdenden (Kassel, 1922): 379–394. {Also in *Das Alter der Kirche* (1928), pp. 729–760, expanded and improved version ("Der Annus Acceptus des Theophrast von Hohenheim (Paracelsus), Lucas 4:17–21.").}
SEE (1928) DAS ALTER DER KIRCHE.

"Die philosophischen Grundlagen des Arbeitsrechts," *Juristische Wochenschrift* 51, Heft 8 (April 15, 1922): 560–562.
REEL 2, ITEM 122.

Die Politik als Lehre vom Staat. 1922. 9 pp. Archiv der Eugen Rosenstock-Huessy Gesellschaft. Unpublished.
REEL 2, ITEM 123.

Werkstattaussiedlung, Untersuchungen über den Lebensraum des Industriearbeiters. In Verbindung mit Eugen May und Martin Grünberg (Berlin: Julius Springer Verlag, 1922), 286 pp.
REEL 2, ITEM 118.

1923

"ABC in Politik," *Neuwerk* 5, Ein Dienst am Werdenden (Kassel, 1923–1924): 181–189. {Also in *Abbau der politischen Lüge* (1924), pp. 7–14, abridged.}
SEE (1924) ABBAU DER POLITISCHEN LÜGE.

"Angewandte Seelenkunde. Anlässlich Karl Haase, *Angewandte Seelenkunde* (Gotha, 1921)," *Die Arbeitsgemeinschaft* 4, Monatsschrift für das gesamte Volkshochschulwesen, ed. Werner Picht, with Robert von Erdberg and A. H. Hollemann (Leipzig: 1923): 129–146. {Used in *Angewandte Seelenkunde* (1924).}
REEL 2, ITEM 126.

Darmstädter Vorträge Wissen und Reden von Staat und Gesellschaft. 1922–1923. 30 pp. Archiv der Eugen Rosenstock-Huessy Gesellschaft. [1. Übersicht; 2. 1. Vorlesung Einführung, 3 pp.; 3. 2. Vorlesung Klassenkampf, 3 pp. + 1 p.; 4. 3. Vorlesung Krieg und Weltfrieden, 3 pp.; 5. 4. and 5. Vorlesung Krieg (Fortsetzung), 1 and 5 pp.; 6. 6. Vorlesung Geisteszerfall u. Menschheitsfrieden, Politik und Zeitgeist; 7. 8. Vorlesung Natur und Politik II. 6 pp.; 9. Gesetz und Volk. 2 pp.; 10. Glaube, Liebe, Hoffnung, 3 pp.] Unpublished.
REEL 2, ITEM 130.

"Deutschlands Kommunisten und Faschisten," *Neuwerk* 5, Ein Dienst am Werdenden (Kassel, 1923–1924): 395–398.
REEL 2, ITEM 127.

Die Erschütterung der Wissenschaft (und das Evangelium). September 28, 1923. Three drafts, 12 pp.; typescript by L. van der Molen, 5 pp. = pp. 2–7. Archiv der Eugen Rosenstock-Huessy Gesellschaft. Unpublished.
REEL 2, ITEM 131.

Eugen Friedrich Moritz Rosenstock. Lebensbericht für die juristische Fakultät in Breslau. Autumn 1923. Manuscript of 2 pp.; typescript by L. van der Molen, 2 pp. Four Wells. Unpublished.
REEL 2, ITEM 132.

"Eine Fahrt ins 'Neuwerk'," *Frankfurter Zeitung und Handelsblatt* (January 17, 1923). {Two half-columns.}
REEL 2, ITEM 128.

"Das Herz der Welt. Ein Maßstab der Politik," *Kirche und Wirklichkeit*, ed. Ernst Michel (Jena: Eugen Diederichs, 1923): 241–265. {Also in *Das Alter der Kirche* (1928), pp. 3–44.}
SEE (1928) DAS ALTER DER KIRCHE.

Leben, Lehre und Wirken. Eine Auslegung der letzten beiden Worte des *Sterns der Erlösung*. March 10, 1923, 40 pp. (incomplete); typescript by L. van der Molen, 8 pp. Four Wells. {= *Das Alter der Kirche* (1928), pp. 111–140; *Die Sprache des Menschengeschlechts*, Bd. 1 (1963), pp. 119–142; and *Die Umwandlung* (1968), pp. 8–31, revised.} Unpublished.
REEL 2, ITEM 133.

Perioden der Geschichte. 1923. 2 pp., fragment; typescript by L. van der Molen, 1 p. Archiv der Eugen Rosenstock-Huessy Gesellschaft. Unpublished.
REEL 2, ITEM 134.

Theophrast von Hohenheim, eds. Richard Koch and Eugen Rosenstock. Introduction by Eugen Rosenstock, pp. 4–15. Fünf Bücher über die unsichtbaren Krankheiten. (Stuttgart: Fr. Fromanns Verlag [H. Kurtz], 1923), 116 pp.
REEL 2, ITEM 125.

"Die Unterrichtsmethode der Akademie der Arbeit in Frankfurt a.M.," *G.A.D. [Gewerkschaft der Angestellten]* 1 (Jablonec, Czechoslovakia, 1923). {= "Die Unterrichtsmethode," *Zentralblatt für die gesamte Unterrichtsverwaltung in Preussen* (1921); = "Die Unterrichtsmethode," *Zentralblatt der christlichen Gewerkschaften Deutschlands* (1921). Also in *Im Kampf* (1926), pp. 122–128.}
SEE (1926) IM KAMPF.

Die Volksordnung. Grundlegung einer Volkswissenschaft in fünf Bänden. [Forerunner to *Soziologie*(1925).] Band 1: Der Ursprung des Gemeinwesens von Eugen Rosenstock Dr. jur. and phil. 1923. 512 pp. Archiv der Eugen Rosenstock-Huessy Gesellschaft. [I. Die Kräfte der Volksleidenschaft pp. 1–242 (pp. 54 and 86 missing; pp. 111a – e and pp. 119a – d added; handwritten. Typescript by L. van der Molen, 1 p.) II. Von den Gewalten des öffentlichen Lebens pp. 243–512 (pp. 383–383a and pp. 448–448a added; handwritten. Typescript by L. van der Molen, 1 p.) (In addition, pp. 196, 197, 199, 207, 208, 208a and b, 290, 212, 216 of the missing 2nd volume, Der Alltag der Arbeit). Table of Contents: Die übrigen Bände sollen enthalten: II. Der Alltag der Arbeit. III. Das Wirken der Sprache. IV. Die Gesetze unserer Zeitrechnung. V. Biographie der Persönlichkeit. With two outlines of contents and 8 pp. Introduction of the 1st volume.] {Volume 1 in the typed manuscript form only.} Unpublished.
REEL 2, ITEM 135.

"Was soll man denn sonst tun?" *Neuwerk* 5, Ein Dienst am Werdenden (Kassel: 1923–1924): 114–119.
REEL 2, ITEM 129.

"Die Welt vor dem Blick der Kirche," *Die Tat* 15, Monatsschrift für die Zukunft deutscher Kultur (1923): 8–20. {= "Die Welt vor dem Blick der Kirche," *Kirche und Wirklichkeit* (1923). Also in *Das Alter der Kirche* (1928), pp. 761–784.}
SEE (1928) DAS ALTER DER KIRCHE.

"Die Welt vor dem Blick der Kirche," *Kirche und Wirklichkeit,* Ein katholisches Zeitbuch, ed. Ernst Michel (Jena: Eugen Diederichs, 1923): 226–240. {= "Die Welt vor dem Blick der Kirche," *Die Tat* (1923). Also in *Das Alter der Kirche* (1928), pp. 761–784.}
SEE (1928) DAS ALTER DER KIRCHE.

"Das Wesen des Fascismus," *Hochland* 20, Bd. 2, Monatsschrift für alle Gebiete des Wissens, der Literatur und Kunst, ed. Karl Muth (1923): 225–234. {Also in *Abbau der politischen Lüge* (1924), pp. 55–61, abridged.}
SEE (1924) ABBAU DER POLITISCHEN LÜGE.

Zerfall und Ordnung des Industrievolks (Frankfurt a.M.: Carolus Druckerei, 1923; reprint, Frankfurt a.M.: *Rhein-Mainischen Volkszeitung,* 1923), 39 pp. {= *Industrievolk* (1924).}
REEL 2, ITEM 124.

Zur Quellenfrage des Sachsenspiegels von Dr. iur. et phil. Eugen Rosenstock. 1923. 9 pp.; typescript by L. van der Molen, 4 pp. Archiv der Eugen Rosenstock-Huessy Gesellschaft. Unpublished.
REEL 2, ITEM 136.

Die Zweischneidigkeit des geistigen Lebens. 1923. 6 pp. Incomplete preliminary study for "Die Welt vor dem Blick der Kirche," *Die Tat* (1923) and "Die Welt vor dem Blick der Kirche," *Kirche und Wirklichkeit* (1923). {= *Das Alter der Kirche* (1928) pp. 761–784 ("Die Welt vor dem Blick der Kirche").} Typescript by L. van der Molen, 2 pp. Archiv der Eugen Rosenstock-Huessy Gesellschaft. Unpublished.
REEL 2, ITEM 137.

1924

Abbau der politischen Lüge (Frankfurt a.M.: Carolus Druckerei, 1924) 81 pp. In der Reihe: *Volk im Werden,* Schriftenreihe der *Rhein-Mainischen Volkszeitung*. {pp. 39–54 also in: *Die Sprache des Menschengeschlechts,* Bd. 2 (1964), pp. 116–134; pp. 15–33 also in: *Die Hochzeit des Krieges* (1920), pp. 83–106.}
REEL 2, ITEM 138.

"Andragogik," *Archiv für Erwachsenenbildung* 1, Organ des Hohenrodter Bundes (1924): 248–276. {Also in *Im Kampf* (1926), pp. 193–219.}
SEE (1926) IM KAMPF.

Angewandte Seelenkunde: Eine programmatische Übersetzung (Darmstadt: Röther-Verlag GmbH, 1924), 79 pp. Bücher der deutschen Wirklichkeit, ed. Wilhelm Henrich. {Also in: *Die Sprache des Menschengeschlechts,* Bd. 1 (1963), pp. 739–810, without Foreword. Cf. *Toegepaste Zielkunde* (1982) and *Practical Knowledge of the Soul* (1988).}
SEE (1963) DIE SPRACHE DES MENSCHENGESCHLECHTS.

"Arbeiterbildung," *Blätter der Volkshochschule Breslau* 3, Nr. 35 (July–September 1924): 13–17. {= "Arbeiterbildung," *Rhein-Mainische Volkszeitung* (1924).}
SEE (1924) "ARBEITERBILDUNG."

"Arbeiterbildung," *Rhein-Mainische Volkszeitung* (November 7, 1924). {= "Arbeiterbildung," *Blätter der Volkshochschule Breslau* (1924), one sentence added.}
REEL 2, ITEM 140.

"Arbeiterfreizeiten," *Pfingstfeuer*, 4, Nr. 1, Zeitschrift für Kultur und Lebenserneuerung, ed. Rudolf Jokil and Neisse Neuland (1924): 34–35.
NOT MICROFILMED.

"Betriebsverfassung des Hochkapitalismus," *Frankfurter Zeitung und Handelsblatt* 68, Nr. 125, Erstes Morgenblatt (February 16, 1924).
REEL 2, ITEM 141.

Die Gesetze unserer Zeitrechnung. Zum Werden und Vergehen der europäischen Volkscharaktere. 1924 (?). 15 pp. (Mit Zahlentafel zu den Gesetzen). Archiv der Eugen Rosenstock-Huessy Gesellschaft. Unpublished.
REEL 3, ITEM 150.

Die Gestalten unserer Zeitrechnung. 1. Die Kirche. 1924 (?). 8 pp. Archiv der Eugen Rosenstock-Huessy Gesellschaft. {= *Das Alter der Kirche* (1928), pp. 81–101 ("Kirche und Menschheit," revised).} Unpublished.
REEL 3, ITEM 151.

"Hegel und unser Geschlecht," *Der Neue Merkur* 8 (1924–1925): 360–362.
REEL 2, ITEM 142.

Industrievolk (Frankfurt a.M.: Carolus Druckerei, 1924), 55 pp. Aus dem Zwischenraum zwischen Technik und Weisheit, Aus der Zwischenzeit zwischen Krieg und Frieden. In der Reihe: *Volk im Werden*, Schriftenreihe der *Rhein-Mainischen Volkszeitung* 2, erweiterte Auflage. {= *Zerfall und Ordnung des Industrievolks* (1923), expanded.}
REEL 2, ITEM 139.

"Des Kaufmanns Dienst am Volke," *Rhein-Mainische Volkszeitung* 183 (August 6, 1924): 1–2.
REEL 2, ITEM 143.

"Die Mittel der Politik," *Rhein-Mainische Volkszeitung* (September 23, 1924). {= *Abbau der politischen Lüge* (1924), pp. 49–55; *Die Sprache des Menschengeschlechts*, Bd. 2 (1964), pp. 127–134.}
SEE (1924) ABBAU DER POLITISCHEN LÜGE; (1964) DIE SPRACHE DES MENSCHENGESCHLECHTS.

"Nachträgliche Erwägungen zu 'Angewandte Seelenkunde.' Zusätze zum psychosozialen Programm," *Rhein-Mainische Volkszeitung* 188 (August 12, 1924). {= "Nachträgliche Erwägungen" (1969), pp. 7–9.}
See (1969) "Nachträgliche Erwägungen."

"Die nackte Arbeit," *Literarische Beilage der Augsburger Postzeitung* 44 (October 29, 1924): 1. {= "Die nackte Arbeit," *Rhein-Mainische Volkszeitung* (1924).}
See (1924) "Die nackte Arbeit."

"Die nackte Arbeit," *Rhein-Mainische Volkszeitung* (December 22, 1924): 298. {= "Die nackte Arbeit," *Literarische Beilage der Augsburger Postzeitung* (1924).}
Reel 2, Item 144.

"Not und Wende in der Arbeiterbewegung," *Neuwerk* 4, Ein Dienst am Werdenden (Kassel: 1924): 437–443.
Reel 3, Item 145.

Review: Ferdinand Ossendowskis *Tiere, Menschen und Götter* (translation of the original American edition), *Literarische Beilage der Augsburger Postzeitung* 15 (April 9, 1924): 59.
Reel 3, Item 146.

Review: Otto Selzes *Die Gesetze der produktiven und reproduktiven Geistestätigkeiten* (Bonn, 1924), *Archiv für Erwachsenenbildung.* Organ des Hohenrodter Bundes 1 (1924): 178.
Reel 3, Item 147.

"Schulreform und Hochschule," *Frankfurter Zeitung und Handelsblatt* 662, Abendblatt, co-author Rudolf Ehrenberg (September 4, 1924): 3–4.
Reel 3, Item 148.

"Die Sprache der Ereignisse," *Rhein-Mainsiche Volkszeitung* (August 11, 1924). {= *Abbau der politischen Lüge* (1924), pp. 39–45; *Die Sprache des Menschengeschlechts*, Bd. 2 (1964), pp. 116–123.}
See (1924) Abbau der politischen Lüge; (1964) Die Sprache des Menschengeschlechts.

"Staatsfamilie oder öffentliches Leben?" *Rhein-Mainsiche Volkszeitung* 188 (August 12, 1924): 1–2.
Reel 3, Item 149.

"Unternehmer und Volksordnung," *Der Neue Merkur* 7 (1924): 997-1004. {Also in *Im Kampf* (1926), pp. 176–182.}
SEE (1926) IM KAMPF.

"Die wahren Eigenschaften des Politikers," *Rhein-Mainsiche Volkszeitung* (September 13, 1924). {= *Abbau der politischen Lüge* (1924), pp. 46–49; *Die Sprache des Menschengeschlechts*, Bd. 2 (1964), pp. 123–127.}
SEE (1924) ABBAU DER POLITISCHEN LÜGE; (1964) *DIE SPRACHE DES MENSCHENGESCHLECHTS*.

Die Wahrhaftigkeit des Hochschullebens. Vortrag. End of May 1924. Outline, 6 pp. + Auszüge aus Gothein, Staat und Gesellschaft des Zeitalters der Gegenreformation und G. Ritter, Spätschriften I, 1921 und Studien I. 4 pp. Typescript by L. van der Molen, 4 pp. = pp. 1–2, 7–9. Archiv der Eugen Rosenstock-Huessy Gesellschaft. Unpublished.
REEL 3, ITEM 151A.

1925

Bericht über die beiden Referate am 9. und 10. Dezember 1925 auf der Berufsschulwoche Frankfurt a.M. 1925. 4 pp. Archiv der Eugen Rosenstock-Huessy Gesellschaft. Unpublished. {= "Die seelischen Wirkungen," *Berufsschule und Leben* (1925).}
REEL 3, ITEM 161.

Englandreise Tagebuch. 1925. 38 pp. Archiv der Eugen Rosenstock-Huessy Gesellschaft. Unpublished.
REEL 3, ITEM 162.

"Freizeiten her!" *Rhein-Mainische Volkszeitung* 48 (February 27, 1925).
REEL 3, ITEM 154.

Für Ursprung der Sprache. Für Freund Technik Mister Creakles System. 1925 (?). 2 pp.; typescript by L. van der Molen, 1 p. Archiv der Eugen Rosenstock-Huessy Gesellschaft. Unpublished.
REEL 3, ITEM 163.

Gesetz oder Sakrament? Für Joseph und Bianka (Wittig), von Eugen und Margrit. (Stuttgart: Union Deutsche Verlagsgesellschaft, 1925). 8 pp. {Forerunner of "Gesetz oder Sakrament? Zur Ehediskussion," *Eckart* (1927) and *Das Alter der Kirche* (1928), pp. 927–936.}
REEL 3, ITEM 164.

Karl der Grosse und das Schicksal der Kirche. 1925 (?). 8 pp.; typescript by L. van der Molen, 3 pp. Archiv der Eugen Rosenstock-Huessy Gesellschaft. Unpublished.
REEL 3, ITEM 165.

Der Lebensweg Fritz Mauthners. 1925. Fragments pp. 6–9, 23–27 of the original introduction to "Das Versiegen der Wissenschaft und der Ursprung der Sprache," *Der Neue Merkur* (1925). Archiv der Eugen Rosenstock-Huessy Gesellschaft. Unpublished.
REEL 3, ITEM 166.

Protestantismus und Volksbildung (Berlin: Eckart-Verlag GmbH, 1925), 24 pp. {Also in: *Das Alter der Kirche* (1928), pp. 675–728 ("Luthers Volkstum und Volksbildung"; expanded version, omits final quotation from John 1:1–5).}
REEL 3, ITEM 152.

Review: H. Hellers *Freie Volksbildung* (Leipzig, 1925), *Archiv für Erwachsenenbildung* 2, Organ des Hohenrodter Bundes (1925): 47–51.
REEL 3, ITEM 155.

Review: Leo Weismantels *Schule der Volkschaft* (Frankfurt a.M.: Carolus Druckerei, 1925), *Archiv für Erwachsenenbildung* 2, Organ des Hohenrodter Bundes (1925): 166–168.
REEL 3, ITEM 158.

"Die seelischen Wirkungen der modernen Arbeitsordnung," *Berufsschule und Leben* (Frankfurt: 1925): 26–31; an elaboration of two lectures given December 9 and 10, 1925, at the Berufsschulwoche, Frankfurt a.M.
REEL 3, ITEM 156, WITH PP. 30–31 REVERSED.

"Sozialpolitik und Arbeitsrecht," *Arbeitskunde*. Grundlagen, Bedingungen und Ziele der wirtschaftlichen Arbeit, ed. Johannes Riedel (Leipzig and Berlin: Druck und Verlag B.G. Teubner, 1925), pp. 64–84.
REEL 3, ITEM 157.

Soziologie I. Die Kräfte der Gemeinschaft (Berlin and Leipzig: Walter de Gruyter & Co., 1925), 264 pp. {= *Soziologie,* Bd. 1 (1956, revised).}
REEL 3, ITEM 153.

"Das Versiegen der Wissenschaft und der Ursprung der Sprache," *Der Neue Merkur* 8, Nr. 10 (July 1925): 814–837. {Also in *Die Sprache des Menschengeschlechts,* Bd. 1 (1963), pp. 655–683.}
SEE (1963) DIE SPRACHE DES MENSCHENGESCHLECHTS.

Versuchslehrgang des Instituts der Arbeit, "Arbeit, Arbeiter, Arbeitsgestaltung." March 1 – October 31, 1925; assisted chiefly by Darmstadt, Frankfurt, and Heidelberg Hochschullehrer. (Plans and program, together with A. Mirgeler). 6 pp. Archiv der Eugen Rosenstock-Huessy Gesellschaft. Unpublished.
REEL 3, ITEM 167.

"Werkstatthygiene," *Die Räder* 6, Nr. 12 (1925): 139–140.
REEL 3, ITEM 159.

"Werkstattkommandite," *Reichsarbeitsblatt* 38, Nichtamtlicher Teil (1925): 615–618.
REEL 3, ITEM 160.

Die Zeitliche Ordnung. Arbeitszeit. 1925. 5 pp. [Belongs to "Die seelischen Wirkungen," *Berufsschule und Leben* (1925)]; typescript by L. van der Molen, 2 pp. Archiv der Eugen Rosenstock-Huessy Gesellschaft. Unpublished.
REEL 3, ITEM 169.

1926

"Der Begriff des Lebensraumes und die Methode der Soziologie," *Die Schildgenossen* 6, Zeitschrift für die katholische Laienbewegung (Würzburg: 1926): 233–246. {From *Werkstattaussiedlung* (1922), pp. 1–16.}
SEE (1922) WERKSTATTAUSSIEDLUNG.

Die europäische Krise in England. 1926. 16 pp., unfinished; typescript by L. van der Molen, 7 pp. Archiv der Eugen Rosenstock-Huessy Gesellschaft. Unpublished.
REEL 3, ITEM 179.

"Der Geist des Menschen ist der heilige Geist." Zu Franz Rosenzweig (Zweistromland: 1926; reprint, Dordrecht: Martinus Nijhoff, 1984, p. 214): 229. {Also found in: "Des Menschen Geist," in *Franz Rosenzweig* (1987), pp. 44–45; and unpublished: 3 pp. (67-line meditation on Franz Rosenzweig's quotation from Hermann Cohen), typescript by L. van der Molen, 1 p. and 2 pp., respectively.} Archiv der Eugen Rosenstock-Huessy Gesellschaft. Unpublished.
REEL 3, ITEM 180.

"Die geistigen Bewegungen der Gegenwart," *Neuwerk* 8, Ein Dienst am Werdenden (Kassel, 1926): 197–205.
REEL 3, ITEM 174.

Im Kampf um die Erwachsenenbildung, 1912–1926, Werner Picht and Eugen Rosenstock. Schriften für Erwachsenenbildung. Im Auftrag der Deutschen Schule für Volksforschung und Volksbildung, ed. Robert von Erdberg, Bd. 1 (Leipzig: Verlag Quelle und Meyer, 1926), 240 pp.
REEL 3, ITEM 170.

"Der Ingenieur im Kampf gegen die Unrentabilität des Betriebes," *Hessische Hochschulzeitung* 15, Heft 4 (1926): 42–45. {Also in *Im Kampf* (1926), pp. 186–193.}
SEE (1926) IM KAMPF.

Lebensarbeit in der Industrie und Aufgaben einer europäischen Arbeitsfront (Berlin: Julius Springer, 1926), 88 pp.
REEL 3, ITEM 171.

"Macht und Schranken der Industrialisierung des Reichs," *Der Arbeitgeber* 16, Nr. 7, Zeitschrift der Vereinigung der Deutschen Arbeitgeberverbände (Berlin: April 1, 1926): 129–134. A lecture at a meeting of the Vereinigung der Deutschen Arbeitgeberverbände, March 12, 1926. {= "Macht und Schranken," *Hessische Hochschulzeitung* (1926). Also in *Politische Reden* (1929), 16–31.}
SEE (1926) "MACHT UND SCHRANKEN" OR (1929) POLITISCHE REDEN.

"Macht und Schranken der Industrialisierung des Reichs," *Hessische Hochschulzeitung* 15, Heft 9, Amtliches Organ der Studentenschaft der Technischen Hochschule Darmstadt (July 7, 1926): 101–104; and *Amtliches Mitteilungsblatt der Kreisleitung des Kreises VI der Deutschen Studentenschaft* 15, Heft 10 (July 20, 1926): 113–115. {= "Macht und Schranken," *Der Arbeitgeber* (1926). Also in *Politische Reden* (1929), pp. 16–31.}
REEL 3, ITEM 175.

Macht und Schranken der Industrialisierung. Vortrag. March 12, 1926. Theme and sketch, 8 pp. Archiv der Eugen Rosenstock-Huessy Gesellschaft. {Cf. "Macht und Schranken," *Der Arbeitgeber* (1926), and "Macht und Schranken," *Hessische Hochschulzeitung* (1926).} Unpublished.
REEL 3, ITEM 181.

Plan einer Deutschen Schule für Volksbildung und Volksforschung. Entwurf einer Denkschrift vorgelegt vom Vorbereitenden Ausschuss des Hohenrodter Bundes (Berlin: Otto Walter, 1926), 16 pp. {Cf. *Die Deutsche Schule für Volksforschung und Erwachsenenbildung* (1927).}
REEL 3, ITEM 172.

"Protestantismus und Volksbildung," *Neuwerk* 7, Ein Dienst am Werdenden (Kassel, 1926): 482–489. {Abridged version of *Protestantismus und Volksbildung* (1925).}
REEL 3, ITEM 176.

Religio Depopulata. Zu Joseph Wittigs Ächtung (Berlin: Verlag Lambert Schneider, 1926), 44 pp. {Also in: *Das Alter der Kirche*, Bd. 3 (1928), pp. 103–132.}
SEE (1928) DAS ALTER DER KIRCHE.

"Robert von Erdberg, 6. Juni 1866 – 6. Juni 1926," *Unterhaltungsbeilage der Schlesischen Zeitung* 45 (June 6, 1926): 1.
REEL 3, ITEM 177.

Dr. Rosenstock's report on his visit to England, September 25th to November 20th, 1925 {invited by the World Association of Adult Education}. 1926. 3 pp., incomplete. Archiv der Eugen Rosenstock-Huessy Gesellschaft. Unpublished.
REEL 3, ITEM 178.

Schiffahrtrecht (a collection of keywords only). 1926 (?). 12 pp. Archiv der Eugen Rosenstock-Huessy Gesellschaft. Unpublished.
REEL 3, ITEM 182.

The Tribes of the Spirit. Manchester College Upton Lectures. Four Lectures on the Ethical Problem of Modern Europe. [Thursday, November 4th: The Need of Simplification; Friday, November 5th: Education and Labour; Thursday, November 11th: Theology and Economics; Friday, November 12th: The Temporal and Eternal.] I. Why Europe Does Not Matter, 25 pp.; II. A New Approach of the Temporal, 23 pp. November 1926, 48 pp., typescript by L. van der Molen, 14 pp. The second and third lectures, in the papers called "Adult Education—A Contradiction in Terms" and "The Economist's Answer to Religion," have not been preserved. In addition, there are 46 pp. of preparational papers, not numbered, of which 40 pp. have been typed by L. van der Molen, 12 pp. Archiv der Eugen Rosenstock-Huessy Gesellschaft. Unpublished.
REEL 3, ITEM 183.

Vom Industrierecht. Rechtssystematische Fragen. Festgabe für Xaver Gretener (Berlin: H. Sack, 1926), 183 pp.
REEL 3, ITEM 173.

"Vom Neuland zwischen Pädagogik und Demagogik," Der Kunstwart 40 (1926–1927): 357–365.
REEL 3, ITEM 197.

Wirkungen der europäischen Krise auf England. 1926. 2 pp. (outline of a book). Archiv der Eugen Rosenstock-Huessy Gesellschaft. Unpublished.
REEL 3, ITEM 184.

1927

"Alphons Maria Ratisbonne, ein neuer Bruder im Herrn, von Theodor de Bussières. Mit einer Einleitung über Nationalsozialismus und Antisemitismus von P. Alois Mager, O.pp.B." (Munich and Rome, 1926), *Una Sancta* 3, Ein Ruf an die Christenheit, ed. Alfred von Martin (1927): 490–491.
REEL 3, ITEM 185.

"Augustinus und Thomas in ihrer Bedeutung für das Denken unserer Zeit," *Una Sancta* 3, Heft 1, Ein Ruf an die Christenheit, ed. Alfred von Martin (1927): 14–22. {Also in *Das Alter der Kirche* (1928), pp. 655–673 ("Augustin und Thomas in ihrer Wirkung auf unser Denken," expanded).}
SEE (1928) DAS ALTE DER KIRCHE.

Die Deutsche Schule für Volksforschung und Erwachsenenbildung. *Das erste Jahr*, ed. the Hohenrodter Bund: Theodor Bäuerle, Robert von Erdberg, Wilhelm Flitner, Walter Hoffmann, Eugen Rosenstock (Stuttgart: Verlag Silberburg GmbH, 1927), 141 pp.
NOT MICROFILMED.

Deutsche Schule für Volksforschung und Erwachsenenbilding sucht zehn Ingenieure. Entwurf eines Vorschlags an die Industriellen zur Gründung des neuen Ausbildungsinstituts (=Deutsche Schule). 1927. 3 pp.; typescript by L. van der Molen, 2 pp. Archiv der Eugen Rosenstock-Huessy Gesellschaft. Unpublished.
SEE REEL 4, ITEM 218.

"Deutscher Stamm, deutsches Volk, deutsches Reich, deutsche Nation." Vortragsreihe 1–10. 1927 (ca.). 8 pp. Archiv der Eugen Rosenstock-Huessy Gesellschaft. Unpublished.
REEL 3, ITEM 194.

"Das dritte Tor noch offen!" 2. Beiblatt des *8 Uhr-Abendblatt* 301 (Berlin), December 24, 1927.
NOT MICROFILMED.

"Die geistige Struktur des deutschen Ostens," *Abendland* 3, Deutsche Monatshefte für europäische Kultur, Politik und Wissenschaft (1927): 75–78.
REEL 3, ITEM 186.

"Gesetz oder Sakrament? Zur Ehediskussion," *Eckart. Blätter für evangelische Geisteskultur* 3 (Berlin: 1927): 249–251. {= Revised version of *Das Alter der Kirche,* (1928), pp. 927–936 ("Die Ehe—Gesetz oder Sakrament?"). See "Gesetz oder Sakrament?" (1925).}
REEL 3, ITEM 187.

"Hochschule und Arbeitslager," *Die gelbe Zeitung* Heft 5–6, Bericht und Botschaft der Bündischen Jugend Deutschlands (Christmas 1927): 81–84. {= "Hochschule und Arbeitslager," *Schlesiche Hochschulblätter* (1927); = "Hochschule und Arbeitslager," *Die Volksgruppe* (1928).}
REEL 3, ITEM 188.

"Hochschule und Arbeitslager," *Schlesiche Hochschulblätter* 2, Amtliches Mitteilungsblatt (June 1927): 17–19. {= "Hochschule und Arbeitslager," *Die gelbe Zeitung* (1927); = "Hochschule und Arbeitslager," *Die Volksgruppe* (1928).}
REEL 3, ITEM 189.

Komburghefte. Protokolle der Vorträge in der Ersten Akademie der Deutschen Schule für Volksforschung und Erwachsenenbildung, Comburg bei Schwäbisch Hall. Gruppe I, "Bildung und Vergehen der europäischen Volkscharaktere, insbesondere in Italien, Deutschland, England, Frankreich und Russland" (Cf. *Die Deutsche Schule für Volksforschung und Erwachsenenbildung* (1927), pp. 56–59), March 14 – April 9, 1927. 30 pp. Pp. 1–17 with Roman numerals, pp. 18–26 not numbered, pp. 28–30 conventionally numbered. One-page synopsis in Rosenstock's handwriting at the beginning. Archiv der Eugen Rosenstock-Huessy Gesellschaft. Unpublished.
REEL 3, ITEM 195.

"Lehrer oder Führer? Zur Polychronie des Menschen," *Die Kreatur* 1, Heft 1, ed. Martin Buber, Joseph Wittig, and Victor von Weizsäcker (Berlin: Verlag Lambert Schneider, 1926–1927; reprint, Nendeln, Liechtenstein: Kraus Reprint, 1969): 52–68. {= *Im Kampf* (1926), pp. 219–224; *Die Sprache des Menschengeschlechts,* Bd. 2 (1964), pp. 136–156 ("Die Sprachalter").}
SEE (1926) IM KAMPF OR (1964) DIE SPRACHE DES MENSCHENGESCHLECHTS.

"Notiz über sich selbst," *Ein neuer Weg* (L. Voggenreiter, 1927): 141–142. REEL 3, ITEM 190.

"Die Polychronie des Volks," *Die Kreatur* 1, Heft 4, ed. Martin Buber, Joseph Wittig, and Victor von Weizsäcker (Berlin: Verlag Lambert Schneider, 1926–1927; reprint, Nendeln, Liechtenstein: Kraus Reprint, 1969): 409–425. {Also in *Die Sprache des Menschengeschlechts,* Bd. 2 (1964), pp. 156–175 ("Die Polyphonie des Volks").}
SEE (1964) DIE SPRACHE DES MENSCHENGESCHLECHTS.

"Religionsphilosophie der Gesellschaft," *Jahresberichte der schlesischen Gesellschaft für vaterländische Cultur* 100 (1927): 106–108. REEL 14, ITEM 619.

Review: Nikolaus Berdjajews *Das neue Mittelalter. Betrachtungen über das Schicksal Russlands und Europas* (Darmstadt, 1927). Die Ostkirche Sonderheft der Vierteljahresschrift *Una Sancta,* ed. Nicolas von Arseniew and Alfred von Martin, *Una Sancta* 3, Ein Ruf an die Christenheit, ed. Alfred von Martin (1927): 125–128. REEL 3, ITEM 191.

"Universität und Technische Hochschule," *Breslauer Hochschul-Rundschau* 18, Nr. 1 (January 1927): 1–3. {= "Die Freizeit des Akademikers," *Freizeitgestaltung* (1927), revised.} REEL 3, ITEM 192.

"Die Verarmung des Typs. Gemeinsamkeiten und Gegensätze der Wesensart," *Der Weisse Ritter* 7 (1927): 142–145. {= "Die Verarmung des Typs," *Ein neuer Weg* (1927). See "The Impoverishment of the Type," *Britain and Germany* (1928).}
SEE (1927) "DIE VERARMUNG DES TYPS."

"Die Verarmung des Typs. Gemeinsamkeiten und Gegensätze der Wesensart," *Ein neuer Weg* (L. Voggenreiter, 1927): 46–49. {= "Die Verarmung des Typs," *Der Weisse Ritter* (1927). See "The Impoverishment of the Type," *Britain and Germany* (1928).} REEL 3, ITEM 193.

Der Weg Europas nach dem Krieg. 1927. 1 p. (notes for a lecture in Bulgaria); typescript by L. van der Molen, 1 p. Archiv der Eugen Rosenstock-Huessy Gesellschaft. Unpublished. REEL 3, ITEM 196.

1928

Das Alter der Kirche. Kapitel und Akten. 3 Bände. Co-author, Joseph Wittig (Berlin: Verlag Lambert Schneider, 1927–1928), Bd. 1 and 2, 977 pp.; Bd. 3, 273 pp.
REEL 4, ITEM 198.

"Ansprache bei der Beerdigung des Vaters Theodor Rosenstock." May 16, 1928. 4 pp. Archiv der Eugen Rosenstock-Huessy Gesellschaft. Unpublished.
REEL 4, ITEM 199.

Arbeitsdienstpflicht in Bulgarien. 1928. 2 pp. (incomplete). Archiv der Eugen Rosenstock-Huessy Gesellschaft. Unpublished.
REEL 4, ITEM 209.

"Das Arbeitslager für Jungarbeiter, Jungbauern und Jungakademiker in Löwenberg vom 14.–31. März 1928," *Freie Volksbildung* (Neue Folge des *Archivs für Erwachsenenbildung)* 3 (1928): 217–224.
REEL 4, ITEM 200.

Arbeitsrecht. Lectures, winter semester, November 6, 1928 – January 31, 1929; 22 classes, 186 pp. (each lecture separately numbered). Four Wells. Unpublished.
REEL 4, ITEM 210.

Arbeitswissenschaft. [I. Inhalt. II. Orte, seine Feinde und seine Beziehungen. Stichwörter zu einer Vortragsreihe.] 1927/1928 (ca.). 3 pp.; typescript by L. van der Molen, 2 pp. Archiv der Eugen Rosenstock-Huessy Gesellschaft. Unpublished.
REEL 4, ITEM 211.

Das europäische Sechstagewerk. Vorwort zu dem im Hohenrodter Bund geplanten Lehrbuch der *Europäischen Revolutionen.* 1928. 10 pp. Archiv der Eugen Rosenstock-Huessy Gesellschaft. Unpublished.
REEL 4, ITEM 213.

"Hochschule und Arbeitslager," *Mitteilungen des Verbandes der deutschen Hochschulen* 8 (1928): 101–105.
REEL 4, ITEM 201.

"Hochschule und Arbeitslager. Zum Arbeitslager der ostelbischen Freischaren Ostern 1927," *Die Volksgruppe* Heft 1, Beiträge zum schlesischen Volksbildungswerk (1928): 6–7. {= "Hochschule und Arbeitslager," *Die gelbe Zeitung* (1927); = "Hochschule und Arbeitslager," *Schlesiche Hochschulblätter* (1927).}
REEL 4, ITEM 201.

"Idealistisches und namentliches Denken," *Archiv für Rechtsphilosophie*, Bd. 21 (1927–1928): 272–274. {= "Idealistisches und namentliches Denken," *Archiv für Rechts- und Wirtschaftsphilosophie* (1928).}
SEE (1928) "IDEALISTISCHES UND NAMENTLICHES DENKEN."

"Idealistisches und namentliches Denken," *Archiv für Rechts- und Wirtschaftsphilosophie*, Bd. 21 (1927–1928): 420–422. {= "Idealistisches und namentliches Denken," *Archiv für Rechtsphilosophie* (1928), expanded.}
REEL 4, ITEM 202.

"The Impoverishment of the Type," *Britain and Germany*, eds. Rolf Gardiner and Heinz Rocholl (William and Norgate, Ltd., 1928): 111–120. {See "Die Verarmung des Typs," *Der Weisse Ritter* (1927); "Die Verarmung des Typs," *Ein neuer Weg* (1927).}
REEL 4, ITEM 203.

"Kirche und Arbeit—Eine Rede," *Die Kreatur* 2, eds. Martin Buber, Joseph Wittig, and Victor von Weizsäcker (Berlin: Verlag Lambert Schneider, 1927–1928; reprint, Nendeln, Liechtenstein: Kraus Reprint, 1969): 158–180.
REEL 4, ITEM 204.

"Leben und Arbeit," *Eine Aussprache zwischen evangelischen Männern und Frauen auf dem 25. kirchlich-sozialen Kongress in Düsseldorf 1927* (A. Deichert, 1928): 36–47.
REEL 4, ITEM 205.

"Leben und Arbeit," *Zeitwende* 4, Erste Hälfte, Kultur, Theologie, Politik (January – June 1928): 341–353. An elaboration of an address at a conference on church and society in Dusseldorf. {Also in *Politische Reden* (1929), pp. 42–55.}
REEL 4, ITEM 205.

Die Lebensalter der Wirtschaft. Vorlesungsnachschriften und Protokolle des 1. Arbeitslagers für Arbeiter, Bauern und Studenten, Löwenberg. March 17–30, 1928: [March 17 – Einleitung; March 19 – Die Entstehung des Bauerntums; March 20 – Bauer, Ritter, Handwerker; March 21 – Die Handwerker; March 22 – Der Arbeiter; March 23 – Dorf, Stadt, Staat; March 24 – Arbeiter, Gruppe (mit Diskussion); March 30 – Führung, Persönlichkeit, Autorität.] 35 pp. Archiv der Eugen Rosenstock-Huessy Gesellschaft. Unpublished.
REEL 4, ITEM 214.

"Die Namen Deutsch und Völkisch," *Die Schildgenossen* 8 (1928): 536–543.
REEL 4, ITEM 206.

Pfarrer und Laie in der Kirchenpolitik. Protokoll eines Vortrags im C.S.V.-Kreis Breslau. February 11, 1928. 10 pp. Archiv der Eugen Rosenstock-Huessy Gesellschaft. Unpublished.
REEL 4, ITEM 217.

Review: M. Värtings *Die Macht der Massen* (Berlin-Friedenau: Verlag Dr. M. Pfeiffer, 1928), 290 pp. I. Band des Gesamtwerkes. 9 pp. Archiv der Eugen Rosenstock-Huessy Gesellschaft. {= "Menschenmacht und Massenmacht." *Zeitwende* (1930).} Unpublished.
REEL 4, ITEM 212; SEE (1930) "MENSCHENMACHT UND MASSENMACHT."

"Symbol und Sitte als Lebensmacht," *Zeitschrift für evangelische Pädagogik* 3, Heft 4 (1928): 145–155. An abridged and garbled stenograph from a lecture delivered at the fifth Religious Pedagogy Conference in Magdeburg, April 11, 1928. {See "Symbol und Sitte als Lebensmächte," *Die Erziehung* (1929).}
SEE REEL 5, ITEM 229.

Unser Volksname Deutsch und die Aufhebung des Herzogtums Bayern (Breslau: Korn, 1928), 66 pp. Also published as an offprint. {= *Der Volksname Deutsch,* Wege der Forschung (1970), pp. 32–102; "Unser Volksname Deutsch," *Mitteilungen der Schlesischen Gesellschaft fur Volkskunde* (1929): 1–66.}
SEE (1929) "UNSER VOLKSNAME DEUTSCH."

"Volksbildung in der Universität," *Rhein-Mainische Volkszeitung,* August 13, 1928. {= "Volksbildung in der Universität," *Blätter der Volkshochschule Breslau* (1929).}
SEE (1929) "VOLKSBILDUNG IN DER UNIVERSITÄT."

Volkskirche und Volkssiedlung. 1928–1929 (ca.). 1 p. (4 theses). Archiv der Eugen Rosenstock-Huessy Gesellschaft. Unpublished.
REEL 4, ITEM 215.

Was geht die Industrie die Erwachsenenbildung an? 1928 (?). 3 pp., from pp. 14–16. This appears to be a part of a brochure (of the Hohenrodter Bund?) with the title: "??aldienst: Die interessante Seite. Erwachsenenbildung—eine Forderung unserer Zeit." Archiv der Eugen Rosenstock-Huessy Gesellschaft. Unpublished.
REEL 4, ITEM 216.

"Ein Wort von Augustin und eins von Goethe," *Aus unbekannten Schriften,* Festgabe für Martin Buber zum 50. Geburtstag (Berlin: Verlag Lambert Schneider, 1928): 53–57.
REEL 4, ITEM 208.

1929

"A magánjog néhány új alapfogalmáról," *Kereskedelmi Jog, Hiteljogi Es Gazdaságpolitikai Folyóirat* (Budapest, November 1, 1929): 245–247, (December 1, 1929): 269–271. {= "Über einige neue Grundbegriffe," *Beiträge zum Wirtschaftsrecht* (1931). Cf. "Über einige neue Grundbegriffe," unpublished item (1929).}
REEL 4, ITEM 220.

"Aphorismus und Kurztitel," *Eckart* 5, Blätter für evangelische Geisteskultur (Berlin, 1929): 197–199. {= "Aphorismen über den Aphorismus," *Mitteilungsblatt der Eugen Rosenstock-Huessy Gesellschaft* (1982).}
REEL 4, ITEM 220A.

Der beschränkte Untertanenverstand, *Die Volkswacht,* Breslau (Eingesandt zur Verfassungsfeier der Universität am 13. Juli gegen einen Artikel "Die Universität rebelliert"). July 1929. 2 pp. Archiv der Eugen Rosenstock-Huessy Gesellschaft.
REEL 5, ITEM 232.

"Dienstpflicht?" *Deutsche Rundschau* 119 (April–May–June 1929): 1–15.
REEL 4, ITEM 221.

Das englische Budget. With a table of contents for the chapter on England. 1929. 11 pp. (pp. 1–9b). Archiv der Eugen Rosenstock-Huessy Gesellschaft. {Preparatory work for *Die Europäischen Revolutionen* (1931), pp. 274–278.} Unpublished.
REEL 5, ITEM 233.

Enttäuschte Wirtschaft. Sketch for the lecture in Bochum. October 30, 1929. 5 pp. Archiv der Eugen Rosenstock-Huessy Gesellschaft. Unpublished.
REEL 5, ITEM 234.

Erwachsenenbildung und Betriebspolitik. Vortrag für das Forschungsinstitut für Sozialwissenschaften. February 27, 1929. 31 pp. Archiv der Eugen Rosenstock-Huessy Gesellschaft. {= "Erwachsenenbildung und Betriebspolitik," *Sozialrechtliches Jahrbuch* (1930).} Unpublished.
REEL 5, ITEM 235.

Erwachsenenbildung und Schlesisches Arbeitslager. 1929. 11 pp. An untitled work. Beginning reads: "Erwachsenenbildung? Wir sind der allgemeinen Bildung etwas müde..." Archiv der Eugen Rosenstock-Huessy Gesellschaft. {= "Erwachsenenbildung und Schlesisches Arbeitslager," *Schlesische Monatshefte* (1929).} Unpublished.
SEE (1929) "ERWACHSENENBILDUNG UND SCHLESISCHES ARBEITSLAGER."

"Erwachsenenbildung und schlesisches Arbeitslager," *Schlesische Monatshefte,* Heft 3 (March 1929): 112–117.
REEL 4, ITEM 222.

"Die Freizeit des Akademikers," *Freizeitgestaltung, Grundsätze und Erfahrungen zur Erziehung berufsgebundener Menschen,* ed Fritz Klatt (1929): 17–26. {= "Universität und Technische Hochschule," *Breslauer Hochschul-Rundschau,* revised.}
REEL 4, ITEM 223, WITH PP. 25–26 REVERSED.

Die Grenzen des Sozialpolitikers. Review of Franz Müller's book, *Franz Hitze und sein Werk.* 1929. 6 pp. Archiv der Eugen Rosenstock-Huessy Gesellschaft. Unpublished.
REEL 5, ITEM 236.

Interview, on *Werkstattaussiedlung,* *Freizeitgestaltung,* ed. Fritz Klatt (1929): 151–156 {Cf. *Werkstattaussiedlung* (1922).}
REEL 4, ITEM 223.

Jugend und Alter. Notes on and excerpts from the lecture in Cologne. 1929. 1 + 9 pp. Archiv der Eugen Rosenstock-Huessy Gesellschaft. {See "Jugend und Alter," *Kölner Blätter für Berufserziehung* (1929), and unpublished item, "Jugend und Alter," (1930).} Unpublished.
SEE REEL 4, ITEM 223A.

Jugend und Alter in der modernen Gesellschaft. 1929. 40 pp. Archiv der Eugen Rosenstock-Huessy Gesellschaft. {Forerunner of "Jugend und Alter in der modernen Gesellschaft," *Kölner Blätter für Berufserziehung,* with revisions, additions, and parts omitted, 1929.} Unpublished.
SEE REEL 4, ITEM 223A.

"Jugend und Alter in der modernen Gesellschaft," *Kölner Blätter für Berufserziehung* 5 (1929): 147–161.
REEL 4, ITEM 223A.

"Kirche und Beruf," *Soziale Praxis* 38 (1929): 468–470.
REEL 4, ITEM 224.

Notiz über "Die Ökonomisierung einiger Privatrechtsbegriffe grundlegender Art." 1929. 1 p. Archiv der Eugen Rosenstock-Huessy Gesellschaft. {Relates to "A magánjog néhány új alapfogalmáról," *Kerskedelmi Jog, Hiteljogi Es, Gazdaságpolitikai Folyóirat* (1929) and "Über einige neue Grundbegriffe," *Beiträge zum Wirtschaftsrecht* (1931).} Unpublished.
SEE REEL 14, ITEM 620.

Politische Reden—Vierklang aus Volk, Gesellschaft, Staat und Kirche (Berlin: Verlag Lambert Schneider, 1929), 55 pp.
REEL 4, ITEM 219.

"Die Presse als Träger und Erzieher der öffentlichen Meinung." Spätsommerkurs im Volkshochschulheim Prerow unter Leitung von Fritz Klatt. August 25 – September 11, 1929. Class notes, 14 pp.; typescript by L. van der Molen, 3 pp. Archiv der Eugen Rosenstock-Huessy Gesellschaft. Unpublished.
REEL 5, ITEM 237.

"Protestantismus und Seelenführung," *Protestantismus als Kritik und Gestaltung*, ed. Paul Tillich. Zweites Buch des Kairos-Kreises (Otto Reichl Verlag, 1929): 219–260. {Partially reprinted as "Protestantismus und Seelenführung," *Deutsches Pfarrerblatt* (1964): 224–228, 248–253.}
REEL 4, ITEM 225.

Recht und Wirtschaft. Eigenbericht der Tagung der Akademie gemeinnütziger Wissenschaften, Abteilung für Erziehungswissenschaften und Jugendkunde. Thema: Wirtschaft und Bildung. Erfurt, November 11 – 18, 1929. 3 pp. Archiv der Eugen Rosenstock-Huessy Gesellschaft. Unpublished.
REEL 5, ITEM 238.

Review: Karl Heldmanns *Das Kaisertum Karls des Grossen.* Theorien und Wirklichkeit. Quellen zur Verfassungsgeschichte des deutschen Reiches in Mittelalter und Neuzeit (Weimar, 1928), *Zeitschrift der Savigny Stiftung für Rechtsgeschichte* 49, Germanistische Abteilung (Weimar: Verlag Hermann Böhlaus Nachfolger, 1929): 509–524.
REEL 4, ITEM 226.

"Die Schranke des Sozialpolitikers," *Zeitwende* 5, Kultur, Theologie, Politik (1929): 97–107. {Also appeared as a reprint.}
REEL 5, ITEM 227.

"Der Sozialismus als Antithese," *Zeitwende* 5, Kultur, Theologie, Politik (1929): 193–203.
REEL 5, ITEM 228.

Soziologie. 1929–1930 (ca.). Notes for 24 lectures, 12 pp. (not numbered). Archiv der Eugen Rosenstock-Huessy Gesellschaft. Unpublished.
REEL 5, ITEM 239.

Soziologie, 1. und 4. Stunde. (Soziologie ist das Wissen, das der Funktionär braucht). 1929–1930 (ca.). 4 pp. Archiv der Eugen Rosenstock-Huessy Gesellschaft. Unpublished.
REEL 5, ITEM 239.

"Symbol und Sitte als Lebenmächte," *Die Erziehung* 4, Monatsschrift für den Zusammenhang von Kultur und Erziehung in Wissenschaft und Leben (1929): 341–361. {See "Symbol und Sitte als Lebensmacht," *Zeitschrift für evangelische Pädagogik* (1928).}
REEL 5, ITEM 229.

Über einige neue Grundbegriffe des Privatrechts. Originalvorlesung. 1929. 17 pp. Archiv der Eugen Rosenstock-Huessy Gesellschaft. {= "A magánjog néhány új alapfogalmáról," *Kerskedelmi Jog, Hiteljogi Es, Gazdaságpolitikai Folyóirat* (1929) and "Über einige neue Grundbegriffe," *Beiträge zum Wirtschaftsrecht* (1931).} Unpublished.
REEL 14, ITEM 620.

"Die ungeschriebene Verfassung," *Akademische Rundschau* 1, Nr. 2, Nachrichtenblatt für die Studierenden der schlesischen Hochschulen, Breslau (1929): 3–12. {Appeared as a reprint. Also in *Politische Reden* (1929), pp. 32–41.}
SEE (1929) POLITISCHE REDEN.

Die ungeschriebene Verfassung. Eine Rede zum 11 August 1928. (Breslau: Breslauer Akademischer Verlag, 1929), 13 pp. {= "Die ungeschriebene Verfassung," *Akademische Rundschau* (1929): 3–12. Also in *Politische Reden* (1929), pp. 32–41.}
REEL 4, ITEM 219A.

"Unser Volksname Deutsch und die Aufhebung des Herzogtums Bayern," *Mitteilungen der Schlesischen Gesellschaft für Volkskunde* 29 (1929): 1–66. {= *Unser Volksname Deutsch* (1928).}
REEL 5, ITEM 230.

"Volksbildung in der Universität," *Blätter der Volkshochschule Breslau* 8, Heft 9/11 (1929/1930): 162–166. {= "Volksbildung in der Universität," *Rhein-Mainische Volkszeitung* (1928).}
REEL 4, ITEM 207.

Vom anderen Ende. (Zur Mission der Kirche im 3. Jahrtausend). 1929 (ca.). 3 pp. Four Wells. {Cf. Die Kirche am Ende der Welt (1930). = *Die Sprache des Menschengeschlechts,* Bd. 1 (1963), pp. 205–220 ("Die Lust am Lästern").} Unpublished.
REEL 3, ITEM 168.

"Vom Staat zum Stamm," *Der Kunstwart* 42 (1929): 377–382.
REEL 5, ITEM 231, WITH P. 378 MISSING.

1930

Die Arbeitslager innerhalb der Erwachsenenbildung (Stuttgart: Verlag Silberberg, 1930), 20 pp. {Reprint of "Die Arbeitslager," *Jahrbuch der Erwachsensenbildung* (1930).}
REEL 5, ITEM 240.

"Die Arbeitslager innerhalb der Erwachsenenbildung," *Jahrbuch der Erwachsenenbildung* 2, Herausgegeben von der Deutschen Schule für Volksforschung und Erwachsenenbildung (Stuttgart, 1930): 28–47. {= *Die Arbeitslager* (1930).}
SEE (1930) DIE ARBEITSLAGER.

Bericht über das dritte schlesische Arbeitslager für Arbeiter, Bauern und Studenten. Berater für Volkshochschulen an der Universität Breslau. July 1930. 19 pp. Archiv der Eugen Rosenstock-Huessy Gesellschaft. [1. Literatur; 2. Bedeutung des dritten Arbeitslagers; 3. Zusammensetzung; 4. Tagesverlauf; 5. Geistige Arbeit; 6. Sondertagung; 7. Fortwirkung; 8. Finanzen; 9. Übertragung in andere Landschaften.] Unpublished.
REEL 5, ITEM 250.

"Deutsche Nation und deutsche Universität. Zur intensiven Seite der Hochschulreform," *Deutsche Rundschau* 225 (October–November–December 1930): 215–225.
REEL 5, ITEM 240A.

"Dringe ein Dringe ein Zion dringe ein in Gott." Andacht. Hörsaal XV der Universität. July 1930. 3 pp. Archiv der Eugen Rosenstock-Huessy Gesellschaft. Typescript by L. van der Molen, 1 p.
REEL 5, ITEM 241.

Erwachsenenbildung in den deutschen Landen. Rundfunkvortrag. June 28, 1930. 12 pp. (p. 8 missing, p. 11 handwritten and, like p. 12, not numbered). Archiv der Eugen Rosenstock-Huessy Gesellschaft. {Translated in part in "Opvoeding der volwassenen in de Duitsche Gewesten," *Jong Dietsland* (1930).}
REEL 5, ITEM 251.

"Erwachsenenbildung und Betriebspolitik," *Sozialrechtliches Jahrbuch* 1 (1930): 135–150.
REEL 5, ITEM 242.

"Erwiderung (auf Dr. Karl Heldmanns Erwiderung S. 625–659)," *Zeitschrift der Savigny Stiftung für Rechtsgeschichte* 31, Germanistische Abteilung (Weimar: Verlag Hermann Böhlaus Nachfolger, 1930): 659–667.
SEE REEL 4, ITEM 226.

"Die Gefangenschaft des Volkes," *Die Kreatur* 3, eds. Martin Buber, Joseph Wittig, and Victor von Weizsäcker (Berlin: Verlag Lambert Schneider, 1929–1930; reprint, Nendeln, Liechtenstein: Kraus Reprint, 1969): 61–68. {Also in *Politische Reden* (1929), pp. 9–15.}
SEE (1929) POLITISCHE REDEN.

Die Heimkehr der Europäer. 1930 (ca.). 5 pp. Completion of the incomplete handwritten manuscripts of 4 and 6 pp. Archiv der Eugen Rosenstock-Huessy Gesellschaft. {Planned foreword to *Die Europäischen Revolutionen* (1931).} Unpublished.
REEL 5, ITEM 252.

"Die Kirche am Ende der Welt," *Credo Ecclesiam*. Festgabe zum 70. Geburtstag D. Wilhelm Zöllners. Im Auftrage des Kampfbundes christlicher Arbeiter und in Verbindung mit Johannes Müller-Schwefe, ed. Hans Ehrenberg (Gütersloh: C. von Bertelsmann, 1930): 161–175. {Also in *Die Sprache des Menschengeschlechts*, Bd. 1 (1963), pp. 205–220 ("Die Lust am Lästern").}
REEL 5, ITEM 243.

"Die Kirche und die Völker. Abriss und Überblick," *Credo Ecclesiam* (1930): 285–295. {See "Die Kirche am Ende der Welt," *Credo Ecclesiam* (1930).}
REEL 5, ITEM 244.

"Menschenmacht und Massenmacht," *Zeitwende* 6, Kultur, Theologie, Politik (January – June 1930): 77–81. {Also appeared as a reprint.}
REEL 5, ITEM 245.

"Opvoeding der volwassenen in de Duitsche Gewesten," *Jong Dietsland, Algemeen Weekblad voor Katholiek Vlaamsch-Nationaalleven* 4, Nr. 32 (Stekene, Belgium: 1930): 505–507. {= Unpublished item "Erwachsenenbildung in den deutschen Landen," in part, (1930).}
REEL 5, ITEM 246.

Das Recht und die rechtswissenschaftlichen Methoden. Rede an der Universität in Breslau. 1930 (??). 13 pp. Archiv der Eugen Rosenstock-Huessy Gesellschaft. Unpublished.
REEL 5, ITEM 253.

"Reverendissime!" Widmungsblatt, *Credo Ecclesiam* (1930). A translation into Dutch by L. van der Molen. {See "Die Kirche am Ende der Welt," *Credo Ecclesiam* (1930).}
REEL 5, ITEM 247.

"Die rückwärts gelebte Zeit. Unsere Erfahrungen von 1918 bis 1928," *Die Kreatur* 3, eds. Martin Buber, Joseph Wittig, and Victor von Weizsäcker (Berlin: Verlag Lambert Schneider, 1926–1927; reprint, Nendeln, Liechtenstein: Kraus Reprint, 1969): 101–117. {Also in *Die Sprache des Menschengeschlechts,* Bd. 2 (1964), pp. 178–197.}
SEE (1964) DIE SPRACHE DES MENSCHENGESCHLECHTS.

"The Social Function of Adult Education," *Bulletin of the World Association for Adult Education* 44 (London: 1930): 10–16.
REEL 5, ITEM 248.

Soziologie. 1930 (ca.). 15 pp. + 4 pp. [1. Universität Kampffeld; 2. Universal qua Singular; 3. Angriffe; 4. Haushalt; 5. Massstab; 6. Statistik; 7. Neuer Willensbegriff; 8. Ökonomie des Wissens.] Archiv der Eugen Rosenstock-Huessy Gesellschaft. {See unpublished items Soziologie, 1929–1930 (1929) and Soziologie 1. und 4. Stunde (1929).} Unpublished.
REEL 5, ITEM 254.

"Über 'Reich,' 'Staat' und 'Stadt' in Deutschland von 1230–1235. Bemerkungen zu Emil Franzel, *König Heinrich VII von Hohenstaufen.* Studium zur Geschichte des Staats in Deutschland, Prag 1929," *Mitteilungen des österreichischen Instituts für Geschichtsforschung* (1930): 401–416.
REEL 5, ITEM 249.

Und dreimal: Die Nation. 1930. 2 outlines of 5 and 18 pp. each (not numbered). Several pages are missing. Typescript by L. van der Molen, 4 pp. Archiv der Eugen Rosenstock-Huessy Gesellschaft. Unpublished.
REEL 5, ITEM 255.

Wandlungen im Recht. Class notes on a lecture by Prof. Dr. Rosenstock, Breslau. September 17, 1930, zu Hohenroth, 8th week. 6 pp. (with notes for the talk). Archiv der Eugen Rosenstock-Huessy Gesellschaft. Unpublished.
REEL 5, ITEM 256.

1931

Das Arbeitslager. Berichte aus Schlesien von Arbeitern, Bauern, Studenten, eds. Eugen Rosenstock and Carl Dietrich von Trotha (Jena: Eugen Diederichs, 1931), 160 pp. [Pp. 87–116, "Das Dritte Lager," and "Stimmen" are condensed and reprinted in: *Bildungsarbeit mit Erwachsenen. Handbuch für selbstbestimmtes Lernen*, eds. Klaus Bergmann and Günther Frank (Reinbeck bei Hamburg: Rowohlt Taschenbuch Verlag GmbH, March 1977), pp. 44–60.] {Polish translation, *Obozy Integracyjne Naślązku* (1993).}.
REEL 5, ITEM 257.

"Arbeitslager als Sonntag," an address recorded in a report by cand. phil. W. Waidelich in "Tübinger Treffen der Teilnehmer des Arbeitslagers Münsingen vom Tübinger stud. Heimatsdienst," *Würtembergische Hochschulzeitung* 35 (1931): 4–5. {Also in *Stimmstein* 2 (1988): 56–60.}
REEL 5, ITEM 260.

Bemerkungen zu Emil Brunner. Concerning the sketch of his 1937 book, *Der Mensch im Widerspruch*. Zürich. With a reproaching letter of July 23, 1937 of 2 pp. March 15, 1931. 10 pp. Four Wells. [1. Sprache; 2. Dogma; 3. Vergessen; 4. Atheismus; 5. 'Und'; 6. Zerstörung des allgemeinen Priestertums: Materie-Mensch, der getretene Tritt, der Erdenkloss.] Unpublished.
REEL 5, ITEM 263.

"Das Dritte Reich und die Sturmvögel des Nationalsozialismus," *Hochland* 28, Bd. 2, Monatsschrift für alle Gebiete des Wissens, der Literatur und Kunst, ed. Karl Muth (June 9, 1931): 193–211. Written under the psuedonym "Ludwig Stahl." {Also in *Tumult* 20 (1995): 16–36.}
REEL 5, ITEM 261.

Erwiderung. Zu Dr. Adolf Scheffbuch über die Preissenkung in: *Volksdienst.* Gezeichnet von Jak. Herbert. February 2, 1931. 2 pp. Archiv der Eugen Rosenstock-Huessy Gesellschaft.
REEL 5, ITEM 264.

Die Europäischen Revolutionen. Volkscharaktere und Staatenbildung (Jena: Eugen Diederichs Verlag, 1931), iv + 554 pp. 2 Zeittafeln. {= *Die Europäischen Revolutionen und der Charakter der Nationen*, 2d ed. (revised), 1951, and *Die Europäischen Revolutionen und der Charakter der Nationen* (revision of previous title), 1961. A different version of this same work is *Out of Revolution: Autobiography of Western Man.*}
REEL 5, ITEM 258.

"Grundsätze über eine Bildungsstätte für erwachsene Arbeiter. Denkschrift, September 1920," *Die Akademie der Arbeit an der Universität Frankfurt a.M., 1921–1931. Zu ihrem zehnjährigen Bestehen im Auftrag des Dozenten-Kollegiums,* ed. Ernst Michel (1931): 31–37. {Also in *Im Kampf* (1926), pp. 92–98; in *Zur Geschichte der Arbeiterbildung* (1968): 85–90, abridged}.
SEE (1926) IM KAMPF.

Der Kampf zwischen Stadt und Land im 17. Jahrhundert. 1931 (?). 13 pp. Archiv der Eugen Rosenstock-Huessy Gesellschaft. Unpublished.
REEL 5, ITEM 265.

Revolution als politischer Begriff in der Neuzeit (Breslau: M. & H. Marcus, 1931), 41 pp. {Reprint of "Revolution als politischer Begriff," *Abhandlungen der schlesischen Gesellschaft* (1931).}
REEL 5, ITEM 259.

"Revolution als politischer Begriff in der Neuzeit," *Abhandlungen der schlesischen Gesellschaft für vaterländische Kultur.* Geisteswissenschaftliche Reihe 5. Heft, Festgabe der Rechts- und Staatswissenschaftlichen Fakultät in Breslau für Paul Heilborn zum 70. Geburtstag, 6. Februar 1931. (M. & H. Marcus, 1931): 83–124. {= *Revolution als politischer Begriff in der Neuzeit* (1931).}
SEE REEL 5, ITEM 259.

Stadt und Land. Zur Breslauer Vortragswoche. July 26 – August 1, 1931. Pp. 8–9 of a radio newsletter. Archiv der Eugen Rosenstock-Huessy Gesellschaft.
REEL 5, ITEM 266.

"Die Stellung der Akademie unter den übrigen Schulen. Aus einem Brief des ersten Leiters," *Die Akademie der Arbeit in der Universität Frankfurt a.M.* (Frankfurt a.M.: 1931): 42–44. {Also in *Im Kampf* (1926), pp. 115–118; in *Zur Geschichte der Arbeiterbildung* (1968): pp. 90–92, abridged}.
SEE (1926) IM KAMPF.

"Über einige neue Grundbegriffe des Privatrechts. Nach einem Vortrag gehalten in der Peter Patmany-Universität in Budapest am 2. Oktober 1929," *Beiträge zum Wirtschaftsrecht* 1, Festschrift für E. Heymann, eds. F. Klausing, H. C. Nipperdey, A. Nussbaum (N. G. Elwertsche Verlagsbuchhandlung, G. Braun, 1931): 213–228. {= "A magánjog néhány új alpfogalmáról," *Kereskedelmi Jog, Hiteljogi Es Gazdaságpolitikai Folyóirat* (1929).}
SEE REEL 14, ITEM 620.

Die Umkehr in der Ausbildung. "Richtlinien zur Lebensgestaltung und Einrichtung der Ausbildung im Zeitalter der permanenten technischen Erneuerung mit seiner inhärenten Arbeitslosigkeit." Denkschrift. December 17, 1931. 3 pp. Akte Deutsche Schule Bd. 4, Bäuerle Archiv, Stuttgart, Germany. Unpublished.
REEL 5, ITEM 267.

Unser Weg. 1930–1931 (ca.). 7 pp. Archiv der Eugen Rosenstock-Huessy Gesellschaft. Unpublished.
REEL 5, ITEM 268.

Urwelt. Zum Ende der grossen europäischen Revolutionen. 1930–1931 (ca.). 7 pp. Four Wells. Unpublished.
REEL 5, ITEM 269.

"Weil der Geist weht, wo er will...Zur Frage Tillichs: Gibt es noch Universität?" *Frankfurter Zeitung und Handelsblatt* 909 (December 6, 1931): 6.
REEL 5, ITEM 262.

Der Zauber des Menschen. 1930–1931 (ca.). 7 pp. Archiv der Eugen Rosenstock-Huessy Gesellschaft. Unpublished.
REEL 5, ITEM 270; REEL 14, ITEM 617.

**"'Abschlag,' 'Abschlagen,' 'abschlägig,' 'abschläglich,' 'Abschlagung'," ***Deutsches Rechtswörterbuch, Wörterbuch der älteren deutschen Rechtssprache* 1, eds. Richard Schröder and Eberhard Freiherr von Künssberg (Weimar: Hermann Böhlaus Nachfolger, 1914–1932): 252–260. The installment number was published in 1919.
REEL 6, ITEM 273.

"Der Arbeitsdienst als Erzieher," *Die Jugendpflege* 9, Zentrale Monatschrift für Jugendpflege, Jugendbewegung und Leibesübungen (1932): 177–181.
REEL 6, ITEM 274.

Arbeitsdienst—Heeresdienst? (Jena: Eugen Diederichs Verlag, 1932), 80 pp.
REEL 6, ITEM 271.

"Arbeitslosenversicherung." Rechenexempel der Soziallasten und der Energieverbrauch im Deutschen Reich und die Überführung des Denkfehlers in der Lohnbuchhaltung. Besteuerung soll nicht nach Kopfteilen vorgehen. 1932. Manuscript of 4 pp. Title and typescript by L. van der Molen, 2 pp. Archiv der Eugen Rosenstock-Huessy Gesellschaft. Unpublished.
REEL 6, ITEM 283.

"Die Arbeitslosenversicherung vermehrt das Übel der Arbeitslosigkeit." 1932. Incomplete manuscript of 6 pp. Title (taken from the first sentence) and typescript by L. van der Molen, 2 pp. Archiv der Eugen Rosenstock-Huessy Gesellschaft {See unpublished item "Arbeitslosenversicherung" (1932). Preliminary study for unpublished items "Sozialaristokratie und Arbeitslosigkeit" (1932) and "Arbeitskraft ohne gestern und morgen" (1933).} Unpublished.
REEL 6, ITEM 284.

"Aus der Geschichte des Arbeitsdienstes," Eine Unterredung mit Prof. Dr. Eugen Rosenstock-Huessy (Breslau) von Gerhard Sappok, *Neues Studententum* 12, Heft 3–4, Zeitschrift des Hochlandverbandes (1932–1933): 2–5.
REEL 6, ITEM 274A.

Denkschrift der Deutschen Schule für Volksforschung und Erwachsenenbildung über die Bedeutung sozialpädagogischer Gesichtspunkte und die Führerbildung beim Freiwilligen Arbeitsdienst. October 20, 1932. *Akte Deutsche Schule* Band 4, Bäuerle Archiv, Stuttgart, Germany. Unpublished.
NOT MICROFILMED.

Denkschrift zur Schliessung der Akademie für Kunst und Kunstgewerbe zu Breslau. January 15, 1932. Breslau, Akademie für Kunst und Kunstgewerbe. 2 pp. Archiv der Eugen Rosenstock-Huessy Gesellschaft. Unpublished.
REEL 6, ITEM 285.

"Les Étudiants et l'université au service de la société. Rôle social de l'université," *I.S.S. Annals, Annales universitaires, Annalen des Weltstudentenwerke* 3 (1932): 60–63. {= "Sozialer Dienst," *I.S.S. Annals* (1932); "Student and University Service," *I.S.S. Annals* (1932).}
REEL 6, ITEM 278.

Führer und Funktionär oder die radikale Wendung der Soziologie. Rede in Stuttgart. 1932. 18 pp. Archiv der Eugen Rosenstock-Huessy Gesellschaft. Unpublished.
REEL 6, ITEM 286.

Die Funktion des Apostel Paulus und die Sendung der Deutschen. (Sketch) 3 pp. Typescript by L. van der Molen. 2 pp., ca. 1932. Four Wells. Unpublished.
REEL 6, ITEM 280A.

"Die Geschichtsnot und die Gefahr der Barbarei," *Gartenlaube,* Illustriertes Familienblatt (Rubrik: Wissenschaft an der Wende, 1932): 831–833. {= "Laodizee," *Frankfurter Zeitung und Handelsblatt* (1954), expanded; see also "Die Geschichtsnot" (1995).}
REEL 6, ITEM 275.

Der heilige Karl und der eiserne Karl. 1931–32 (ca.). 7 pp., incomplete. Archiv der Eugen Rosenstock-Huessy Gesellschaft. Unpublished.
REEL 6, ITEM 287.

"Henrich Steffens," *Schlesische Lebensbilder* 4 (Breslau: 1932): 264–280.
REEL 6, ITEM 276.

"Judas Ischariot und die preussischen Konservativen. Zum Auftreten der politischen Diabolik," *Hochland* 29, Bd. 2, Monatsschrift für alle Gebiete des Wissens, der Literatur und Kunst, ed. Karl Muth (April 1932): 1–16.Written under the pseudonym "Ludwig Stahl."
REEL 6, ITEM 277.

"Die Judenemanzipation," *Bayerische Israelitische Gemeindezeitung* 8, Nr. 1 (1932): 3–6. {From *Die Europäischen Revolutionen Volkscharaktere und Staatenbildung* (1931): 372–377}.
REEL 6, ITEM 278.

Kriegsheer und Rechtsgemeinschaft. Rede, gehalten zur Verfassungsfeier der Friedrich-Wilhelms-Universität und Technischen Hochschule am 23. July 1932 (Breslau: Trewendt & Granier, 1932), 31 pp.
REEL 6, ITEM 272.

"Mannwerdung. Zur Initiative des Reiches in der 'Jugendertüchtigung'," *Die Erziehung* (November 1932): 102–118.
REEL 6, ITEM 279.

Politische Geschichte als Heilsgeschichte. Rede. July 1, 1932. 21 pp. (fragmentary record). Archiv der Eugen Rosenstock-Huessy Gesellschaft. {See "Laodizee," *Frankfurter Allgemeine Zeitung* (1954). "Die Geschichtsnot," *Gartenlaube* (1932), and unpublished item "Theodizee oder Laodizee?" (1932).} Unpublished.
REEL 6, ITEM 288.

Rede des Herrn Prof. Rosenstock-Huessy gehalten in der Protestversammlung gegen die Schliessung der Akademie (für Kunst und Kunstgewerbe zu Breslau). January 27, 1932. 15 pp. Archiv der Eugen Rosenstock-Huessy Gesellschaft. Unpublished.
REEL 6, ITEM 289.

"Sklaverei oder Regeneration? Gedanken zur Gefährdung des Arbeitsdienstes," *Hannoversche Landeszeitung, Deutsche Volkszeitung, Niedersächsische Zeitung, Neue Hannoversche Zeitung*—2 editions: 65. Jg., Nr. 54 (June 21, 1932): 1; and 65. Jg., Nr. 55 (June 22, 1932): 1.
REEL 6, ITEM 280.

Sozialaristokratie und Arbeitslosigkeit. Aus Anlass des gleichnamigen Buches von Franz Schürholz (Berlin: Junker und Dünnhaupt, 1931). 1932. 8 pp. Archiv der Eugen Rosenstock-Huessy Gesellschaft. Unpublished.
REEL 6, ITEM 290.

"Sozialer Dienst der Universität und ihrer Studenten," *I.S.S. Annals, Annales universitaires, Annalen des Weltstudentenwerkes* 3 (1932): 46–48. {= Abridged translation of "Student and University Service," *I.S.S. Annals* (1932); "Les Étudiants et l'université," *I.S.S. Annals* (1932).}
SEE REEL 6, ITEM 278.

"Student and University Service to the Community," *I.S.S. Annals, Annales universitaires, Annalen des Weltstudentenwerkes* 3 (1932): 4–10. {= "Sozialer Dienst," *I.S.S. Annals* (1932); "Les Étudiants et l'université," *I.S.S. Annals* (1932).}
SEE REEL 6, ITEM 278.

Theodizee oder Laodizee? Die Zukunft der Geschichtschreibung. 1932. 8 pp. Archiv der Eugen Rosenstock-Huessy Gesellschaft. {See "Laodizee," *Frankfurter Allgemeine Zeitung* (1954); "Die Geschichtsnot," *Gartenlaube* (1932); and unpublished item "Politische Geschichte als Heilsgeschichte" (1932).} Unpublished.
REEL 6, ITEM 291.

"Das Volk zwischen Himmel und Erde," *Das evangelische Deutschland* 9, Kirchliche Rundschau (1932): 219–220. {From *Arbeitsdienst—Heeresdienst?* (1932), pp. 37–46 ("Die religiös-philosophische Dialektik. Das Volk zwischen Himmel und Erde").}
SEE (1932) ARBEITSDIENST—HEERESDIENST?

"Weshalb heissen wir Deutsche?" *Kölnische Zeitung* Nr. 468, Unterhaltungsblatt (August 27, 1932).
REEL 6, ITEM 281.

"Zur Strategie des Arbeitsdienstes," *Freie Volksbildung* 7 (1932): 275–284.
REEL 6, ITEM 282.

1933

Das Amt der Jugend. Early 1933. Manuscript of 23 pp. numbered 1–18 and a–e; typescript by L. van der Molen, 8 pp. Four Wells. Unpublished.
REEL 6, ITEM 293.

Apologia pro vita mea. Early 1933. Manuscript of 4 pp.; typescript by L. van der Molen, 2 pp. Four Wells. Unpublished.
REEL 6, ITEM 294.

"Arbeitskraft ohne gestern und morgen. Die falsche Sozialpolitik und die falsche Betriebspolitik kulminieren in die Unmoral der Arbeitslosigkeitsversicherung." Title by L. van der Molen. An article that starts with the words: Sozialisieren heisst nicht verstaatlichen. 1933. 21 pp. Archiv der Eugen Rosenstock-Huessy Gesellschaft. Unpublished.
REEL 6, ITEM 295.

"Arbeitslager," *Handwörterbuch des deutschen Volksbildungswesens*, eds. Heinrich Becker, Georg Adolf Narciss, and Rudolf Mirbt (1933): columns 138–145. {Also in: *Stimmstein* 2 (1988): 61–69.}
REEL 6, ITEM 292.

Militia Academica. For the World Student Movement / Für das Weltstudentenwerk. 1933. 13 pp. Archiv der Eugen Rosenstock-Huessy Gesellschaft. {Related to "Sozialer Dienst," "Student and University Service," and "Les Etudiants et l'université" in *I.S.S. Annals* (1932). = "Militia Academica," Eugen Rosenstock-Huessy Gesellschaft (1980).} Unpublished.
REEL 6, ITEM 296.

Sieger und Besiegte. Deutschland zwischen französischer und russischer Revolution. "Geschrieben in einem kleinen Hotel in der Linkstrasse, beim Potsdamer Platz, an dem Tag, an dem ich Urlaub für das Sommersemester nachsuchte und wusste, es war alles vorbei, für mich selber" is written above the title. March 21, 1933. 20 pp. Four Wells. Archiv der Eugen Rosenstock-Huessy Gesellschaft. {= Sieger und Besiegte (1994). Also in *Mitteilungsblätter der Eugen Rosenstock-Huessy Gesellschaft* 2. Halbjahr (1994): 20–49.} Unpublished.
REEL 6, ITEM 296A.

Volk. Ein Beitrag zur Vertiefung des Begriffes "Volk" in leiblichem und geistigem Sinne. Vortrag im Convivium Viadrinum, Musikheim in Frankfurt a/d Oder. Written as if they were class notes from the lecture and discussion. February 6 and 21, 1933. 9 pp. Archiv der Eugen Rosenstock-Huessy Gesellschaft. Unpublished. {= Vortrag von Professor Rosenstock (1995).]}
REEL 6, ITEM 297.

1934

Address delivered before Parent Teacher Association of Shady Hill School. November 19, 1934. 16 pp. + 3 pp. Questions and Answers. Four Wells. Unpublished.
REEL 6, ITEM 299.

"The Army Enlisted against Nature," *Journal of Adult Education* (formerly *Journal of the American Association for Adult Education;* Philadelphia: 1934): 271–274.
REEL 6, ITEM 298.

Model of Emperors. 8 pp. without numbers. Typescript by L. van der Molen. 2 pp. ca. 1934. Four Wells. Unpublished.
REEL 6, ITEM 301.

The Rhythm of Society: Life and Learning Coordinated. At Wellesley College Reunion, Second Informal Session. 1934. 10 pp. With a report on the two sessions (Lucy Wright) 10 pp. Four Wells. Unpublished.
REEL 6, ITEM 300.

The Role of the Apostle Paul in the Papal Revolution of the Eleventh Century. (A chapter in the posthumous life of the doctor gentium.) Speech to the Medieval Academy of America, Cambridge, Massachusetts. April 28, 1934. 46 pp. Four Wells. {Emendated, transcribed, and reprinted by Lise van der Molen, 1994, 39 pp.} Unpublished.
REEL 6, ITEM 301.

1935

"Franz Rosenzweig und Eugen Rosenstock. Judentum und Christentum," *Briefe: Franz Rosenzweig.* Selected and edited by Edith Rosenzweig, with the assistance of Ernst Simon (Berlin: Schocken Verlag, 1935): 637–720. {See *Judaism Despite Christianity* (1969), pp. 77–170, with prologue and epilogue. In the later edition, *Franz Rosenzweig: Briefe und Tagebücher,* Raphael Rosenzweig and Edith Rosenzweig-Scheinmann, eds. (The Hague: Martinus Nijhoff, 1979), the letters are separated and inserted between letters to other correspondents.}
REEL 6, ITEM 302.

In Defence of the Grammatical Method. 27 pp. 1935 and expanded in 1955. Four Wells.{= *Speech and Reality* (1970): 9–44. Translation in *Friedensbedingungen* (1988): 287–325, and unpublished item, In Verteidigung der grammatischen Methode (1986).}Unpublished.
SEE (1970) SPEECH AND REALITY.

The Inheritors of Industry. Ecodynamics of a Mechanized World. Lowell Lectures. 1935. 200 pp. [*First Part: The World of Dead Time.* 1. The Black Magic of the Twenty-four Hour Day; 2. Modern Technique a Restitution of Nature; 3. Factory Force and Legal Personality; 4. The Waste of Power in Industry. *Second Part: Ecodynamics of Human Time.* 5. The Social Body Rebelling against Dead Time; 6. First Ecodynamic Law: The Group in Production; 7. Second Ecodynamic Law: The Responsibility for Reproduction; 8. Third Ecodynamic Law: The New Roots of Personality.] Four Wells. {Basic to *The Multiformity of Man—Economics of a Mechanized World* (1936), *The Multiformity of Man* (1949), and *Der unbezahlbare Mensch* (1955).} Unpublished.
REEL 6, ITEM 304.

"The Predicament of History," *Journal of Philosophy* 32, no. 4 (February 14, 1935): 93–100.
REEL 6, ITEM 303.

"The Role of Language." Notes for a lecture on April 9, 1935. 2 pp. Title by L. van der Molen. Four Wells. Unpublished.
REEL 6, ITEM 307.

Syllabus, Kuno Francke Lectures 1934–1935. The Constitutional History of Germany from Otto I to Charles V (936–1555) or The Defence of the Roman Empire by the Germans. 1935. 4 pp. Four Wells. Unpublished.
REEL 6, ITEM 305.

The University of Logic, Language and Literature. An Address to the Philosophy Club at Dartmouth College. 1935. 17 pp. Four Wells. {= *Speech and Reality* (1970), pp. 61–97, *Die Sprache des Menschengeschlechts*, Bd. 1 (1963), pp. 525–567 ("Die Einsinnigkeit von Logik, Linguistik und Literatur. Zum Andenken an Wilhelm von Humboldt").} Unpublished.
REEL 6, ITEM 306.

1936

"Dr. Johnson's Cat and the Assimilation of Reality." An Exercise in the Functioning of The Cross of Reality. 8 pp. numbered a – g, one page not numbered. Typescript and title by L. van der Molen 5 pp. With a letter to Mr. Cohn 2 pp. Four Wells. Unpublished.
REEL 6, ITEM 311.

Ends and Beginnings of Philosophy. Crux of Philosophy versus Cross of Reality. The Soil of Thought and The Country of the Thinker. Father Henson or the University of Adversity (An introduction). Between 1936 and 1939 (?). Manuscript of 5 pp.; typescript by L. van der Molen, 2 pp. Four Wells. Unpublished.
REEL 6, ITEM 309.

The Multiformity of Man—Economics of a Mechanized World (Norwich, Vt.: Beachhead, 1936), 39 pp. {Reprinted as *The Multiformity of Man* (1949), with Chapter 1 added; German edition: *Der unbezahlbare Mensch* (1955).}
REEL 6, ITEM 308.

1937

Articulated Speech. 1937. 17 pp. (12a–12o). Four Wells. {= *Speech and Reality* (1970), pp. 45–66.} Unpublished.
REEL 6, ITEM 312A.

A Classic and a Founder (Hanover, N.H.: Dartmouth College, 1937 and 1943), 73 pp. [Part 1, "The Scientific Grammar of Michael Faraday's Diaries." Part 2, "The Tripartition in the Life of Theophrastus Paracelsus."] Contributions to the Philosophy of the Sciences.
REEL 6, ITEM 312.

The One and the Many. No Theology without Trinity. February 8, 1937. Manuscript of 15 pp., numbered a – n; p. i written on both sides; interruption within pp. d – f: p. e two lines; typescript by L. van der Molen, 4 pp. Four Wells. Unpublished.
REEL 6, ITEM 313.

"The Singular and the Plural in the Sciences." Original crossed-out title: "The axiological significance of Singular and Plural in the Sciences." 47 pp. numbered 4–48, with pp. 11a, 11b, and 39a inserted. Title and typescript by L. van der Molen, 10 pp. Four Wells. Unpublished.
REEL 6, ITEM 310.

1938

Articulated Speech (follow-up to 1937 unpublished item?). Ch. 4 - Equations in time; 5 - The Survival of The Imperative; 6 - Grammatical Diagnosis. 1938 (?). 8 pp. (pp. a – h.) Four Wells. Unpublished.
SEE REEL 6, ITEM 312A. "EQUATIONS IN TIME" CAN BE FOUND ON REEL 13, ITEM 610.

Eugen Rosenstock-Huessy (On *Out of Revolution*), 1938. 1 p. Dartmouth College Library. Unpublished.
REEL 6, ITEM 315.

The Future of Natural Law. Speech before Jurists. With a postscript and a letter, his "depositum fidei," to Hans Thieme from March 31, 1955. 1938. 25 pp. Archiv der Eugen Rosenstock-Huessy Gesellschaft. Unpublished.
REEL 6, ITEM 316.

Mythical Grammar. 1938–1939. 10 pp. numbered vii–xvi. Four Wells. Unpublished.
REEL 6, ITEM 317.

On the *De Magistro* of St. Augustine. Paper read before the Augustinian Society at Harvard University. December 17, 1938. 10 pp. Pamphlet in Argo Books Archive. [1. Augustine's effect on sociology; 2. Former evaluations of the *De Magistro*; 3. Repentance for a Social Situation: The Distemporaneity of Teacher and Student; 4. The biographical place of *De Magistro*.] Unpublished.
REEL 6, ITEM 318.

Our Means of Resistance. Richard Cabot Lectures. 1938–1939. 6 pp. [1. Nine Theses; 2. Our System of Coordinates; 3. Four Demands.] Four Wells. Unpublished.
REEL 6, ITEM 318A.

Out of Revolution: Autobiography of Western Man (New York: William Morrow & Co., 1938; reprint, London: Jarrolds, 1939; Norwich, Vt.: Argo Books, 1969, with introductions by Page Smith, Bastian Leenman, and Col. A. A. Hanbury Sparrow, xxii pp.; Providence: Berg Publishers, 1993, with an introduction by Harold Berman), 795 pp. {A different version of: *Die Europäischen Revolutionen. Volkscharaktere und Staatenbildung* (1931), *Die Europäischen Revolutionen und der Charakter der Nationen* (1951), *Die Europäischen Revolutionen und der Charakter der Nationen* (revision, 1961; reprint, 1987).}
REEL 6, ITEM 314.

The Patience for Liberty. 1937–1938 (ca.). 3 pp. Four Wells. {Cf. unpublished items "Articulated Speech" (1937) and "Articulated Speech" (follow-up? 1938).} Unpublished.
REEL 6, ITEM 319.

Privilege and Future Opportunity of the University. Richard Cabot Lectures. October 7, 14, 21, and 28, 1938. 113 pp. Four Wells. [Lecture 1 - *The German University*. Parents, scholars, students, administrators; The human side of thought; "Mr. Dick" and the end of the German University. Lecture, pp. 1–15; discussion, pp. 16–24. / Lecture 2 - *The American University*. Woodrow Wilson's legacy to American universities, Princeton, Chicago, Dartmouth; The modern confusion between ideas, sciences, education and knowledge, exemplified by A. E. Housman's "Introductory Lecture"; The proper relations between birth, growth, spread and death of thought; Economy of the mind. Lecture, pp. 1–19; discussion, pp. 20–29. / Lecture 3 - *Ideas*. The opportunities of parents; The ten commandments of education: Listen, read, think, play; doubt, protest, suffer; return, teach, designate; The institutional representation of these commandments in society. Lecture, pp. 1–21b; discussion, pp. 22–28. / Lecture 4 - *Facts*. The opportunities of scholars: the question of their trustworthiness; How ideas are changed into sciences; The transition from faith to science through work, which must be 1) of universal significance, 2) detached from the environment, 3) vouched by concrete persons, 4) exposed to constant criticism; The forgotten principle of the occidental universities: Paris, Bologna, Salerno and their secret (postponed to a later session due to lack of time). Lecture, pp. 1–20; discussion, pp. 21–32.)] Four of six lectures. Missing are Lecture 5 - *Men*, The fellowship of students, and Lecture 6 - *Administrative Measures*. For their content see next entry: *Privilege and Future Opportunity of the University* (Summaries, summary of the whole series) Four Wells. Unpublished.
REEL 6, ITEM 320.

Privilege and Future Opportunity of the University. Six lectures on, and three from within, The Future University. (For the last three, see *The Brattle Street Lectures*, 1939.) Summaries of: the whole series 2 pp.; Lecture 2, 2 pp.; Lecture 3, 2 pp.; Lecture 4, 2 pp; + Theses, 1 p. 9 pp. 1938. Four Wells. Unpublished.
NOT MICROFILMED.

Revolution as a political concept. 1936–1939 (ca.). 20 pp. handwritten, numbered a–t, incomplete; typescript by L. van der Molen, 6 pp. Four Wells. Unpublished.
REEL 6, ITEM 321.

St. Augustine, *De Magistro* (four chapters) Summary. 1938. 3 pp. Four Wells. Unpublished.
SEE REEL 6, ITEM 318.

Science, Superstition, Education and The Three Storeys of a University. 1938 (ca.). 6 pp. Four Wells. [I. Summary of the four attitudes of man in time; II. Development of the four attitudes in politics and science; III. The superstitions of the scientist and his destruction of education; IV. The three storeys of a university; V. The terminology of a Science of Time.] {= Science, Superstition, Education (1996).} Unpublished.
REEL 6, ITEM 323.

1939

The Brattle Street Lectures. Jan. 13, 20, and 27, 1939. [I – 1. Introduction, pp. 1–3; 2. The Luther of Physics—Diagnosis of Research or the Redirection of Scientific Problems, pp. 3–16. The Luther of Physics, and the re-embedding of the natural sciences. The situation of the theology in 1500 similar to the situation of physics today. The important scientific parties today. The Richard Cabot Lecture, *The Science of Bodies and The Appeal to Somebody* (1939). / II – *Language, Logic, Literature*. 1. Language as nature, pp. 1–3; 2. Language as social organizer, pp. 3–6; 3. Sentence and act; 4. Their four possible combinations; 5. When to change from one combination to the other; (4 and 5 not marked). Scepticism and Mystification. The modern Sophists and the university machinery and monopolies. The three scientific processes: designing, enumerating, articulating. The growth of logic and mathematics. The lack of a science of articulation. Popular substitutes. The disease of self-expression. Proper remedies.] 17 pp. {Cf. unpublished item, The University of Logic, Language and Literature (1935), not identical.} / III - A. *Diagnosis of Education and Redirection of the Mind;* B. *The Religion of the Scientist*, pp. 1–2; C. *Personal Education*, pp. 2–6; D. *Buddha*, pp.6–8; E. *Lao-tzu*, pp. 8–11; F. *Abraham, Jesus, Buddha, Laotse*, 19 pp. {= Unpublished item, The Penetration of the Cross. Abraham, Jesus, Lao-tzu, Buddha (1939), II, pp. 2–55.} Unpublished.
NOT MICROFILMED, BUT SEE REEL 6, ITEM 327A, "LANGUAGE, LOGIC, LITERATURE."

Christmas 1939, First Advent. Introduction to a planned new edition of *Out of Revolution*. 1939. 8 pp. Four Wells. Unpublished.
REEL 6, ITEM 325.

Education in the Third Phase of the Industrial Era. Applied Science versus Representative Education. 1939. 14 pp. Four Wells. [1. Is it: Time and Space, or: When and Where? 2. Modern Man, Inc.; 3. Timeless Man; 4. The Theological Residue in Science; 5. Timely Education, or Woodrow Wilson at Dartmouth; 6. Conclusion: The Staff of a College.] Unpublished.
REEL 6, ITEM 326.

The Happy Guilt. Some miscellaneous pages on the Sabbath between Crucifixion and Easter. Meant for some 6 lectures during 8 days, organized by the Quakers at Dartmouth College. 1939 or 1940. 13 pp. Four Wells. [1. The Church and the churches; 2. The individual and the makro-anthropos; 3. The history of man in prophesies; 4. The consecration of the water; 5. The felix culpa; 6. The crucifixion of the cross. With a separate piece of 4 unnumbered pages: On the Great Saturday, Israel lost her secret. For this, see *Out of Revolution* (1938), pp. 483f., 763.] Unpublished.
REEL 6, ITEM 327.

Modern Man's Disintegration and the Egyptian Ka. 1939. 15 pp. Four Wells. {= *I Am an Impure Thinker* (1970), pp. 35–52. Later included in The First Cycle of Letters to Cynthia (1943).} Unpublished.
SEE (1970) I AM AN IMPURE THINKER.

On the Renaissance and Revolution of Medieval Studies. Conclusion of a paper reflecting on the new Institutes of Medieval Studies in Montreal and Toronto. 1939 (ca.), 3 concluding pages: 23–25. Four Wells. Unpublished.
NOT MICROFILMED.

The Pacification of the New Nationalism (Proposal to the Carnegie Institute by the Organisation of German Scholars Abroad—Notgemeinschaft deutscher Wissenschaftler). 1939. 4 pp. Four Wells. Unpublished.
REEL 6, ITEM 328.

The Penetration of the Cross. Abraham, Jesus, Lao-tzu, Buddha. I. The Cross of Reality, pp. 1–17; II. The Redirection of the Mind: a. Soul and Mind of the Scientist, pp. 1–2; b. – i, 1939. {= Brattle Street Lecture III, B: The Religion of the Scientist. pp. 1–55.} Unpublished.
REEL 6, ITEM 329.

Perpetual Features of Education. (Deleted heading: Philosophy 10, Eugen Rosenstock-Huessy I.U.D. Dr. Phil. Dartmouth College. Universities, Past and Present or The Imperatival Logic of Education. A Philosophy of Science.), 1939. Manuscript of 83 pp.; typescript by L. van der Molen, 21 pp. Four Wells. [Introduction, p. 1; / I part: Perpetual features of education. The quantities of education, p. 9; The basic situation: History versus nature, p. 19; The first commandment of education, p. 27; Some Analyses of the first commandment, p. 38; The first commandment as Man's Magna Charta, p. 53; Journalism and education, p. 60.] Unpublished.
REEL 6, ITEM 330.

Review: Crane Brinton's *The Anatomy of Revolution* [New York, 1938] and Roger Bigelow Merriman's *Six Contemporaneous Revolutions* [New York, 1938], *American Historical Review* (July 24, 1939): 882–884.
REEL 6, ITEM 324.

The Rise and Fall of Nationalism and Internationalism. April 21, 1939. 6 pp. Four Wells. Unpublished.
REEL 6, ITEM 331.

The Science of Bodies and The Appeal to Somebody. Richard Cabot Lectures on the Future of the University (Cambridge, Mass., 1939). 15 pp. Four Wells. {From *The Brattle Street Lectures*, I, 2: The Luther of Physics. Also in: *Rosenstock-Huessy Papers, Vol. 1* (1981), Ch. 2.} Unpublished.
REEL 6, ITEM 322.

The Spirit of Recognition. On Rhythm, Time-Span, Accent and Emphasis. Christmas 1939. 10 pp. Four Wells. Unpublished.
REEL 6, ITEM 332.

1940

The Antidote to Teaching. Conference on Science, Philosophy and Religion, Education, The Strategy of Peace. May 23, 1940. 13 pp. [Antidote to Teaching; Social Regeneration; Why Teaching must be Free; America's Creed.] George Allen Morgan, private collection. Unpublished.
REEL 7, ITEM 343.

The Artist and His Community. Commencement Exercises at the Stuart School of the Creative Arts, Boston: June 1, 1939 (Ann Arbor, Mich.: Edward Brothers, Inc., 1940), 16 pp.
REEL 7, ITEM 333.

The Atlantic Revolution. 1940–1941 (ca.). Two versions: 11 pp. and 6 pp. Related to unpublished item, "A Township College" (1940) ("Immigration without End.") Four Wells and Dartmouth College Library. Unpublished.
REEL 7, ITEM 344.

Attack on My Generation. For Granville Clark in the dark days of 1940. 1940. Two versions, 3 pp. and 1 pp. Four Wells. Unpublished.
REEL 7, ITEM 345.

The Battle Against Segregation. Memorandum on The Potentialities of Council and Camp, Inc. 1940. 6 pp. Four Wells. Unpublished.
REEL 7, ITEM 338.

"A Common Vocabulary for Teachers and Students," *The Dartmouth* (Hanover, N.H.), March 13, 1940.
NOT MICROFILMED.

"Correction on Paying the Price," Letter to *The Dartmouth* (February 23, 1940): 2–3.
REEL 7, ITEM 334.

The Credentials of Teaching. Survey Theses. List of papers used in the Richard Cabot Lectures on the Future of the University (Cambridge, Mass.: 1938–1939) and in the Professional Seminar at Dartmouth College (1930–1940). 1939 and 1940. Two versions, 5 pp. and 9 pp. {Cf. unpublished item, *A Township College* (1940), pp. 49–55 (not identical).} Unpublished.
SEE REEL 7, ITEM 353.

The Creed. 1940 (ca.). 21 pp. Dartmouth College Library. {Forerunner of *The Christian Future* (1946), pp. 98–100.} Unpublished.
NOT MICROFILMED.

A Draft of a Petition to His Excellency The President of the United States. September 25, 1940, Tunbridge Town Hall. 2 pp. Four Wells. {= *Dienst auf dem Planeten* (1965), p. 132.} Unpublished.
REEL 7, ITEM 346.

Faculty Seminar with Dr. Rosenstock-Huessy. 1939–1940. 12 pp. Reports. Four Wells. Unpublished.
SEE REEL 7, ITEM 353.

Forerunner of *The Christian Future* (1946), 1940. pp. 24–73, pp. 26–51 {= Unpublished items "The Religion of the Scientist" and "The Penetration of the Cross" II, pp. 52–73, "The Soul on the Highway." George Allen Morgan, private collection. Unpublished.
REEL 7, ITEM 347.

The German Plan of War for 1940. 1940. 8 pp. Four Wells. Unpublished.
REEL 7, ITEM 348.

God in America or Survival Values for Americans. 1940. Outline of 2 pp. Four Wells. Unpublished.
REEL 7, ITEM 349.

Man Must Teach. 1940. 69 pp. Pamphlet in Argo Books Archive. {= Unpublished item "Supertime, or The Correspondences of Society" without the introduction. Also in: *Rosenstock-Huessy Papers, Vol. 1* (1981), Ch. 3; *Der Atem des Geistes* (1951), pp. 95–166 ("Der Sohn des Augustinus oder die Zeit in der zweiten Potenz"); and *Die Sprache des Menschengeschlechts*, Bd. 2 (1964), pp. 368–427 ("Die Arbeiter lehren zu wenig und die Lehrer lehren zuviel," later changed to: "Jeder muss lehren: Augustin der erste Metanomiker.") The latter two expanded and revised.} Unpublished.
REEL 7, ITEM 350.

The Meaning of Morale. 1940 (ca.) 2 pp. Four Wells. Unpublished.
REEL 7, ITEM 339.

Minutes of CCC [Civilian Conservation Corps] Meeting May 23, 1940. 4 pp. Four Wells. Unpublished.
REEL 7, ITEM 341.

Our Stand Against the Current Fallacies. 1940. 3 pp. (In conjunction with a Professional Seminar at Dartmouth College 1939–40. Summary by a participant.) Four Wells. Unpublished.
NOT MICROFILMED.

"A Peace Within," *American Youth: An Enforced Reconnaissance,* ed. Thatcher Winslow and Frank P. Davidson (Cambridge, Mass.: Harvard University Press, 1940): 197–206. {= translation of *Im Kampf* (1926), pp. 3–9 ("Ein Landfrieden. Eine Denkschrift von 1912").}
REEL 7, ITEM 336.

Purpose of Camp William James. 1940 4 pp. Four Wells. Unpublished.
REEL 7, ITEM 340.

The Question of the Empty Grave. 1940–1941. 3 pp. Four Wells. {Probably related to unpublished item, The Creed (1940).} Unpublished.
REEL 7, ITEM 352.

"Rendering Accounts," *The Dartmouth*; in three parts: (March 5, 1940): 1, 3; (March 6): 1, 3; (March 7): 1, 3.
REEL 7, ITEMS 335A, 335B, AND 335C.

Time and Space in Education. A Method for Determining the Process of Integration for an Industrial Society. 1940. 1 p. Outline for the Faculty Seminar with Dr. Rosenstock-Huessy 1939–1940. Four Wells. Unpublished.
SEE REEL 7, ITEM 353.

A Township College. Materials for Staff Colloquia, used in the Richard Cabot Lectures on the Future of the University (Cambridge, Mass., 1938–1939) and in the Professional Seminar at Dartmouth College (1939–1940). 1940. 26 pp. (pp. 33–57). Four Wells. An Argo Books pamphlet, 1970. {"A Township College" was the title for the second part of the two-part series, Teaching too Late, Learning too Early. Part 1 contained the series title. In *I Am an Impure Thinker* (1970) pp. 91–114. [Our Singleness of Purpose / The Time and Space Horizon of Dartmouth College. Our System of Coordinates / A Common Vocabulary for Teachers and Students / The Credentials of Teaching. Fourteen Theses on the Meaning of Academic Freedom / Immigration without End. (From a speech to the Educational Advisers of the Civilian Conservation Corps in the First Corps Area, at their annual conference held at Dartmouth, May 23, 1940) / List of Papers used in the Richard Cabot Lectures on the Future of the University (Cambridge, Mass., 1938–1939), and in the Professional Seminar at Dartmouth College in 1939–1940.} Unpublished.
REEL 7, ITEM 353.

"What They Should Make Us Think" and "What We Should Make Them Do." Two addresses given May 21 and 23, 1940, respectively. *Annual Conference of CCC Educational Advisers*, First Corps area, Dartmouth College (1940): 35–43.
REEL 7, ITEM 337.

"Youth and Authority," *American Youth: An Enforced Reconnaissance*, ed. Thatcher Winslow and Frank P. Davidson (Cambridge, Mass.: Harvard University Press, 1940): 3–25. {Also printed as a booklet by Harvard University Press (1940).}
REEL 7, ITEM 342.

1941

"A Balance Sheet. Confidential Report on Camp William James," (Norwich, Vermont: Argo Books Archive, February 15, 1941), 30 pp. REEL 7, ITEM 354.

***The Cross of Reality,* Draft preface to,** A planned work consisting of *Out of Revolution* (1938) and *The Full Count of Times* [see *Soziologie,* Bd. 2 (1958)]. 1941. Manuscript of 6 pp. numbered a–f; typescript by L. van der Molen, 3 pp. Four Wells. Unpublished.
REEL 7, ITEM 355.

Eastern and Western Christendom. 1941. 18 pp. Four Wells and Dartmouth College Library. {Cf. *The Christian Future* (1946), pp. 138–164 (not identical).} [Introduction; First Picture: Chalcedon; Second Picture: Frankfurt; Third Picture: Florence; Fourth Picture: Stockholm; Conclusion: Eastern and Western Christendom Dates; Sources.] Unpublished.
REEL 14, ITEM 621.

The End of the World or When Theology Slept. 1941. In two versions, one of 20 and one of 10 pp. Meant for the magazine *Christendom* as a response to Fred. S. Grant's "Realized Eschatology" (Spring 1941), but apparently not accepted for publication. Four Wells and Argo Books Archive. Unpublished.
REEL 7, ITEM 356.

Faculty Address on The Future of Christianity. 1941. 39 pp. Pp. 20 and 30 are missing. Four Wells. {Cf. *The Christian Future* (1946), Ch. III ("The Creation of Future,") which draws upon this material.} Unpublished.
REEL 7, ITEM 357.

Faculty address on "The Potential Christians of the Future" (title by L. van der Molen). 1941. 21 pp., of which p. 16 is missing. Dartmouth College Library. {Cf. *The Christian Future* (1946), Ch. III, pp. 100–112 ("The Creed of the Living God"), which draws upon this lecture.} Unpublished.
REEL 7, ITEM 358.

God's Peace. Christmas Greetings, 1941. Translation of Dionysios the Areopagite. 1941. 1 p. Four Wells. Unpublished.
NOT MICROFILMED.

History makes sense. (On Nietzsche). 1941 (ca.). Manuscript of 4 pp., not numbered; typescript by L. van der Molen, 2 pp. Four Wells. Unpublished.
REEL 7, ITEM 359.

Hölderlin and Nietzsche. 1941 (ca.). Manuscript of 12 pp. not numbered; typescript by L. van der Molen, 4 pp. Four Wells. Unpublished.
REEL 7, ITEM 360.

Letter to *The Christian Newsletter*, *The Christian Newsletter* 101, ed. J. H. Oldham (October 1, 1941): 3–4.
NOT MICROFILMED.

***Out of Revolution,* A preface to a planned new edition of,** 1941. 3 pp. (incomplete). Four Wells. Unpublished.
NOT MICROFILMED.

Peace in Deed. For the Harvard *Guardian*. August 28, 1941. 6 pp. Written March 7, 1940. Four Wells. Unpublished.
REEL 7, ITEM 351.

Rules for the Second World War. December 15, 1941. 2 pp. Four Wells. Unpublished.
REEL 7, ITEM 361.

The Three Sciences. Preface to the planned two-volume set, *The Cross of Reality*, containing *Out of Revolution* (1938) and *The Full Count of Times* [see *Soziologie*, Bd. 2 (1958)]. 1941. 4 pp. Four Wells. Unpublished.
REEL 7, ITEM 362.

"Workproject." Incomplete notes on Camp William James. 1941. 7 pp. Title and typescript by L. van der Molen 2 pp. Four Wells. Unpublished.
NOT MICROFILMED.

1942

"Charge to Rev. Roy Chamberlain." Four Wells (April 25, 1942), 9 pp. Unpublished.
REEL 7, ITEM 363.

Comments on the Document by Emil Brunner, "The Ethical Reality and Function of the Church." For the Ecumenic Council of Churches, letter to Dr. Bennet (December 2, 1942), 8 pp. Four Wells. Unpublished.
REEL 7, ITEM 366.

"The Domestic Parallel to War. As told to George F. Havell," *Free America* (January 1942): 14–15.
REEL 7, ITEM 364.

For Prof. John U. Nef (on the method of sociology). 1942 (ca.). 6 pp. Four Wells. Unpublished.
REEL 7, ITEM 367.

Friedrich Nietzsche's Function in the Church and the Crisis of Theology and Philosophy. Prepared for the joint meeting of the American Association of Church History and the American Historical Association. December 1942. 28 pp. Four Wells. [I. The Unity of Health and Madness as a new historical phenomenon / II. The conquest of space from 1100–1900; Thomas, Cusanus, Paracelsus, Descartes / III. Nietzsche's program for the conquest of time / IV. and V. Nietzsche's masks as the price for his program; The Deification of Man in the Church / VI. and VII. Blasphemy and Madness; Theology and Philosophy have changed rapiers.] {See unpublished item, Nietzsche's Masks (1944).} Unpublished.
REEL 7, ITEM 368.

The Future Way of Life. Christmas 1942. 13 pp. Argo Books Archive. {= *Rosenstock-Huessy Papers, Vol. 1* (1981), Ch. 4.} Unpublished.
REEL 7, ITEM 371.

How Leadership May Be Taught without Doing More Harm than Good. By Prof. Eugen Rosenstock-Huessy, ca. 1942. 7 pp., not numbered. Four Wells. Unpublished.
REEL 7, ITEM 372.

Nietzscheana. 1942. 9 pp. Four Wells. {Preparatory pages to unpublished item, Friedreich Nietzsche's Function in the Church and the Crisis of Theology and Philosophy (1942).} Unpublished.
REEL 7, ITEM 369.

"Nietzsche's Untimeliness." 1941–1942 (ca.). Manuscript of 12 pp. numbered a–l. Title and typescript by L. van der Molen, 4 pp. Four Wells. Unpublished.
REEL 7, ITEM 370.

Philosophy and The Social Sciences. December 1942 (possibly 1943). Conference of the American Philosophers. (Most likely the annual December meeting of the American Philosophical Association, although the APA does not have proceedings from those dates to confirm this.) 68 + 2 pp.; typescript by L. van der Molen, 12 pp. Four Wells. Unpublished.
REEL 7, ITEM 373.

"Population Trends and Economic Changes," *Know Your Town, The Survey of Norwich, Vt.* Produced through Community Cooperation, The Norwich Women's Club (together with and under the names of Carrie Barret and Margrit Rosenstock-Huessy, 1942): 10–17.
REEL 7, ITEM 365.

Sex and Sequence. 1942 (ca.). Manuscript of 3 pp.; typescript by L. van der Molen, 2 pp. Four Wells. Unpublished.
REEL 7, ITEM 374.

Soldiers in the Larger Sense. Comments on the address of William James, "A Soldier in the Larger Sense." February 25, 1942. 39 pp. (incomplete). George Allen Morgan private collection. [1. Conversation; 2. Genius; 3. The Heroic; 4. Science, Consciousness, Conscience; 5. Philosophies, a Plural; 6. The Impossible. Hercules' Choice? 7. The Soul; 8. Importance; 9. Infinity; 10. Fear; 11. Thinkers versus Soldiers. 10 and 11 are missing. For 11, see *The Christian Future* (1946), pp. 216ff.] Unpublished.
SEE REEL 8, ITEM 401.

Soldiers of the Impossible. Lecture at Shady Hill School. May 2, 1942. 37 pp. Four Wells and Dartmouth College Library. [1. Our way of thinking; 2. Our way of acting; 3. Our way of transmitting.] Unpublished.
REEL 7, ITEM 375.

The Soul of William James. Metalegomena on the Pragmatic Significance of the term "soul." An address delivered at Dartmouth College. January 11, 1942. 22 pp. With an appendix of Notes, not in the published versions, pp. 20–22. {= *I Am an Impure Thinker* (1970), pp. 20–34. Translated into German in unpublished item, "William James," (1947); condensed in "William James," *Thema* (1950). Translated in "Die Seele von William James," *Beiheft Stimmstein* (1995).} Unpublished.
REEL 7, ITEM 376.

Supertime, or The Correspondences of Society. Investigations in the Field of Biography, Time, Politics and Education. 1942. 42 pp., with 2-page Introduction, "Space and Time are 'unnatural,' social data." Four Wells. {= Unpublished item, Man Must Teach (1940) and *Rosenstock-Huessy Papers, Vol. 1* (1981), Ch. III, both without the introduction. Cf. unpublished item, Education in the Third Phase of the Industrial Era (1939).} Unpublished.
REEL 7, ITEM 377.

1943

Letters to Cynthia (Harris), The First Cycle of, *On Tribe, Egypt and Israel in order to find direction in our Era.* 1943–1944. With insertions from 1939, 1946, 1947, and 1950. [1. Geography and History or Spaces and Times (February 7, 1943), 10 pp. / 2. The Family: Male and Female create Home or Space; Old and Young create Epoch or Time (February 13, 1943), 11 pp. / 3. Government, the Viscera of the Body Politic; The vital goal of history is the creation of one common speech; History is the triumph of the Singular over the Plural (February 22, 1943), 15 pp. / 4. History as the enlarged Self; You learn history, you cannot learn anything from history (March 11 and 12, 1943), 17 pp. / 5. The Future of our Era: I. "Truth, Trust, True. The Belonging to an Era is demanding a Decision between Traject and Preject"; II. Our Era (March 21 and 25, 1943), 31 pp.

6. The Era of Department-history is coming to an end; The real pressures to become an understanding individual and the finality of history (April 5, 1943), 26 pp. / 7. War and Art ; The graven images of the victors; The Body an Army at the price of death; Idealism and Materialism as Fire and Ashes; Tribe - Empire - Israel and the inverted sequence, Church - State - Society (April 21, 1943), 14 pp. / 8. Any order for which nobody is willing to die is doomed; The Historian's Obligation" (April 28, 1943), 9 pp. (5 + 4 inserted pp.) / 9. The Yaruros of the Capanaparo River; Using and commenting on the published materials of Vincenzion Batrulle (May 4, 1943), 38 pp. / 10. ENVOY (July 9, 1943), 2 pp. with insertion: I. The Secret of the Temple or Underwriting the Sky (ca. 1947), 29 pp., and II. Modern Man's Disintegration and the Egyptian Ka. (1939), 15pp.

11. On Method (July 9, 1943), pp. 2–21, with insertion: 1. Generalisations. The Calendar. Metanoia [originally 23rd letter] (February 24, 1946), 22 pp. (There is an earlier version with 9 pp.

The insertion in this version is on pp. 12–19); 2. 24th letter (May 27, 1946), Church and State, 5 pp.; 3. Two Reflections on the Role of Egypt [Preface, p. 2: I. Sun or Horizon. The Distribution of Cosmic and of Historical Facts in Egypt's Orientation, pp. 2–24; II. Eye of Horus? Eye for Osiris? The Dialectics between Clans and Empire in Egypt's Liturgy, pp. 24–38 (March 1950)]; 4. Superbody, Supermind, Supersoul [originally 22nd letter], no date, 21 pp. / 12(a). Catastrophe as Origin of Society (July 14, 1943), 4 pp.; 12(b). The Cross of Reality. Tribe, Empire, and Israel (July 21, 1943), 12 pp. / 13. Introduction to the Origin of Civilisation (July 22, 1943), 5 pp. / 14. Speech and Writ overcoming Death and Distance (August 10, 1943), 27 pp. (23 + 4 inserted pp.: 8a, 9a, 11a, 19a). / 15. The Task of Settlement (Fall 1943), 24 pp. (21 + 3 insert pp.: 9a, 10a, 10b). /

16. Patience. I. 4 questions answered. II. 1. Set, the indispensable (p. 8); 2. The Djed Pillar (p. 12); 3. Set's Place in Egypt (p. 24); 4. Set, the d.....d. (p. 32) (November 11, 1943), 45 pp. (42 + 3 inserted pp.: 16a, 18a, 41a) / 17. A World of Gods (November 11, 1943), 8 pp. / 18. Writing versus Speaking (November 19, 1943), 5 pp. / 19. How the Skyworld became observable (no date), 21 pp. with an appendix of 11 pp. / 20. Chapter on Israel (February 25, 1944), 31 pp. / 21. Hitler and Israel, or On Prayer (October 19, 1944), 21 pp. (17 + 4 inserted pp.: a, 1a, 2a, 3a).
REEL 7, ITEM 378.

Premises for Thought at Dartmouth about the Future of Dartmouth. 1943 (ca.). 3 pp. Four Wells. Unpublished.
NOT MICROFILMED.

The "quarters" of speech. 1943 (ca.). Manuscript of 10 pp.; typescript by L. van der Molen, 4 pp. Four Wells. Unpublished.
REEL 7, ITEM 379.

1944

Demons of Peace or The Soul at War. A table of contents and two prefaces for a planned book. 1944. 6 pp. Four Wells. [1. Mad Economics or Polyglot Peace; 2. The Next Homer; 3. The Multiformity of Man; 4. A Saint of Pluralism: William James. Address at his Centenary before the Members of Camp William James.] Unpublished.
REEL 7, ITEM 382.

"The Law of Liberty. A Fourth of July Sermon." Congregational Church, Norwich, Vermont. July 2, 1944. 6 pp. {See "Predigt eines Laien," *Christ und Welt* (1948, translation). Also in *Die Sprache des Menschengeschlechts*, Bd. 2 (1964), pp. 304–310. See *The Law of Liberty* (1975)} Unpublished.
REEL 7, ITEM 381.

The Listener's Tract. 1944. 2 versions: 31 pp and 26 pp. (1–24, 24a, 25), respectively. Four Wells. {= *Speech and Reality* (1970), pp. 134–154 (not identical).} Unpublished.
REEL 7, ITEM 383.

Mad Economics or Polyglot Peace. 1944. 32 pp. Four Wells and Argo Books Archive; also at Dartmouth College Library. {= Unpublished item, "Verrückt gewordene Ökonomie oder mehrsprachiger Friede" (1984, translation).} [1. The Moral Crisis of 1944; 2. America's Future; 3. 1914 and 1944; 4. Germany, World Power or World Organ? 5. Alternatives; 6. An Economy of Economies; 7. Personal Record; 8. Military versus Economic Order.] {*Stimmstein* 4 (1993)}. Unpublished.
REEL 7, ITEM 384.

The Next Homer. Also under the titles: Homeric Man and The Creation of Humanism, and The Release of Poetry. Easter 1944. 22 pp. Four Wells. {= Unpublished items, The Next Homer (1947), after 1. "Transition" and "Der nächste Homer," ca. 1954.} Unpublished.
REEL 7, ITEM 385.

Nietzsche's Masks. 1944. 16 pp. {Intended to have been inserted in unpublished item, Friedrich Nietzsche's Function in the Church and the Crisis of Theology and Philosophy (1942)}. Four Wells. Unpublished.
REEL 7, ITEM 368.

Surrender to Whom? (On Germany after the War). 1944. 12 pp. Four Wells and Dartmouth College Library. {Related to unpublished item, Mad Economics or Polyglot Peace (1944).} Unpublished.
REEL 8, ITEM 386.

There are no Synonyms. 1944. 11 pp. Four Wells. {An inadequate German translation exists in *Die Sprache des Menschengeschlechts*, Bd. 1 (1963), pp. 568–578.} Unpublished.
REEL 8, ITEM 387.

"War-Election-Genius" or "The Threefold Inspiration" (titles by L. van der Molen). April 29, 1944. 3 pp. Four Wells. Unpublished.
REEL 8, ITEM 388.

1945

The achievements of the various persons. 1945 (ca.). 3 pp. {Probably the conclusion to "Grammar as Dogma or as Social Science?" See below. Handwritten above the title is "f."} Four Wells. Unpublished.
NOT MICROFILMED.

Establishing Relations. 1945. 21 pp. Argo Books Archive. {= *Speech and Reality* (1970), Ch. 5, pp. 115–133, *Die Sprache des Menschengeschlechts*, Bd. 1 (1963), pp. 441–464 ("In-Beziehung-Treten. Die soziale Gruppierung durch die Grammatik (Neufassung).")} Unpublished.
REEL 8, ITEM 391.

"God is Free," *Advance* (July 1945): 5. {Also in *Stimmstein* 3 (1990): 60–62. Related to: The Law of Liberty (1944). = "Predigt eines Laien," *Christ und Welt* (1948). Also in *Die Sprache des Menschengeschlechts*, Bd. 2 (1964), pp. 304–310.}
REEL 8, ITEM 389.

Grammar as Dogma or as Social Science? 1945. 21 pp. Argo Books Archive. {= *Speech and Reality* (1970), pp. 98–114 ("Grammar as Social Science"); *Die Sprache des Menschengeschlechts*, Bd. 1 (1963), pp. 419–440 ("In-Beziehung-Treten [Neufassung].")} Unpublished.
REEL 8, ITEM 393.

"Hitler and Israel, or, On Prayer," *Journal of Religion* 2 (April 25, 1945): 129–139. {Also in *Judaism Despite Christianity* (1969), pp. 178–194.} {Translation: "Hitler und Israel oder Vom Gebet" (1987, a much larger version). Also in "Hitler und Israel oder Vom Gebet," *Beiheft Stimmstein* (1992), with translations into German, Dutch, and Polish.}
REEL 8, ITEM 390.

How Is New Speech Created? 1945 (ca.). 5 pp. numbered a–e. Four Wells. Unpublished.
REEL 8, ITEM 394.

In answer to a request of Sgt. Albert (Joe) de Vivo to explain how the same people who crowded the churches in Germany, could be accused of having had Hitler as their only religion. May 22, 1945. 3 pp. Four Wells. Unpublished.
REEL 8, ITEM 395.

The Individual's Right to Speak and Some Final Terms of Grammar. 1945. Four Wells, 35 pp. {= *Speech and Reality* (1970), pp. 155–189. Also in: *Die Sprache des Menschengeschlechts*, Bd. 1 (1963), 711–735 ("Des Individuums Recht auf Sprache [Neufassung].")} Unpublished.
REEL 8, ITEM 396.

The Life of Life. A Prologue. 1945. 18 pp. Four Wells. {Forerunner of *Die Sprache des Menschengeschlechts*, Bd. 1 (1963), pp. 269–294 ("Ein Komma").} Unpublished.
REEL 8, ITEM 397.

The New Nature of Christianity. A Task for Drafted Thinkers and Free Soldiers. (An exchange of letters between Irving and Rosenstock-Huessy, meant to be included in a book. The letters are from August 25 and September 15, 1943). 1945. 32 pp., numbered vii–xii and 171–194. Four Wells. Unpublished.
REEL 8, ITEM 398.

"The New Re-production Economy after the World Wars." 1945 (originally 1943). 21 pp. Title by L. van der Molen. Four Wells. Unpublished.
REEL 8, ITEM 392.

"Our Raft in Time" and "World History, Church History, History of Society." 1945. 8 pp. (i–viii). Titles and typescript by L. van der Molen, 3 pp. Four Wells. Unpublished.
REEL 8, ITEM 399.

The Renaissance of Mind and Body. The Grammar of Physics. 1945. 30 pp. Four Wells. {Forerunner of unpublished item, The Metabolism of Science, with the Carmen Arvale in translation (1947), included in *Der Atem des Geistes* (1951): 167–235; *Die Sprache des Menschengeschlechts*, Bd. 2 (1964), pp. 221–275. Related to "A Classic and a Founder," in *Rosenstock-Huessy Papers, Vol. 1* (1981), Ch. 1, First Part. [1. The Scientific Grammar of Michael Faraday's Diaries; 2. A Physicist's Work Sheet; 3. Experience versus Experiment; 4. The Three Dimensions of Time; 5. The Real Mind and the Real Body, or "The Nature of the Physical World."]} Unpublished.
REEL 8, ITEM 399A.

The Wooer's Fate. 1945. 15 pp. (no further page numbers after 9a). Incomplete. Four Wells. {Cf. *Soziologie*, Bd. 1 (1956), pp. 144f. and 184ff.} [Le Langage de l'amour p. 1; The wooer p. 6.] Unpublished.
REEL 8, ITEM 400.

1946

Biology and the Life of Life. Between 1946 and 1950, or even possibly between 1936 and 1940. Manuscript of 19 pp. One page with a German hymn added. Typescript by L. van der Molen, 5 pp. Four Wells. Unpublished.
REEL 8, ITEM 404; REEL 8, ITEM 433.

The Christian Future—or The Modern Mind Outrun (New York: Charles Scribner's Sons, 1946; reprint, London: S.C.M. Press, Ltd., 1947, with a foreword by J. H. Oldham and a soliloquy by the author; New York: Harper & Row Publishers, Harper Torchbooks TB 143, 1966, with an introduction by Harold Stahmer, pp. vii–lv), 248 pp. {German edition: *Des Christen Zukunft oder Wir überholen die Moderne* (1955).}
REEL 8, ITEM 401.

Jungfrauengeburt. Between 1946 and 1950. Manuscript of 4 pp. not numbered, incomplete; typescript by L. van der Molen, 2 pp. Four Wells. Unpublished.
REEL 8, ITEM 405.

Life and death or death and life? Philosophy 58 (final lecture), June 13, 1946. Manuscript of 10 pp., nine of which are numbered a–i; typescript by L. van der Molen, 3 pp. Four Wells. Unpublished.
NOT MICROFILMED.

Our Faith in Science (prepared for *The Journal of Religion*, but not published). 1946. 24 pp. Four Wells. [1. The Academic Treatment of Faith; 2. Science Corrects Grammar; 3. The Nature of the Physical World.] Unpublished.
REEL 8, ITEM 406.

Planetary Man: In Memoriam Oswald Spengler (Southend-on-sea, England: W. H. Houldershaw, Ltd. 1946), 14 pp. {Reprinted from *New English Weekly* (May 30, June 6, and June 13, 1946.}
REEL 8, ITEM 402.

"Planetary Man. In memoriam Oswald Spengler," *New English Weekly* (May 30, 1946): 68–69, (June 6, 1946): 77–78, and (June 13, 1946): 88–89. {= *Planetary Man* (1946).}
REEL 8, ITEM 402.

The United States and Communism. [I. Torn-to-pieceshood and Class War. II. The United States and Russia]. 1946 (ca.). 6 pp. Four Wells. Unpublished.
REEL 8, ITEM 403.

Untragic America. Our Democratic Faith Needs Correcting If We Are To Produce Great Tragic Drama (for editorial in *Life, or Religion and Politics,* Birmingham). December 2, 1946. 4 pp. Four Wells. [What is Tragedy? The Idea of Progress; Reversal of Values.] Unpublished.
REEL 8, ITEM 407.

Vitamine. Between 1946 and 1950 (?). Manuscript of 10 pp., numbered a–k, no page j.; typescript by L. van der Molen, 3 pp. Four Wells. {Cf. unpublished item, The Science of Bodies (1939). = *Rosenstock-Huessy Papers, Vol. 1* (1981), Ch. 2, ("The Science of Bodies and The Appeal to Somebody").} Unpublished.
REEL 8, ITEM 408.

1947

Antwort oder Anruf an den Verfasser der Rede: "Warum ich gerne ein Nihilist sein möchte" (written by an author who was unknown at the time, a young Catholic priest, Otto Eichler). 1947. 3 pp. with a handwritten appendix, "Mehraltrigkeit." 2 pp. Typescript by L. van der Molen, 1 p. Four Wells. Unpublished.
REEL 8, ITEM 412.

"Ascent of Taurus," by E. F. Little and Prof. Eugen Rosenstock-Huessy, *Canadian Alpine Journal* 30 (Chicago: 1947): 15–28.
REEL 8, ITEM 409.

Autobiographic note on his youth. 1947 (?). 2 pp. Typescript by L. van der Molen 1 p. Four Wells. Unpublished.
NOT MICROFILMED.

Autobiography by Eugen Rosenstock-Huessy. A Partner on Patmos. The Plan of the Book Survey and Chapter Headings. 1947. 3 pp. Four Wells. Unpublished.
REEL 8, ITEM 413.

Christ Moses Pharao. 1947. 28 pp. Four Wells. [1. Christ Moses Pharao; 2. Four Steps; 3. The Shattering Experience of Pharao; 4. Stalin.] Unpublished.
REEL 8, ITEM 414.

The Egyptian Ka and Mythical Man. 1947 (originally 1944). 76 pp. Four Wells. {A first-draft translation into German appears in unpublished item, Dich ruft dein Stern (1954).} [1. Egyptian in Us; 2. The Egyptian Constitution; 3. The Literature on Ka; 4. Pronoun versus Noun; House versus Tribe; 5. Pharaoh and Taboo; 6. Osiris and Isis; 7. The Homeric World.] Unpublished.
REEL 14, ITEM 613.

Epilogue to The Spirit of the Alphabet. 1947. 3 pp. Four Wells. {Cf. "The Spirit of the Alphabet," *Catholic Art Quarterly* (1947) and *Die Sprache des Menschengeschlechts*, Bd. 2 (1964), pp. 346–353.} Unpublished.
SEE REEL 8, ITEM 411.

Letter to Richard Koch, Essentuki, Caucasus. November 4, 1947. 10 pp. Argo Books Archive. {= *I Am an Impure Thinker* (1970), pp. 53–64.} Unpublished.
SEE (1970) I AM AN IMPURE THINKER.

The Metabolism of Science, with the Carmen Arvale in translation. 1947. 25 pp. Argo Books Archive. {Cf. "A Classic and a Founder," *Rosenstock-Huessy Papers, Vol. 1* (1981), Ch. 1, First Part; and unpublished item, The Renaissance of Mind and Body (1945). Basic to *Der Atem des Geistes* (1951), pp. 167–235 ("Unser Anspruch auf Wissenschaft oder der Rechtstitel der Physik,") and *Die Sprache des Menschengeschlechts*, Bd. 2 (1964), pp. 221–275 ("In die Zahlensprache der Physik").} [1. The Nature of the Physical World; 2. The Laboratory of Mind and Body; 3. Michael Faraday's Superiority; 4. Invitation to Science; 5. Mars in Rome and World War III, with a laboratory worksheet, excerpts from Faraday's diaries, the Carmen Arvale in translation.] Unpublished.
REEL 8, ITEM 415.

The Next Homer. 1. Transition. 1947. 4 pp. Four Wells. {Links unpublished item, The Next Homer (1944). The Egyptian Ka and Mythical Man, The Secret of the Temple or Underwriting the Sky, and this item were all meant to be grouped together. A first-draft translation exists in unpublished item, Der nächste Homer (1954).} Unpublished.
SEE REEL 7, ITEM 385.

Revolution. (Possibly planned for *Politisches Wörterbuch*). 1947 (ca.). Two versions of 3 and 4 pp. Four Wells. Unpublished.
REEL 8, ITEM 416.

"Rückblick auf die *Kreatur*," *Deutsche Beiträge zur Geistigen Überlieferung* 1 (Chicago: University of Chicago Press, 1947): 208–216. {= "Rückblick auf die *Kreatur*," (1965), *Ja und Nein* (1968): 107–118.}
SEE (1968) JA UND NEIN.

The Secret of the Temple or Underwriting the Sky. 1947 (ca.). 29 pp. Four Wells. {A first-draft translation in unpublished item, Unterschreibe den Himmel! (1954).} Unpublished.
SEE REEL 7, ITEM 380 (PART OF TWO REFLECTIONS ON THE ROLE OF EGYPT).

"The Spirit of the Alphabet," *Catholic Art Quarterly* (1947): 80–85. {= *Die Sprache des Menschengeschlechts*, Bd. 2 (1964), pp. 346–353.}
REEL 8, ITEM 411.

Staat. (Possibly planned for *Politisches Wörterbuch*). 1947 (ca.). 4 pp. Four Wells. Unpublished.
REEL 8, ITEM 417.

William James der Philosoph des modernen Amerikanischen Lebens. Eine Rede vor den Mitgliedern von Camp William James bevor sie zur Armee abgingen, an William James' hundersten Geburtstag, January 11, 1942. 1947. 14 pp. Four Wells. {Translation of unpublished item, The Soul of William James (1942), for *Prisma* (Munich: Verlag Kurt Desch); it is uncertain whether this appeared in *Prisma*. Abridged version, "William James," *Thema* (1950). = *I Am an Impure Thinker* (1970), pp. 20–34. Unpublished.
REEL 8, ITEM 418.

Die Wollust, Die Syphilis, Die Eifersucht. Drei Terrassen der Liebe durch drei Jahrtausende. 1947 (?). 5 pp. handwritten; typescript by L. van der Molen, 2 pp. Four Wells. Unpublished.
REEL 8, ITEM 419.

Zum Patmos Datum, Phaenomeno-nomie oder Epiphanio-nomie. [A. Das Gesetz der Wahrnehmbarkeit einer geistigen Erscheinung (Teilhard de Chardin); B. Hölderlin; C. "The Circulation of Thought: From Idea to Common Place."] 1947. 1 p. Four Wells. Unpublished.
NOT MICROFILMED.

"Der barmherzige Samariter des Denkens (über Ernst Michel)," *Christ und Welt* 17 (September 25, 1948): 12–13. {= "Review of Ernst Michel's *Renovatio*," *German Books* (1948).}
SEE REEL 8, ITEM 410.

The Multiformity of Man. The Notes for the Lectures. October 4, 1948 – January 26, 1949. 35 pp. Four Wells. Unpublished.
NOT MICROFILMED.

Our Urban Goggles. An analysis of the future relation between The City of God and the cities of men. 1948. 14 pp. Argo Books Archive. {= "What Is the City Doing?" *Religion in Life* (1948); "Was bedeutet die Stadt?" *Zeitwende* (1949, translation); *Rosenstock-Huessy Papers, Vol. 1* (1981), Ch. 6; *Die Sprache des Menschengeschlechts*, Bd. 1 (1963), pp. 221–234.} Unpublished.
REEL 8, ITEM 422.

"Outside the Church," *The Parish Messenger*, Church of Saint James the Less (New York: December 1948).
REEL 8, ITEM 420.

"Predigt eines Laien in Amerika. Zum Unabhängigkeitstag. Das Gesetz der Freiheit," *Christ und Welt* (December 3, 1948): 11. {Also in *Die Sprache des Menschengeschlechts*, Bd. 2 (1964), pp. 304–310. Translation of The Law of Liberty (1944).}
SEE REEL 7, ITEM 381.

Review: Ernst Michels *Renovatio*. Zur Zwiesprache zwischen Kirche und Welt (Stuttgart, 1947), *German Books* (Chicago: University of Chicago Press, 1948): 10–14. {= "Der barmherzige Samariter des Denkens," *Christ und Welt* (1948).}
REEL 8, ITEM 410.

"Symblysma oder Überschwang der Jesuiten," *Frankfurter Hefte*, Zeitschrift für Kultur und Politik 3, Heft 11, ed. Eugen Kogon, with assistance from Walter Dirks (November 1948): 1023–1032. {Also in *Der Atem des Geistes* (1951), pp. 275–293 (expanded); *Der Atem des Geistes* (reprint, 1991).}
REEL 8, ITEM 421.

Symprochoresis or The Jesuits Come Home. March 22, 1948. 5 pp. Argo Books Archive. {Translation in: "Symblysma oder Überschwang der Jesuiten," *Frankfurter Hefte* (1948). Also in *Der Atem des Geistes* (1951, and 1991 reprint), pp. 275–293.} Unpublished.
SEE REEL 8, ITEM 421.

"What Is the City Doing to Christian Life? An Analysis of the Future Relation between the City of Man and the City of God," *Religion in Life*. A Christian quarterly of opinion and discussion (Spring 1948): 171–181. {See "Was bedeutet die Stadt?" *Zeitwende* (1949, translation). Also in *Die Sprache des Menschengeschlechts,* Bd. 1 (1963), pp. 221–234 ("Die Grossstadt"); *Rosenstock-Huessy Papers, Vol. 1* (1981), Ch. 6, ("Our Urban Goggles").}
SEE REEL 8, ITEM 425.

1949

America's Contribution to Philosophy (Philosophy 17). Notes for the lectures, prepared by a student. September 27 – September 20, 1949. 25 pp. Four Wells. Unpublished.
NOT MICROFILMED.

The Circulation of Thought – 1949, The Eugen Rosenstock-Huessy Lectures, Vol. 1; Dartmouth College, May 9 – May 25, 1949 (Jericho, Vt.: Argo Books, 1994): 114 pp. in transcription, 6 lectures on audio cassettes. College catalog title: Philosophy 10.
REEL 15, ITEM 626.

Circulation of Thought: Mental Biology (Philosophy 10). Notes for the lectures, prepared by a student. February 16 – May 25, 1949. 25 pp. Four Wells. Unpublished.
NOT MICROFILMED.

"Liturgical Thinking," *Orate Fratres* 23, no. 12 (November 6, 1949): 529–537, and *Orate Fratres* 24, no. 1 (January 1950): 63–69. {Also in *Der Atem des Geistes* (1951), pp. 277–293; *Die Sprache des Menschengeschlechts,* Bd. 1 (1963), pp. 465–492; *Rosenstock-Huessy Papers, Vol. 1* (1981), Ch. 7.}
REEL 8, ITEM 424.

Liturgical Thinking. Joseph Wittig in Memoriam. August 22, 1949. 15 pp. Four Wells. {= "Liturgical Thinking." *Orate Fratres* (1949), *Rosenstock-Huessy Papers, Vol. 1* (1981), Ch. 7. Also in *Der Atem des Geistes* (1951), pp. 239–273; and *Die Sprache des Menschengeschlechts,* Bd. 1 (1963), pp. 465–492 (without Introduction).} Unpublished.
SEE REEL 8, ITEM 424.

The Multiformity of Man (Norwich, Vt.: Beachhead, 1949), 71 pp. {Reprint of *The Multiformity of Man* (1936), Chapter 1 added, with a foreword by The Beachhead (Rosenstock-Huessy) of 5 pp., not numbered. The foreword is not in the Argo Books 1973 reprint. Also without page numbers is the Theme: 3 pp., in Argo Books reprint, pp. iii–v. German edition: *Der unbezahlbare Mensch* [1955, 1957, 1962, and 1964 (paperback)]. See also unpublished item, Whom Money Cannot Buy (1966).}
REEL 8, ITEM 423.

Prolegomena for Ursula and Walter Seemann. July 4, 1949. 6 pp. Argo Books Archive. Unpublished.
REEL 8, ITEM 426.

Universal History – 1949, The Eugen Rosenstock-Huessy Lectures, Vol. 2; Dartmouth College, May 10 – May 26, 1949 (Jericho, Vt.: Argo Books, 1994), 141 pp. in transcription, 6 lectures on audio cassettes. College catalog title: Philosophy 58, "Eternal Horizons of Mankind: Diversity in History."
REEL 15, ITEM 627.

"Was bedeutet die Stadt für das christliche Leben? Über die künftige Beziehung zwischen der Stadt des Menschen und der Stadt Gottes," *Zeitwende* 21, Heft 4, Kultur, Theologie, Politik (October 1949): 241–251. {Translation of "What Is the City Doing to Christian Life?" *Religion in Life* (1948). Also in *Die Sprache des Menschengeschlechts*, Bd. 1 (1963), pp. 221–234 ("Die Grossstadt"); *Rosenstock-Huessy Papers, Vol. 1* (1981), Ch. 6 ("Our Urban Goggles").}
REEL 8, ITEM 425.

1950

The Driving Power of Western Civilization: The Christian Revolution of the Middle Ages. Preface by Karl W. Deutsch, with selected bibliography. (Boston: The Beacon Press, 1950), xiv + 126 pp. {= *Out of Revolution: Autobiography of Western Man* (1938), pp. 453–561.}
SEE (1938) OUT OF REVOLUTION.

"Das Geheimnis der Universität," Eine Rede vor der Universität Göttingen am 5. Juli 1950, *Die Sammlung* 5, Heft 9, Zeitschrift für Kultur und Erziehung Göttingen (1950): 523–539. {Reprinted. Also in *Das Geheimnis der Universität* (1958), pp. 17–37.}
REEL 8, ITEM 428.

Indivisibillimus. 1950. 6 pp. Four Wells. {Probably new conclusion for unpublished item, Establishing Relations (1945).} Unpublished. REEL 8, ITEM 431.

Das Kreuz der Wirklichkeit. Eine nachgöthische Soziologie Erster Band. Druckfahnen für die geplante Neuausgabe der *Soziologie* bei Klett Verlag, Stuttgart. 1950, 312 pp. Portions of this work are with George Allen Morgan (private collection), and Four Wells. The entire work is with L. van der Molen. {Forerunner of *Soziologie,* Bd. 1 (1956); see also *Soziologie I* (1925).} Unpublished. REEL 8, ITEM 432.

Das Kreuz der Wirklichkeit. Eine nachgöthische Soziologie in zwei Bänden. Band II Die Gewalt der Zeiten. 1950. 773 pp. Typewritten manuscript. Four Wells. {= *Soziologie,* Bd. 2 (1958). A 1949 version also exists, containing a chapter 20, "Die Akademische Muse" [A. Goethes Weltgeschichte; B. Giuseppe Ferrari (1811–1876) und der Datierungszwang (later slightly altered and published in *Das Geheimnis der Universität,* 1958: 35–43; C. Musik und Meduse; D. Die jüdischen Antisemiten (Die akademische Form der Judenfrage): 801–880.] Also in: *Das Geheimnis der Universität* (1958): 44–55. The first part, "Der Gang der Ereignisse," contains a first chapter, Die Zeitrechnung, pp. 1–49, which is not found in *Soziologie,* Bd. 2 (1958). The same is also true of Ch. 18, "Heilige, Revolutionäre, Nihilisten," Cf. Im Rückblick mit Polybius, pp. 691–733.} Unpublished.
SEE (1958) SOZIOLOGIE, BD. 2.

Das Kreuz der Wirklichkeit. Eine Nach-Göthische Soziologie in zwei Bänden. 3 Inhaltsübersichten, Vorspruch 2 pp. 1950. 9 pp. Four Wells. Unpublished. REEL 14, ITEM 624.

Die Ordnung unseres geistigen Lebens. Rede in Göttingen. (In der Nachschrift von Prof. Dr. Hans Thieme). 1950. Archiv der Eugen Rosenstock-Huessy Gesellschaft. {See unpublished item, Die Ordnung unseres geistigen Lebens von 1100–2000 (1950).} Unpublished. REEL 8, ITEM 436.

Die Ordnung unseres geistigen Lebens von 1100–2000. Six lectures in Göttingen. 1950. 20 pp. Archiv der Eugen Rosenstock-Huessy Gesellschaft. {See unpublished item, Die Ordnung unseres geistigen Lebens (1950).} From lecture notes by Richard W. McFalls, pp. 1–4; Heinz Hanke, pp. 1–5; W. D. Stüben, pp. 5–8, Karl Heinz Grossmann, pp. 8–16. Unpublished.
REEL 8, ITEM 436.

Planetary Man. [An elaboration of Planetary Man. In Memoriam Oswald Spengler (1946).] 1950 (ca.). 28 pp. (Incomplete; pp. 1, 13, 23, and the end are missing.) Four Wells. Unpublished.
REEL 8, ITEM 402.

"Salamis und die Thermopylen. Ein Beitrag zur Erneuerung der Universität," *Deutsche Universitätszeitung* 5, Heft V/3 (1950): 4–5. {= "Akademik oder Argonautik," *Mitteilungen der Eugen Rosenstock-Huessy-Gesellschaft* (1981, expanded).}
REEL 8, ITEM 429.

Saturnalien. Vorlesungen in Zusammenfassung. June 9, 13, 16, and 20, 1950. 13 pp. Four Wells. Unpublished.
REEL 8, ITEM 437.

The Secret of the University [translation of "Das Geheimnis der Universität," *Die Sammlung* (1950): 523–539]. 1950. 35 pp. (Incomplete; pp. 1–22 and 35 are missing.) Chap. 20 D. Four Wells. Unpublished.
SEE REEL 8, ITEM 428.

Sun and Horizon: The Distribution of Cosmic and of Historical Facts in Ancient Egypt. (À Monsieur le Dr. Drioton, Caire.) April 5, 1950. 27 pp. (A handwritten p. 19 is missing on p. 15.) Four Wells. Unpublished.
REEL 8, ITEM 434.

V. Der Vollständige und der Selbstständige Mensch. {Probably a new paragraph for *Soziologie*, Bd. 1 (1956), Part III. A. paragraph 4: Die Todesüberwinder: Seele, pp. 213–226. It might follow p. 226. It is also not found in an unpublished 1950 version that had been planned for publication by Klett Verlag.} 1950 (ca.). 14 pp., numbered 1–13, with 12 a double page). Typescript by L. van der Molen, 5 pp. Four Wells. Unpublished.
REEL 8, ITEM 435.

What is new about sociology? Conference on The Significance of Sociology for the Strategy of the Church. Ecumenical Institute, Chateau de Bossey, Céligny, Vaud, Switzerland. August 29 – September 5, 1950. 10 pp. Four Wells. {= *Soziologie I* (1925), pp. 41–56, *Soziologie*, Bd. 1 (1956), pp. 48–56.} Unpublished.
REEL 8, ITEM 438.

"William James. Der Philosoph des amerikanischen Lebens." *Thema,* Zeitschrift für die Einheit der Kultur (Gauting bei München) (February 1950): 3–5. {Abridged translation of *I Am an Impure Thinker* (1970), pp. 20–34 ("The Soul of William James"). For an appendix of notes see unpublished item, The Soul of William James (1942).}
REEL 8, ITEM 430.

1951

"Armistice Day. Zachariah 1:11c, 13, 15, 2:12c," Congregational Church, Norwich, Vermont. November 11, 1951. 6 pp. Four Wells. Unpublished.
REEL 9, ITEM 441.

Der Atem des Geistes (Frankfurt a.M.: Verlag der Frankfurter Hefte, 1951; reprint, with foreword and index by Bas Leenman, Moers: Brendow Verlag/Vienna: Amandus, 1991), 293 pp.
REEL 8, ITEM 439.

"Der dritte Weltkrieg," *Frankfurter Hefte* 6, Heft 1, Zeitschrift für Kultur und Politik, ed. Eugen Kogon, with assistance from Walter Dirks (1951): 796–800. {Also in *Die Europäischen Revolutionen und der Charakter der Nationen* (1951), pp. 517–522.}
SEE REEL 8, ITEM 440.

Die Europäischen Revolutionen und der Charakter der Nationen, 2d ed. (Stuttgart: W. Kohlhammer Verlag, 1951), 584 pp. {= *Die Europäischen Revolutionen. Volkscharaktere und Staatenbildung* (1931); *Die Europäischen Revolutionen und der Charakter der Nationen* (1961). Different version of *Out of Revolution: Autobiography of Western Man* (1938).}
REEL 8, ITEM 440.

"Die jüdischen Antisemiten oder die akademische Form der Judenfrage," *Frankfurter Hefte* 6, Heft 1, Zeitschrift für Kultur und Politik, ed. Eugen Kogon, with assistance from Walter Dirks (1951): 8–17. {Also in *Das Geheimnis der Universität* (1958), pp. 44–55. Cf. unpublished item, *Das Kreuz der Wirklichkeit.* Eine nachgöthische Soziologie in zwei Bänden (1950) Ch. 20 ("Die Akademische Muse") D., pp. 864–880; and unpublished item, The Jewish Anti-Semites or the Academic Vocabulary for Judaism (1955).}
REEL 9, ITEMS 442 AND 442A (TRANSLATION).

Memorandum on Books and Manuscripts by Eugen Rosenstock-Huessy, May 16, 1951, 2 pp. Four Wells. Unpublished.
REEL 9, ITEM 444.

Universal History – 1951, The Eugen Rosenstock-Huessy Lectures, Vol. 3; Dartmouth College, May 1951 (Jericho, Vt.: Argo Books, 1994), 22 pp. in transcription, 1 lecture on audio cassette. College catalog title: Philosophy 58, "Eternal Horizons of Mankind: Diversity in History."
REEL 15, ITEM 628.

"Vivit Deus," *In Memoriam Ernst Lohmeyer* (Evangelisches Verlagswerk GmbH: 1951): 250–260. {Also in *Das Geheimnis der Universität* (1958): pp. 274–282.}
REEL 9, ITEM 443.

1952

"Baptism the entry to a new corporality," To a new ecumenical understanding of church-life. Incomplete paper for an unknown conference in response to the Lund conference. Title by L. van der Molen. 1952 (ca.), 15 pp. (numbered 11–25). Four Wells. Unpublished.
NOT MICROFILMED.

Creed; The Power of the Pentecostal Sects; Jehovah's Witnesses; Armageddon. 1952 (ca.). 11 pp. (only Creed exists; the other topics were planned but not written); typescript by L. van der Molen, 3 pp. Four Wells. Unpublished.
REEL 9, ITEM 449.

Death by Abstractions. 1952 (ca.). 11 pp. Four Wells. {= *I Am an Impure Thinker* (1970) Ch. 7, pp. 77–90 ("Heraclitus to Parmenides").} Unpublished.
REEL 9, ITEM 450.

Funeral Prayer. January 6, 1952. 1 p. Four Wells. Unpublished.
REEL 9, ITEM 446.

"Das Gesetz der Technik," *Darmstädter Gespräch, Mensch und Technik.* Neue Darmstädter Verlagsanstalt, ed. Hans Schwippert (1952): 49–52, 173–179. {See "Mensch und Technik," *Die Herausforderung, Darmstädter Gespräche* (1963). Also in *Friedensbedingungen* (1988), pp. 97–106.}
REEL 9, ITEM 447.

Heilkraft und Wahrheit. Konkordanz der politischen und der kosmischen Zeit (Stuttgart: Evangelisches Verlagswerk GmbH, 1952; reprint, with foreword and index by Bas Leenman, Moers: Brendow Verlag / Vienna: Amandus, 1991), 215 pp.
REEL 9, ITEM 445.

Die "Hundert Tage." Das Ende oder Die Hundert Tage. Korea oder die Hundert Tage. Die Hundert Tage und Korea. Three attempts on the meaning of the Korean War. 1951/1952. 1: 7 + 4 pp., not counting pp. a1 and a2, not numbered; 2: 8 pp. a–h; 3: 11 pp. not numbered. Typescript by L. van der Molen: 1: 5 pp.; 2: 3 pp.; 3: 4 pp. Four Wells. Unpublished.
REEL 9, ITEM 451.

Liturgical Thinking versus Theology, or, Escape from or Entry to History. Eden Seminary Lectures, St. Louis. 1952. 29 pp. Argo Books Archive. [I. The Mind Outside History, or The Nature of Man in 1750, 1850 and 1950; II. Experienced Epoch: 1905–1950 or Time as Revelation; III. Experienced Generations, 1811–1910, or Father and Son in the Family of William James.] Unpublished.
REEL 9, ITEM 452; AND REEL 14, ITEM 612.

"Original Grace. A Sermon on Good Friday." Good Friday, 1952. 6 pp. Four Wells. Unpublished.
REEL 9, ITEM 448.

Potential Teachers – 1952, The Eugen Rosenstock-Huessy Lectures, Vol. 4; Air Force Academy at Colorado Springs, Colo., August 5 and 6, 1952 (Jericho, Vt.: Argo Books, 1994), 34 pp. in transcription, 2 lectures on audio cassettes.
REEL 15, ITEM 629.

U.S. Specialist Report. Assignment—Bavarian Adult Education Association, by Prof. Dr. Eugen Rosenstock-Huessy (in Bavaria from August 27 to November 28, 1952). November 1952. 17 pp. American Consulate General Munich. Office of Public Affairs Community Activities—Adult Education. Unpublished.
REEL 9, ITEM 453.

"Die Weltzeituhr," *Hinterländer Geschichtsblätter* 5, Mitteilungen aus Geschichte und Heimatkunde des Kreises Biedenkopf Vereinsblatt des Geschichtsvereins für den Kreis Biedenkopf (1952?): 4. Available at Four Wells. {= *Die Europäischen Revolutionen und der Charakter der Nationen* (1951), pp. 525–527.}
SEE (1951) EUROPÄISCHEN REVOLUTIONEN.

1953

The Cross of Reality – 1953, The Eugen Rosenstock-Huessy Lectures, Vol. 5; Dartmouth College; October 7, 1953 – January 22, 1954 (Jericho, Vt.: Argo Books, 1994), 520 pp. in transcription, 24 lectures on audio cassettes. College catalog title: Philosophy 9.
REEL 15, ITEM 630.

The Crusade of the Star-spangled Banner, a 1918 document written after the first attack by the Americans at Marne. Dartmouth College, Philosophy 57 (1953), 9 pp. {= Rosenstock-Huessy's translation of "Der Kreuzzug des Sternenbanners," *Hochland* (1918).} Unpublished.
REEL 9, ITEM 460.

"Der Gast," *Nutzen und Ordnung* 4, Heft 8, Gegenwartsfragen der Forschung, Lehre und Beratung für Wirtschaft, Haushalt und Familie (1953): 229–230. {Also in *Friedensbedingungen* (1988), pp. 283f.}
REEL 9, ITEM 454.

The Hinge of Generations – 1953, The Eugen Rosenstock-Huessy Lectures, Vol. 6; Dartmouth College; before October 8, 1953 – January 21, 1954 (Jericho, Vt.: Argo Books, 1994), 201 pp in transcription, 14 lectures on audio cassettes. College catalog title: Philosophy 57, "Eternal Horizons of Mankind: The Unity of History."
REEL 15, ITEM 631.

"Ich bin ein unreiner Denker. Vom Töchterlich-Werden des Denkens," *Neues Abendland* 8, Heft 1, Zeitschrift für Politik, Kultur und Geschichte (1953): 11–24. {Also in *Out of Revolution* (1938), pp. 740–750 ("Farewell to Descartes"); *Das Geheimnis der Universität* (1958), pp. 97–112; *I Am an Impure Thinker* (1970), pp. 1–19 ("Farewell to Descartes"); and *Stimmstein* 1 (1987): 27–44.}
REEL 9, ITEM 455.

"Jakob Grimm und unser Erlebnis der deutschen Sprache," *Der Evangelische Erzieher* 5, Zeitschrift für Pädagogik und Theologie (Frankfurt a.M.: 1953): 98–108. {Also in *Das Geheimnis der Universität* (1958), pp. 113–128 ("Jakob Grimms Sprachlosigkeit").}
REEL 9, ITEM 456.

Make Bold To Be Ashamed – 1953, The Eugen Rosenstock-Huessy Lectures, Vol. 7; Dartmouth College, 1953 (Jericho, Vt.: Argo Books, 1994), 37 pp. in transcription, 1 lecture on audio cassette. {Cf. "Make Bold To Be Ashamed" (1956).}
REEL 15, ITEM 632.

"Partner und Stämme der Industrie. Der Marxismus hat seine Zugkraft als Heilswahn eingebüsst," *Neues Abendland* 8, Heft 1, Zeitschrift für Politik, Kultur und Geschichte (1953): 323–337. {Altered in *Der unbezahlbare Mensch* (1955): 139–181, and 1964 paperback ed.: 121–156 ("Die Wirtschaft im Großen und Ganzen").}
REEL 9, ITEM 457.

"Reflexionen über das Thema Quatember," *Quatember* 2, Evangelische Jahresbriefe (Kassel: 1953): 122–125. {Also in *Das Geheimnis der Universität* (1958), pp. 129–133 and reprinted in *Stimmstein* 1 (1987): 45–50.}
REEL 9, ITEM 458.

"Was ist der Mensch? Eine Laienabwehr," *Neues Abendland 8,* Zeitschrift für Politik, Kultur und Geschichte (1953): 707–718. {Also in *Das Geheimnis der Universität* (1958), pp. 134–145.}
REEL 9, ITEM 459.

Before and after Karl Marx, Prophesies Fulfilled and Unfulfilled: The Four Disangelists—Marx, Nietzsche, Darwin, Freud – 1954, The Eugen Rosenstock-Huessy Lectures, Vol. 10; Union Theological Seminary (Forum Committee Lectures), New York, November 30 – December 1, 1954 (Jericho, Vt.: Argo Books, 1994), 23 pp. in transcription, 2 audio cassettes.
REEL 16, ITEM 635, UNDER "FOUR DISANGELISTS."

The Circulation of Thought – 1954, The Eugen Rosenstock-Huessy Lectures, Vol. 9; Dartmouth College, February 10 – May 28, 1954 (Jericho, Vt.: Argo Books, 1994), 570 pp. in transcription, 26 lectures on audio cassettes. College catalog title: Philosophy 10.
REEL 16, ITEM 634.

The Co-creators. Preface to I and II of *Soziologie,* Bd. 1 (1956), and *Soziologie,* Bd. 2. 1954. 4 pp. (pp. a–d). Four Wells and Archiv der Eugen Rosenstock-Huessy Gesellschaft. {Poor translation in "Die Mitschöpfer, eine Einführung in die Universalgeschichte," *Mitteilungen der Eugen Rosenstock-Huessy-Gesellschaft* (1977).} Unpublished.
REEL 9, ITEM 468.

Comparative Religion – 1954, The Eugen Rosenstock-Huessy Lectures, Vol. 8; Dartmouth College, September 23, 1954 – January 6, 1955 (Jericho, Vt.: Argo Books, 1994), 638 pp. in transcription, 25 lectures on audio cassettes. College catalog title: Philosophy 40.
REEL 15, ITEM 633.

Die Deutschen im Gespräch. 1954. 30 pp. Four Wells. {Forerunner of *Frankreich-Deutschland*} [1. Erbbrüder-Erbfeinde; 2. Frankenerde, Frankenheer; 3. "Deutsch" und "Römisch"; 4. Dreifacher Wahn; 5. Friedlose Aufklärung; Schlusswort.] Unpublished.
REEL 9, ITEM 469.

Dich ruft dein Stern. Das ägyptische Ka und der mythische Mensch. 1954. 63 pp. Archiv der Eugen Rosenstock-Huessy Gesellschaft. {A first-draft translation of "The Egyptian Ka and Mythical Man."} [1. Der Ägypter in uns; 2. Die ägyptische Verfassung; 3. Literatur über den Ka; 4. Pronomen und Nomen; 5. Das Haus des Horus; 6. Isis und Osiris; 7. Die homerische Welt.] Unpublished.
NOT MICROFILMED.

"Dich und Ich. Was folgt aus der empirischen Grammatik?" *Neues Abendland* 9, Heft 12, Zeitschrift für Politik, Kultur und Geschichte (December 1954): 719–727. {Also in *Das Geheimnis der Universität* (1958), pp. 160–168.}
REEL 9, ITEM 461.

"Dich und mich. Lehre oder Mode?" *Neues Abendland* 9, Heft 11, Zeitschrift für Politik, Kultur und Geschichte (November 1954): 643–652. {Also in *Das Geheimnis der Universität* (1958), pp. 149–159.}
REEL 9, ITEM 462.

"Glückhafte Schuld," *Quatember* 2 (1954): 94–96. {Also in *Das Geheimnis der Universität* (1958), pp. 146–148 and *Die Sprache des Menschengeschlechts*, Bd. 1 (1963), pp. 251–255.}
REEL 9, ITEM 463.

"Die Heimkehr der Gesellschaft," *Adult Education, Erwachsenenbildung*, 1952 UNESCO International Conference, Hamburg, 1952 (1954): 76–81.{= "The Homecoming of Society" in the same publication (in part).}
REEL 9, ITEM 464.

History Must Be Told – 1954 Draft, The Eugen Rosenstock-Huessy Lectures, Vol. 11; Dartmouth College (Jericho, Vt.: Argo Books, 1994), 14 pp. in transcription, 1 lecture on audio cassette. {First studio take. Content different from 1955 LP disk, *History Must be Told – 1955.*}
REEL 16, ITEM 636.

"The Homecoming of Society. Remarks on the UNESCO Institutes Conference on Adult Education," *Adult Education, Erwachsenenbildung*, UNESCO International Conference, Hamburg, 1952 (1954): 76–83. {= "Die Heimkehr der Gesellschaft" in the same publication (in part).}
REEL 9, ITEM 464.

"Laodizee—Wie rechtfertigt sich ein Volk?" *Frankfurter Zeitung und Handelsblatt* (August 14, 1954). {= Expanded version of "Die Geschichtsnot und die Gefahr der Barbarei" in *Gartenlaube* (1932).}
REEL 9, ITEM 465.

Letter to Mr. Herberg. (On Natural Law. Against Strauss and Hobbes). October 1954, Four Wells. 2 pp. Four Wells. Unpublished.
REEL 9, ITEM 471.

Der nächste Homer. (Title by L. van der Molen; original title was "Homer am Nächsten.") Mit einer neuen Einleitung pp. 1–3. 1954 (ca.). 39 pp. Archiv der Eugen Rosenstock-Huessy Gesellschaft. {A first-draft translation of unpublished items, "The Next Homer" (1944) and "The Next Homer. 1. Transition" (1947).} Unpublished.
NOT MICROFILMED.

"Pentecost and Mission," *Hartford Seminary Foundation Bulletin* 18 (Winter 1954–1955): 17–25. {German translation in "Drei Gaben des Heiligen Geistes," *Christ und Welt*. Also in *Das Geheimnis der Universität* (1958), pp. 236–243 ("Pfingsten und Mission").}
REEL 9, ITEM 466.

Time Bettering Days —A paper read in the Tucker Fellowship at Dartmouth College at the Spring Equinox of 1954. 23 pp. Argo Books Archive. {= *Rosenstock-Huessy Papers, Vol. 1* (1981), Ch. 8, and "Zeitbessernde Tage?" *Antaios* (translation, 1959). Also *Die Sprache des Menschengeschlechts*, Bd. 1, pp. 493–524 ("Was proklamieren unsere Kalender?").} Unpublished.
REEL 9, ITEM 472.

Two Reflections on the Role of Egypt. 1953/1954 (ca.). 38 pp. Four Wells. {Retroactively included in The First Cycle of Letters to Cynthia (1943f). 3rd insertion after the 11th letter. Cf. *Das Geheimnis der Universität* (1958), pp. 179–213 ("Die Zeit im Raum"). New expanded version.} [Preface; I. Sun or Horizon. The Distribution of Cosmic and of Historical Facts in Egypt's Orientation; II. Eye of Horus? Eye for Osiris? The Dialectics between Clans and Empire in Egypt's Liturgy.] Unpublished.
REEL 7, ITEM 380.

Universal History – 1954, The Eugen Rosenstock-Huessy Lectures, Vol. 12; Dartmouth College, February 9 – May 27, 1954 (Jericho, Vt.: Argo Books, 1994), 540 pp. in transcription, 25 lectures on audio cassettes. College catalog title: Philosophy 58, "Eternal Horizons of Mankind: Diversity in History." {Cf. "Tribalism," *Exodus* (1959).}
REEL 16, ITEM 637.

Unterschreibe den Himmel! I. Das Geheimnis des Tempels. 1954 (ca.). 22 pp. Archiv der Eugen Rosenstock-Huessy Gesellschaft. {A first-draft translation of "The Secret of the Temple or Underwriting the Sky" (1947).} Unpublished.
NOT MICROFILMED.

William Stanley, the Sixth Earl of Derby's Sonnets for Elizabeth de Vere 1591–1598. After Forty Years. Quadragesimo Anno. February 24–25, 1954. 74 pp. Four Wells. {German translation in unpublished item, "William Stanleys—des sechsten Grafen von Derby—Sonette für Elisabeth de Vere 1591–1598. Übersetzt von Eckart Wilkens" (1980).} Unpublished.
REEL 9, ITEM 473.

1955

(6) Die ältesten amtlichen Berichte über die Evangelien. (7) Das Wort selbst. (8) Offenbarung. Übersetzungen der drei Schlusskapitel des Buches: *The Fruit of Lips or Why Four Gospels* (1978). September 24, 1955. pp. 70–83. Archiv der Eugen Rosenstock-Huessy Gesellschaft. Unpublished.
REEL 9, ITEM 487.

Bible Study Peter-Paul-John. Ephesians and Colossians (with a letter in German to Dick, 22.3.1955). 1955. 13 pp. Four Wells. Unpublished.
REEL 9, ITEM 482.

Des Christen Zukunft oder Wir überholen die Moderne, trans. Christoph v.d. Bussche and Konrad Thomas, a German revised edition of *The Christian Future* (1946), with the introduction by J. H. Oldham in the 1947 edition (Munich: Kaiser Verlag, 1955; second ed., 1956; paperback ed., Munich and Hamburg: Siebenstern Taschenbuchverlag, no. 57/58, 1965, 288 pp.; reprint, paperback edition, Moers: Brendow Verlag, 1985), 351 pp.
REEL 9, ITEM 475.

"Drei Gaben des Heiligen Geistes," *Christ und Welt* 8 (May 1955). {Translation of "Pentecost and Mission," *Hartford Seminary Foundation Bulletin* (1954). Also in *Das Geheimnis der Universität* (1958), pp. 236–243 ("Pfingsten und Mission").}
REEL 9, ITEM 476.

"Ehe auf Vertrag," *Hochland* 47, Heft 5, 1954/55, Monatsschrift für alle Gebiete des Wissens, der Literatur und Kunst, ed. Karl Muth (June 1955): 495–496. {Sections from *Der unbezahlbare Mensch* (1955), pp. 108–109, 110, 118; = paperback ed., 94–95, 96, 103.}
REEL 9, ITEM 477.

"Glaube und Hoffnung. Ein Nachwort zu Evanston. Korrespondenz zwischen Gerhardt Bartning und Eugen Rosenstock-Huessy," *Neue Deutsche Hefte* 2, Beiträge zur europäischen Gegenwart (November 1955): 625–633. {Also in *Das Geheimnis der Universität* (1958), pp. 262–273.}
REEL 9, ITEM 478.

History Must be Told, LP record jacket, 1 p. of 2 columns entitled "The Universal History of Mankind." Four Wells.
REEL 9, ITEM 470.

History Must Be Told – 1955, The Eugen Rosenstock-Huessy Lectures, Vol. 13; Dartmouth College (Jericho, Vt.: Argo Books, 1994), 14 pages, 1 lecture on audio cassette, originally on LP disk.
REEL 16, ITEM 638.

"Hitler und Israel oder Vom Gebet" (first translation of "Hitler and Israel, or On Prayer," *Journal of Religion,* 1945.) 1955. 19 pp., numbered 2–20. Four Wells. {Cf. "Hitler und Israel oder Vom Gebet," *Jenseits all unseres Wissens wohnt Gott,* 1957.} Unpublished.
REEL 9, ITEM 483.

The Jewish Anti-Semites or the Academic Vocabulary for Judaism. 1955 (ca.). 22 pp., missing four sentences at the end. Translation of "Die jüdischen Antisemiten oder die akademische Form der Judgenfrage," *Frankfurter Hefte* 1 (1951): 8–17, and *Das Geheimnis der Universität* (1958): 44–55. Four Wells. Unpublished.
SEE REEL 9, ITEM 442A.

Lecture on "The Driving Power of Western Civilization" (at Dartmouth College). 1955 (ca.). 16 pp. Four Wells. Unpublished.
REEL 9, ITEM 484.

Myth, Saga, Legend and Necessity. A Preface to Liturgy. 1955 (ca.). 18 pp. Four Wells. [Jupiter and Vediovis; Poplifugia and Refugium; The Naming of the gods.] Unpublished.
REEL 9, ITEM 485.

Primus Sermo Secundus Sermo Tertius Sermo. On the role of Negation and on the Paradox: the three Phases of Speech. Originally written for *Magna Carta Latina* (1967 and 1975), 1955 (ca.). 6 pp. Four Wells. Unpublished.
REEL 9, ITEM 486.

"Raumzeit oder Zeitraum?" *Neue Deutsche Hefte* 1 (March 1955): 939–944. {Also in *Das Geheimnis der Universität* (1958), pp. 262–273.}
REEL 9, ITEM 479.

"Die Sprache des Westens," *Geschichte in Wissenschaft und Unterricht* 6, Zeitschrift des Verbandes der Geschichtslehrer Deutschlands (1955): 22–29. {Also in *Das Geheimnis der Universität* (1958), pp. 56–63.}
REEL 9, ITEM 480.

The Terms of the Creed. With an insertion of 2 pp. for p. 17: How Jesus became the heir of the past eras and the founder of the Christian era. Originally written for *Magna Carta Latina* (1967 and 1975). September 12, 1955. 22 + 2 pp. Four Wells and Archiv der Eugen Rosenstock-Huessy Gesellschaft. {= *Das Geheimnis der Universität* (1958), pp. 244–261, faulty translation without the insertion.} Unpublished.
REEL 9, ITEM 488.

360 + 5 and The Year as Period. 1955. 14 pp. Argo Books Archive. {Revised version in *Das Geheimnis der Universität* (1958), pp. 201–213 ("Der Sinn des Kalenders in Rom").} [1. The Ten Month Year in Ancient Rome; 2. The Latin Year; 3. The Sopdit year; 4. Survey.] Unpublished.
REEL 9, ITEM 489.

Der unbezahlbare Mensch, trans. Gertie Siemsen (first 8 chapters). Preface by Walter Dirks (Berlin: Käthe Vogt Verlag, 1955; paperback ed., Freiburg, Basel, Vienna: Herder Bücherei Bd. 187, 1964, 173 pp.), 201 pp. {German edition of *The Multiformity of Man* (1949), a revision of *The Multiformity of Man: Economics of a Mechanized World* (1936).}
REEL 9, ITEM 474.

Universal History – 1955, The Eugen Rosenstock-Huessy Lectures, Vol. 14; Dartmouth College, February 10 – 14, 1955 (Jericho, Vt.: Argo Books, 1994), 91 pp. in transcription, 4 lectures on audio cassettes. College catalog title: Philosophy 58, "Eternal Horizons of Mankind: Diversity in History."
REEL 16, ITEM 639.

Von einer Grammatik der benannten Menschen. Der Erste Adam. Der Zweite Adam. An earlier sketch of the contents of *Die Sprache des Menschengeschlechts* (1963 and 1964). 1955 (ca.). 1 p. Four Wells. Unpublished.
REEL 13, ITEM 607.

Was kostet die Geschichte? May 4, 1955. 4 pp. Archiv der Eugen Rosenstock-Huessy Gesellschaft. {= *Die Sprache des Menschengeschlechts,* Bd. 1 (1963), pp. 348–353 ("Das Auf beim Hören und das Los beim Sagen"), "Was kostet die Geschichte?" *Mitteilungsblatt der Eugen Rosenstock-Huessy-Gesellschaft* (1985), pp. 2–5.} Unpublished.
REEL 9, ITEM 490.

"Why do good people suffer? The Bible asks and answers." Congregational Church, Norwich, Vt. June 26, 1955. 3 pp. Argo Books Archive. Unpublished.
REEL 9, ITEM 481.

1956

"Das Christentum inkognito," *Evangelische Welt* 10, Nr. 4 (1956): 84–85. {From *Des Christen Zukunft* (1955), pp. 185–189; paperback ed., pp. 152–155.}
REEL 9, ITEM 492.

The Circulation of Thought – 1956, The Eugen Rosenstock-Huessy Lectures, Vol. 15; Dartmouth College, May 11, 1956 (Jericho, Vt.: Argo Books, 1994), 21 pp. in transcription, 1 lecture on audio cassette. College catalog title: Philosophy 10.
REEL 16, ITEM 640.

Die Einheit des menschlichen Schicksals in Kriegsheer und Friedenswirtschaft. 2. Lehrgang der Offiziere in Sonthofen. 1956. 15 pp. Four Wells and Archiv der Eugen Rosenstock-Huessy Gesellschaft. {= *Friedensbedingungen* (1988), pp. 191–207.} Unpublished.
SEE (1988) FRIEDENSBEDINGUNGEN.

Epochenteilung – Epochenbildung. A transcript, with many gaps, of the taped lecture at the Evangelische Akademie Berlin. June 17, 1956. 25 pp. The tape itself is lost. Four Wells. Unpublished.
REEL 9, ITEM 497.

Evozieren und Revozieren oder Die Auflockerung der sozialen Fronten als christliche Aufgabe. June 10, 1956. Bad Boll. 28 pp., or 17 pp. revised transcript of the tape. Four Wells and Archiv der Eugen Rosenstock-Huessy Gesellschaft. {= *Friedensbedingungen* (1988), pp. 121–143.} Unpublished.
REEL 9, ITEM 497A.

Greek Philosophy – 1956, The Eugen Rosenstock-Huessy Lectures, Vol. 16; Dartmouth College, September 27, 1956 – January 24, 1957 (Jericho, Vt.: Argo Books, 1994), 664 pp. in transcription, 26 lectures on audio cassettes. College catalog title: Philosophy 11.
REEL 16, ITEM 641.

"Herakleitos von Ephesos schreibt an Parmenides von Elea," *Arzt im Irrsal der Zeit, Viktor von Weizsäcker. Eine Freundesgabe zum 70. Geburtstag am 21.4.1956,* Prof. Dr. Paul Vogel, ed. (Vandenhoeck & Ruprecht, 1956). {= Expanded version of *I Am an Impure Thinker* (1970), pp. 77–90 ("Heraclitus to Parmenides").}
REEL 9, ITEM 493.

"Heraklit an Parmenides," *Evangelische Unterweisung* 11, Heft 6, Monatsblatt für kirchliche pädagogische Arbeitsgemeinschaften (June 1956): 94–95. {= *Zurück in das Wagnis der Sprache* (1957), pp. 26–30 ("Logos und Schule").}
REEL 9, ITEM 493.

Holy Holy Holy. Our Father Dear Lord and Father of Mankind (On The Lord's Prayer). 1956 (ca.). Typescript by L. van der Molen, 3 pp. Four Wells. Unpublished.
REEL 9, ITEM 498.

"Praise Him Above, Ye Heavenly Hosts. Ephesians 6:12." Congregational Church, Norwich, Vt. October 28, 1956. 4 pp. (with a pastoral prayer). Four Wells.
REEL 9, ITEM 494.

Shame, Self-knowledge and Freedom. 1956. 59 pp. Archiv der Eugen Rosenstock-Huessy Gesellschaft. {Part of *Greek Philosophy – 1956* and *Universal History – 1957*.} Unpublished.
NOT MICROFILMED.

"Soziologie. Auszüge," *Wissen und Leben* 7 (Stuttgart: Kohlhammer Verlag, 1956): 5–6.
REEL 9, ITEM 495.

Soziologie,* Bd. 1, *Die Übermacht der Räume (Stuttgart, Berlin, Köln, Mainz: W. Kohlhammer Verlag, 1956), 335 pp. {= Revised version of *Soziologie I. Die Kräfte der Gemeinschaft* (1925).}
REEL 9, ITEM 491.

Universal History – 1956, The Eugen Rosenstock-Huessy Lectures, Vol. 17; Dartmouth College, April 17 – May 17, 1956 (Jericho, Vt.: Argo Books, 1994), 218 pp. in transcription, 9 lectures on audio cassettes. College catalog title: Philosophy 58, "Eternal Horizons of Mankind: Diversity in History."
REEL 17, ITEM 642.

"Der Verrat im 20. Jahrhundert," *Die Gegenwart* 11 (November 3, 1956): 697–700. {Also in *Das Geheimnis der Universität* (1958), pp. 64–69.}
REEL 9, ITEM 496.

Zeitgeist, Mythos, Krieg. September 15, 1956. 16 pp. Archiv der Eugen Rosenstock-Huessy Gesellschaft. {Related to *Frankreich-Deutschland* (1957). = "Zeitgeist, Mythos, Krieg" (1980).} Unpublished.
REEL 10, ITEM 500.

1957

Arbeitstagung mit Prof. Eugen Rosenstock-Huessy in der Evangelischen Akademie Arnoldshain. July 6–7, 1957. 61 pp. Four Wells. [Einleitendes Referat pp. 1–14, Diskussion über Referat und Thesen, pp. 15–61.] {Related to unpublished item, "Die Weggelaufene Eschatologie" (1957).} Unpublished.
REEL 10, ITEM 508.

"Europa ist nicht mehr die nette Mitte der Welt. Wir denken immer noch in längst überholten Begriffen—Zum Beispiel, was ist schon: der Staat?" *Die Welt* (July 6, 1957): 154. {= "Künftige Widersacher der Kirche," *Mitteilungen der Eugen Rosenstock-Huessy-Gesellschaft* (1983). Also in *Friedensbedingungen* (1988), pp. 181–189.}
SEE (1988) FRIEDENSBEDINGUNGEN.

"Die Europäische Wandlung oder Die Lebensalter müssen ihr angenehmes Mass wiederbekommen." Title by L. van der Molen. Eine unvollständige Vorlesung in Bochum oder Münster. 1957. pp. 6–19. Four Wells. Unpublished.
REEL 10, ITEM 509.

Frage und Antwort. Meant as an insertion in *Zurück in das Wagnis der Sprache* (1957) after the heading, "Der destillierte Geist," and before the heading, "Die neuen Kentauren" (p. 66). 1957. 2 pp. Archiv der Eugen Rosenstock-Huessy Gesellschaft. {Revision of unpublished item, "Die Kunst der Frage" (1957).} Unpublished.
REEL 10, ITEM 510.

Frankreich-Deutschland— Mythos oder Anrede? (Berlin: Käthe Vogt Verlag, 1957), 106 pp.
REEL 10, ITEM 501.

"Gast und Geist oder Stammeszunge und Geisteszunge." 1957 (ca.). Manuscript of 9 pp. Title and typescript by L. van der Molen, 3 pp. Four Wells. {Cf. *Soziologie,* Bd. 2 (1958), pp. 323–333 ("Die Sekte," "Feuer und Geist," "Pfingsten," "Gastfreundschaft.").} Unpublished.
REEL 10, ITEM 511.

"Eine Generation allein ist nicht geschichtsmächtig. Zum Generationsproblem (Zitate ausgewählt von Fritz Vilmar)," *Ansätze,* Eine Semesterzeitschrift der Evangelischen Studentengemeinde in Deutschland (November 11, 1957), 3 pp.
REEL 10, ITEM 504.

Die Kunst der Frage. Insertion for *Zurück in das Wagnis der Sprache.* January 25, 1957. 10 pp. (a–j); typescript by L. van der Molen, 3 pp. Four Wells. {See unpublished item "Frage und Antwort" (1957).} Unpublished.
REEL 10, ITEM 510.

Make Bold To Be Ashamed. On freedom, growth and self-knowledge. Mass Media's New Methodism. 1957 (ca.). 1 p. 4 columns. Four Wells. {Cf. *Make Bold To Be Ashamed – 1953.*} Unpublished.
NOT MICROFILMED.

Review: Henri Pirenne, *Mohammed and Charlemagne*, trans. Bernard Miall (New York), *The Muslim World,* Hartford Seminary Bulletin 47, no. 1 (January 1957): 74–75.
REEL 10, ITEM 505.

"Sermon on Philippians 3:20, 21, 4:4, 5c." Methodist Church, Morrisville, Vt., at the invitation of the Lamoille County Ministers Association. Reformation Sunday, 1957. 4 pp. Argo Books Archive. Unpublished.
REEL 10, ITEM 506.

"Sprache und Geschichte. Vortrag in der Pädagogischen Akademie Dortmund am 20. Juli 1957," *Evangelische Unterweisung* 12, Heft 10 (October 1957): 153–159. {Also in *Das Geheimnis der Universität* (1958), pp. 86–93.}
SEE (1958) DAS GEHEIMNIS DER UNIVERSITÄT.

"Tutilo of St. Gallen, and the Origin of Drama," *Catholic Art Quarterly* 20 (1956–1957): 57–59. {Also in *Die Sprache des Menschengeschlechts*, Bd. 2 (1964), pp. 212–216 (German translation).}
REEL 14, ITEM 622.

Two letters: "An Bürkle" and "An Achim" (on the rejection of a Festschrift as a strike against the academic world), *Ansätze*, Eine Semesterzeitschrift der Evangelischen Studentengemeinde in Deutschland (November 11, 1957), 1 p.
REEL 10, ITEM 502.

Universal History – 1957, The Eugen Rosenstock-Huessy Lectures, Vol. 18; Dartmouth College, February 11 – April 23, 1957 (Jericho, Vt.: Argo Books, 1994), 595 pp. in transcription, 29 lectures on audio cassettes. College catalog title: Philosophy 58, "Eternal Horizons of Mankind: Diversity in History."
REEL 17, ITEM 643.

Der Verlust der Kontinuität und Integration in der modernen Gesellschaft. 1957. 14 pp. Four Wells. [1. Vom gehörigen und ungehörigen Unterbrechungen; 2. Wo ist der Zeitzerstäuber aufgestellt?; 3. Wo wird der Zeitzerstäuber konstruiert?; 4. Vom Rhythmus oder vom rechten Gang in die Zeit.] {Cf. *Soziologie*, Bd. 2 (1958), 712–720. Also in: *Friedensbedingungen* (1988), pp. 145–157.} Unpublished.
REEL 10, ITEM 512.

"Vorwort," preface to Helmuth von Moltke, *Die beiden Freunde* (Berlin: Karl H. Henssel Verlag, 1957): 5–13.
REEL 10, ITEM 507.

Die Weggelaufene Eschatologie. Thesen für eine Arbeitstagung zur Frage der geschichtlichen Heilserwartung. Arbeitstagung mit Eugen Rosenstock-Huessy. July 6–7, 1957. 5 pp. Four Wells. {= "Die weggelaufene Eschatologie," *Mitteilungen der Eugen Rosenstock-Huessy-Gesellschaft* (1975). Also in *Friedensbedingungen* (1988), pp. 327–329.} Unpublished.
REEL 10, ITEM 513.

Zur Verteidigung der grammatischen Methode. Auszug in Thesen aus dem Originalvortrag von Dr. Georg Müller. "Als Grundlage für die Aussprache mit den Ordinarien der Münsterschen Universität." June–July 1957, 5 pp. Archiv der Eugen Rosenstock-Huessy Gesellschaft. {A translation of unpublished item, "In Defence of the Grammatical Method" (1962), expanded in *Speech and Reality* (1970), Ch. 1 and translated in *Friedensbedingungen* (1988), pp. 287–325.} Unpublished.
REEL 10, ITEM 514.

Zurück in das Wagnis der Sprache—Ein aufzufindender Papyrus. Introduction by Georg Müller (Berlin: Käthe Vogt Verlag, 1957), 81 pp. {See *Au risque du langage* (1997).}
REEL 10, ITEM 503.

1958

"Bestimmung der Wirtschaft in einer revolutionierten Welt," *Offene Welt* 57, Zeitschrift für Wirtschaft, Politik und Gesellschaft (Köln and Opladen: Westdeutscher Verlag, October 1958): 447–458. {Also in *Friedensbedingungen* (1988): 145–157.}
REEL 10, ITEM 517.

Bestimmung der Wirtschaft in einer revolutionierten Welt. Referat auf der Arbeitstagung in Arnoldshain. Diskussionsbeitrag. July 12–14, 1958. 50 pp. and 32 pp. Four Wells and Archiv der Eugen Rosenstock-Huessy Gesellschaft. {See "Bestimmung der Wirtschaft in einer revolutionierten Welt," *Offene Welt* (1958). = *Friedensbedingungen* (1988), pp. 145–157.} Unpublished.
SEE REEL 10, ITEM 517.

Entwurf Vorwort zur 2. Auflage der Vollzahl der Zeiten. 1958. 4 pp. Four Wells. Unpublished.
REEL 14, ITEM 625.

Das Geheimnis der Universität—Wider den Verfall von Zeitsinn und Sprachkraft. Essays and addresses, 1950–1957, ed. Georg Müller, with a contribution by Kurt Ballerstedt, "Leben und Werk Eugen Rosenstock-Huessys," (Stuttgart: W. Kohlhammer Verlag, 1958), 320 pp. Includes bibliography compiled by Edward F. Little; Bernhard E. Bergesen; C. Russell Keep, Jr.; and Matthias Rang.
REEL 10, ITEM 515.

"Die Gesetze der christlichen Zeitrechnung," Die Münsteraner Vorlesungen. Sommersemester der Theologischen Fakultät der Universität Münster. 1958. 20 two-period sessions. {= Unpublished item, "Die Gesetze der Christlichen Zeitrechnung" (1982).} Tape.
SEE REEL 18, ITEM 660.

"Ich bin ein unreiner Denker," *Wissen und Leben* 11, Werbeheft (W. Kohlhammer Verlag, 1958): 4–6. {Parts from *Das Geheimnis der Universität* (1958), pp. 97–112.}
REEL 10, ITEM 518.

Interview in Münster, Radio Bremen (1958). {= *Ja und Nein* (1968), pp. 127–147; *I Am an Impure Thinker* (1970) pp. 166–181; "Interview, Radio Bremen (Irmgard Bach, 1958)," *Bremer Beiträge* (1962).} Tape.
SEE (1968) JA UND NEIN AND (1970) I AM AN IMPURE THINKER.

Lebende Gegenwart. 1958. 25 pp. Four Wells and Archiv der Eugen Rosenstock-Huessy Gesellschaft. [I. Lebende Gegenwart. {= *Die Sprache des Menschengeschlechts,* Bd. 1 (1963), pp. 684–703, "Die Zeitweiligkeit der Sprache"}; II. Philonomie oder Die Höhere Grammatik {Die erste Neufassung des Artikels "Das Versiegen der Wissenschaft und der Ursprung der Sprache" in *Die Sprache des Menschengeschlechts,* Bd. 1 (1963), pp. 655–683}.] Unpublished.
SEE (1963) DIE SPRACHE DES MENSCHENGESCHLECHTS.

Die menschlichen Voraussetzungen einer produktiven Wirtschaft. Excerpt from the lecture by Prof. Rosenstock-Huessy, recorded on tape by Volker Hagen. July 12, 1958. 22 pp. Four Wells. {= "Bestimmung der Wirtschaft," *Offene Welt* (1958, expanded and improved, several omissions). Also in: *Friedensbedingungen* (1988), pp. 145–157.} Unpublished.
SEE REEL 10, ITEM 517.

"Saint-Simon—der erste Soziologe," *Quatember* 3 (1958): 139–145. {From *Soziologie,* Bd. 1 (1956), pp. 44–51. Also in *Stimmstein* 2 (1988): 179–186.}
REEL 10, ITEM 519.

Soziologie,* Bd. 2, *Die Vollzahl der Zeiten (Stuttgart: W. Kohlhammer Verlag, 1958), 774 pp.
REEL 10, ITEM 516.

Talk by Eugen Rosenstock-Huessy at Four Wells. September 19 (Friday evening), 1958. 4 pp. (incomplete). Four Wells. {Cf. *Die Sprache des Menschengeschlechts,* Bd. 2 (1964), p. 438.} Unpublished.
REEL 11, ITEM 522.

There is more time than you think. Free Treatment for Journalism of *Out of Revolution* (1938). ca. 1958. 14 pp. Four Wells. Unpublished.
REEL 9, ITEM 499.

"Theorien von gestern—Praktiken von wann?" *Junge Wirtschaft* 10, Zeitschrift für fortschrittliches Unternehmertum (1958): 426–428. {Also in *Mitteilungsblatt der Eugen Rosenstock-Huessy-Gesellschaft* (1986): 13–18. Also in *Friedensbedingungen* (1988), pp. 211–215.}
REEL 10, ITEM 520.

1959

"Abseitige" Gedanken zur Soziologie nach Schelskys "Ortsbestimmung der Soziologie." 1959. 5 pp. (incomplete). Four Wells. Unpublished.
REEL 11, ITEM 532.

Afterglow. 1959 (?). 2 pp. Four Wells. Unpublished.
REEL 11, ITEM 533.

American Social History – 1959, The Eugen Rosenstock-Huessy Lectures, Vol. 19; University of California at Santa Cruz, February 2 – May 25, 1959 (Jericho, Vt.: Argo Books, 1994), 622 pp. in transcription, 41 lectures on audio cassettes. College catalog title: History 180.
REEL 17, ITEM 644.

"An die Russen—Naturforschung oder Gesellschaftslehre?" *Frankfurter Hefte* 14, Heft 2, Zeitschrift für Kultur und Politik, ed. Eugen Kogon, with assistance from Walter Dirks (1959): 97–102. {= "Revolution, Soziologie und Universität," *Werbeheft* (1960), pp. 3–6. Also in "Orientierung des dritten Jahrtausends," 4/5 (1986): 6–11.}
SEE REEL 10, ITEM 518.

"Die Bemannung der Hochschule," *Frankfurter Hefte* 14, Heft 1, Zeitschrift für Kultur und Politik, ed. Eugen Kogon, with assistance from Walter Dirks (January 1959): 55–66. {= Abridged version of *Soziologie*, Bd. 2 (1958), pp. 683–709.}
REEL 11, ITEM 525.

Bibliography–Biography, including a mediation entitled "Biblionomics" (Binghamton, N.Y.: Vail Ballou Press, private printing, 1959), 38 pp. {Includes bibliography from *Das Geheimnis der Universität* (1958).}
REEL 11, ITEM 524.

"Epilog zu: Furor Teutonicus oder Furor Classicus?" *Geschichte in Wissenschaft und Unterricht* 10, Nr. 7, Zeitschrift des Verbandes der Geschichtslehrer Deutschlands (1959): 431–432. {Also in *Die Sprache des Menschengeschlechts,* Bd. 2 (1964), together with "Furor Teutonicus oder Furor Classicus?" *Geschichte in Wissenschaft und Unterricht* (1959), pp. 357–367.}
REEL 11, ITEM 526.

"Die Fortschritte der Gesellschaft und die Soziologie. Universität oder Schule?" *Frankfurter Hefte* 14, Heft 3, Zeitschrift für Kultur und Politik, ed. Eugen Kogon, with assistance from Walter Dirks (1959): 183–192. {= "Revolution, Soziologie und Universität," *Werbeheft* (1960), pp. 6–11 and "Revolutionen oder Revolutionäre?" *Alma Mater Joachimica* (1964): 270–275.}
SEE REEL 10, ITEM 518.

"Friedensbedingungen einer Weltwirtschaft," *Offene Welt* 59, Zeitschrift für Wirtschaft, Politik und Gesellschaft (Köln and Opladen: Westdeutscher Verlag, January–February 1959): 34–48, 60. {Also in *Friedensbedingungen* (1988), pp. 159–180.}
REEL 11, ITEM 527.

"Funeral Service for Margrit Rosenstock-Huessy." Congregational Church, Norwich, Vt., September 4, 1959. 7 pp. Four Wells. Unpublished.
REEL 11, ITEM 528.

"Furor Teutonicus oder Furor Classicus?" *Geschichte in Wissenschaft und Unterricht* 10, Heft 3, Zeitschrift des Verbandes der Geschichtslehrer Deutschlands (1959): 133–137. {Also in *Die Sprache des Menschengeschlechts,* Bd. 2 (1964), together with "Epilog zu: Furor Teutonicus oder Furor Classicus?" *Geschichte in Wissenschaft und Unterricht* (1959), pp. 357–367.}
SEE REEL 11, ITEM 526.

"Die Götter des Landes und der Götze Raum," *Werk und Zeit* 8, Nr. 12, Monatszeitung des deutschen Werkbundes (December 1959): 7–10. {Also in *Die Sprache des Menschengeschlechts,* Bd. 1 (1963), pp. 172–193.}
REEL 11, ITEM 529.

Historiography – 1959, The Eugen Rosenstock-Huessy Lectures, Vol. 20; University of California at Santa Cruz, February 24 – May 26, 1959 (Jericho, Vt., Argo Books, 1994), 581 pp. in transcription, 13 lectures on audio cassettes. College catalog title: History 198, "Bible and History, The Study of History Using the Bible."
REEL 17, ITEM 645.

Man Must Teach – 1959, The Eugen Rosenstock-Huessy Lectures, Vol. 21; Roosevelt School, Santa Monica, California, 1959 (Jericho, Vt.: Argo Books, 1994), 20 pp. in transcription, 1 lecture tape on audio cassette.
REEL 18, ITEM 646.

"Tribalism," transcribed and emended from the course, "Eternal Horizons of Mankind," Philosophy 58, Dartmouth College (March 9, 1954), *Exodus* (New York: Autumn 1959): 9–24. {Also in *I Am an Impure Thinker* (1970), pp. 121–136. Cf. *Universal History – 1954.*}
REEL 11, ITEM 530.

"Wer sind die Götter?" *Evangelische Unterweisung* Heft 1 (1959): 4–8, and Heft 2 (1959): 25–29. {Also in *Das Geheimnis der Universität* (1958), pp. 283–294.}
SEE (1958) DAS GEHEIMNIS DER UNIVERSITÄT.

"Zeitbessernde Tage? Eine Frage an die akademische Welt wegen 'ihrer' Zeit," *Antaios*. Zeitschrift für eine freie Welt 1, Nr. 3 (September 1959): 267–292. {Also in *Die Sprache des Menschengeschlechts*, Bd. 1 (1963), pp. 493–524 ("Was proklamieren unsere Kalender?"); *Rosenstock-Huessy Papers, Vol. 1* (1981), Ch. 8 ("Time Bettering Days" (1954).}
REEL 11, ITEM 531.

1960

"Die Ausbildung des Volksbildners (1920–1921)," *Die Neue Richtung in der Weimarer Zeit*, ed. Jürgen Henningsen. (Ernst Klett Verlag, 1960): 88–102. {= Abridged version of "Die Ausbildung des Volksbildners," *Die Arbeitsgemeinschaft* (1922) and *Im Kampf* (1926), pp. 150–167.}
SEE (1926) IM KAMPF.

"Aussprachen zu dem Vortrag: Ökonomen," Heidelberg (July 2, 1960). Tape.

"Das Dreigestirn der Bildung 1920," *Die neue Richtung in der Weimarer Zeit,* ed. Jürgen Henningsen, Dokumente und Texte von Robert von Erdberg, Wilhelm Flitner, Walter Hoffmann, Eugen Rosenstock-Huessy (Ernst Klett Verlag, 1960): 61–87. {= "Das Dreigestirn der Bildung," *Die Arbeitsgemeinschaft* (1921). Also in *Im Kampf* (1926), pp. 20–42.}
SEE (1926) IM KAMPF.

Der Glaube der Ökonomen und die Ökonomie des Glaubens. Vortrag. July 1, 1960. Heidelberg. 9 pp. (incomplete). Four Wells. {= Unpublished item, Ökonomen (1960).} Unpublished.
SEE REEL 11, ITEM 534.

Lebende Gegenwart. I. Das Versiegen der Wissenschaft und Der Ursprung der Sprache (nicht dabei). II. Philonomik oder Im Kampf um eine höhere Grammatik. Überzetzung Anna Siemsen des In Defence of The Grammatical Method. 1939 and 1955. 1960 (ca.). 59 pp. (p. 44 missing). Archiv der Eugen Rosenstock-Huessy Gesellschaft. {See unpublished item, In Verteidigung der grammatischen Methode (1986). = *Friedensbedingungen* (1988), pp. 287–325.} Unpublished.
SEE (1988) FRIEDENSBEDINGUNGEN.

Liberal Arts College – 1960, The Eugen Rosenstock-Huessy Lectures, Vol. 22; Barnard College, New York, March 3, 1960 (Jericho, Vt.: Argo Books, 1994), 26 pp. in transcription, 1 lecture on audio cassette.
REEL 18, ITEM 647.

"Ökonomen—Vortrag gehalten in der Heidelberger Universität," Heidelberg University (July 1, 1960). {= *Ökonomen* (1980). Also in *Friedensbedingungen* (1988), pp. 237–254.} Tape.
SEE (1988) FRIEDENSBEDINGUNGEN.

Ökonomen. Vortrag in der Aula der Heidelberger Universität. July 1, 1960. 19 and 21 pp. manuscripts in 2 versions. Archiv der Eugen Rosenstock-Huessy Gesellschaft. {= *Ökonomen* (1980) and unpublished item, Der Glaube der Ökonomen und die Ökonomie des Glaubens (1960). Also in *Friedensbedingungen* (1988), pp. 237–254.} Unpublished.
REEL 11, ITEM 534.

"Revolution, Soziologie und Universität," *Werbeheft* (W. Kohlhammer Verlag, 1960): 3–11. {= "An die Russen. Naturforschung oder Gesellschaftslehre?" and "Die Fortschritte der Gesellschaft und die Soziologie," *Frankfurter Hefte* (1959). Cf. "Revolutionen oder Revolutionäre?" *Alma Mater Joachimica* (1964).}
REEL 10, ITEM 518.

Der Ton der fehlt. Überarbeitete Rede vor 300 Offiziere der deutschen Bundeswehr in Sonnthofen. 1960. 24 pp. (not used in: *Friedensbedingungen* (1988) pp. 191–207). Four Wells. {See unpublished item, Die Einheit des menschlichen Schicksals in Kriegsheer und Friedenswirtschaft (1956). = *Friedensbedingungen* (1988), pp. 191–207.} Unpublished.
REEL 11, ITEM 535.

What Future for the Professions? – 1960, The Eugen Rosenstock-Huessy Lectures, Vol. 23; Aspen, Colorado, January 25–28, 1960 (Jericho, Vt.: Argo Books, 1994); 93 pp. in transcription, 4 lectures on audio cassettes.
REEL 18, ITEM 648. SEE ALSO REEL 14, ITEM 623.

Die Wiedergeburt der Wissenschaft aus der Vollmacht der Sprache. [I. Zeitweiligkeit der Sprache; II. Philonomik oder Grammatik.] 1960 (ca.). 51 pp. Four Wells. {I. = *Die Sprache des Menschengeschlechts,* Bd. 1 (1963), pp. 684–703. II. = Unpublished item, Lebende Gegenwart (1958), and 2nd revision of "Das Versiegen der Wissenschaft und Der Ursprung der Sprache," *Die Sprache des Menschengeschlechts,* Bd. 1 (1963), pp. 655–683.} Unpublished.
REEL 11, ITEM 536.

1961

Die Europäischen Revolutionen und der Charakter der Nationen (Stuttgart: W. Kohlhammer Verlag, 1961), xix + 584 pp. {= Revised version of *Die Europäischen Revolutionen und der Charakter der Nationen* (1951). See *Out of Revolution* (1938).}
NOT MICROFILMED.

"Eine Friedenswoche," *Züricher Woche* 13, Nr. 42, Schweizerische illustrierte Wochenzeitung für Politik, Kultur und Wirtschaft (October 20, 1961): 1. {Also in *Friedensbedingungen* (1988), pp. 93–96.}
SEE (1988) FRIEDENSBEDINGUNGEN.

"The Generations of the Faith," *Hartford Quarterly* 3 (1961): 95–111. {Also in *Die Sprache des Menschengeschlechts,* Bd. 2 (1964), pp. 276–300 ("Der Ton der zweiten Stimme. Erster Teil: Jean Calvin, Eine Festrede"); *Rosenstock-Huessy Papers, Vol. 1* (1981), Ch. 9.}
REEL 11, ITEM 537.

Francis L. Lieber (18. März 1800 – 2. Oktober 1872). Referat für das Seminar: Die Dialektik zwischen Europa und Amerika im Gegensatz zur marxistischen Dialektik. Im Amerika-Institut der Universität zu Köln. November 29, 1961. 5 pp. Four Wells. Unpublished.
REEL 11, ITEM 540.

"Stalins Einebnung und die Chronologie der Weltkriegsrevolution," *Züricher Woche* 13, Nr. 48, Schweizerische illustrierte Wochenzeitung für Politik, Kultur und Wirtschaft (December 1, 1961): 1, 28.
REEL 11, ITEM 538.

Stomatology. A Luncheon Address at an R.M. [Rocky Mountain] Orthodontic Product and Film and Demonstration Program, Milwaukee, Wisc. January 19, 1961. 8 pp. (incomplete from tape). Four Wells. Unpublished.
REEL 11, ITEM 541.

"Universitäten oder Schulen?" *Nobis,* Mainzer Studentenzeitung (May 1961): 10–11.
SEE REEL 11, ITEM 518.

"Das Volk Gottes in Vergangenheit, Gegenwart, Zukunft," *Juden, Christen, Deutsche,* ed. Hans Jürgen Schultz (Olten: Kreuz-Verlag, and Freiburg i.Br.: Walter-Verlag, 1961): 198–220. {= "Das Volk Gottes," *Freiburger Rundbrief* (1965). Part II: "Die Dreieinigkeit in beiden Israel," pp. 206–213; = "The Jewish and the Christian Trinity" (1966), with some revisions).}
REEL 11, ITEM 539. {Includes two pages of aphorisms by Rosenstock-Huessy, as printed in *The Viking Book of Aphorisms* (1966).}

"Vom Staatsbürger zum Flüchtlingsstaat," *Evangelische Unterweisung* 16, Heft 8 (August 1961): 121–122. {Also in *Die Europäischen Revolutionen und der Charakter der Nationen* (1961), pp. 530–532.}
NOT MICROFILMED.

Die Weigerung des Quintaners. Vom Anerkennen. 1961 (ca.). 45 pp. Archiv der Eugen Rosenstock-Huessy Gesellschaft. {Third version of the article "Das Versiegen der Wissenschaft und Der Ursprung der Sprache," *Die Sprache des Menschengeschlechts*, Bd. 1 (1963), pp. 655–683.} [With one-page titles for the margin: 1. Lebendiges Sprechen entmächtigt den Quintaner in uns; 2. Über jeden von uns ergeht dreifache Rede; 3. Wer spricht, wird abgewandelt; 4. Der Teufel verachtet die Leibhaftigkeit der Grammatik; 5. Menschliche Gruppen sind Tonfallgemeinschaften; 6. Sprechen schafft Weilen der Zeit; 7. Jede Epoche ist Schöpfung aus dem Nichts; 8. Ständig muss Totes ausgeschieden werden; 9. Ereignisse werden ausgerufen; 10. Der Vokativ ist die grammatische Form der Zukunft; 11. Die grammatischen Formen rufen einander hervor; 12. Sogenannte Übersichten verdecken die Aggregatzustände der Seele.] Unpublished. REEL 11, ITEM 542.

"Wer ist Gottes Volk?" Süddeutscher Rundfunk (April 9, 1961). {= "Das Volk Gottes," *Juden, Christen, Deutsche* (1961); "Das Volk Gottes," *Freiberger Rundbrief* (1965).} Tape.

Die zwölf Töne des Geistes. Auszüge für die Bibelstunde von St. Augustine by the Sea. 1961. 5 pp. (Incomplete. Probably Rosenstock-Huessy's own translation). Archiv der Eugen Rosenstock-Huessy Gesellschaft. {= Translated from *I Am an Impure Thinker* (1970), pp. 69–76.} Unpublished. REEL 11, ITEM 543.

1962

The following entries appeared in *The American People's Encyclopedia* (Grolier, Inc., 1962). The first number following the entry title refers to the volume number; the numbers after the colon are page numbers.

"Abélard, Pierre," 1: 22–23. {Unsigned. Francis Squibb, co-author.} REEL 11, ITEM 545, FRAME 6681.

"Conceptualism," 5: 1022–1023. {Unsigned. Francis Squibb, co-author.} REEL 11, ITEM 545, FRAME 6693.

"Concordance," 6: 5–6. {Unsigned. Francis Squibb, co-author.} REEL 11, ITEM 545, FRAME 6696.

"Confessions of Saint Augustine," 6: 35–36. {Unsigned. Francis Squibb, co-author.}
REEL 11, ITEM 545, FRAME 6698.

"Dante Alighieri," 6: 775–780.
REEL 11, ITEM 545, FRAME 6704.

"David," 6: 806–807. {Unsigned.}
REEL 11, ITEM 545, FRAME 6707.

"Descartes, René," 6: 1000–1003.
REEL 11, ITEM 545, FRAME 6710.

"Dialectic," 7: 47–48.
REEL 11, ITEM 545, FRAME 6714.

"Dialogue," 7: 48–49.
REEL 11, ITEM 545, FRAME 6716.

"Dionysius the Areopagite," 7: 122–123. {Unsigned.}
REEL 11, ITEM 545, FRAME 6719.

"Divine Comedy, The," 7: 176–178.
REEL 11, ITEM 545, FRAME 6722.

"Duns Scotus," 7: 410.
REEL 11, ITEM 545, FRAME 6725.

"Edwards, Jonathan," 7: 615–617.
REEL 11, ITEM 545, FRAME 6727.

"Emerson, Ralph Waldo," 7: 859–861.
REEL 11, ITEM 545, FRAME 6730.

"Existentialism," 8: 201–204. {Unsigned. Francis Squibb, co-author.}
REEL 11, ITEM 545, FRAME 6733.

"Faraday, Michael," 8: 310–313. {Unsigned. Francis Squibb, co-author.}
REEL 11, ITEM 545, FRAME 6736.

"Homer," 10: 573–574. {Unsigned. Francis Squibb, co-author.}
REEL 11, ITEM 545, FRAME 6741.

"Name," 13: 1064–1068. {Unsigned. Francis Squibb, co-author.}
REEL 11, ITEM 545, FRAME 6743.

"Newman, John Henry Cardinal," 14: 304–306. {Unsigned.}
REEL 11, ITEM 545, FRAME 6747.

"Nietzsche, Friedrich Wilhelm," 14: 448–450. {Unsigned. Francis Squibb, co-author.}
REEL 11, ITEM 545, FRAME 6750.

"Nominalism," 14: 500–501. {Unsigned. Francis Squibb, co-author.}
REEL 11, ITEM 545, FRAME 6753.

"Paracelsus," 15: 26–27. {Unsigned.}
REEL 11, ITEM 545, FRAME 6756.

"Plato," 15: 650–657. {Unsigned.}
REEL 11, ITEM 545, FRAME 6759.

"Republic," 16: 429–430. {Unsigned. Francis Squibb, co-author.}
REEL 11, ITEM 545, FRAME 6764.

"Republic," (of Plato) 16: 430–431. {Unsigned. Francis Squibb, co-author.}
REEL 11, ITEM 545, FRAME 6766.

"Research," 16: 438–439. {Unsigned. Francis Squibb, co-author.}
REEL 11, ITEM 545, FRAME 6769.

"Revolution," 16: 466–468. {Unsigned. Francis Squibb, co-author.}
REEL 11, ITEM 545, FRAME 6772.

"Saint-Simon, Claude Henri de," 16: 914–915. {Unsigned.}
REEL 11, ITEM 545, FRAME 6775.

"Social Sciences," 17: 524–526. {Unsigned. Francis Squibb, co-author.}
REEL 11, ITEM 545, FRAME 6778.

"Socrates. Plato, Socrates, and Athens," 17: 546–547. {Unsigned.}
REEL 11, ITEM 545, FRAME 6781.

"Sudhoff, Karl," 17: 1051. {Unsigned. Francis Squibb, co-author.}
REEL 11, ITEM 545, FRAME 6785.

"Swedenborg, Emmanuel," 18: 101–102. {Unsigned. Francis Squibb, co-author.}
REEL 11, ITEM 545, FRAME 6787.

"Timaeus," 18: 546–548. {Unsigned. Francis Squibb, co-author}
REEL 11, ITEM 545, FRAME 6789.

"Vahlen, Johannes," 19: 144.
REEL 11, ITEM 545, FRAME 6795.

"Vaihinger, Hans," 19: 144–145.
REEL 11, ITEM 545, FRAME 6797.

"Valentinius," 19: 152–153.
REEL 11, ITEM 545, FRAME 6800.

"Vampire," 19: 164.
REEL 11, ITEM 545, FRAME 6803.

"Ventris, Michael George Francis," 19: 239–241.
REEL 11, ITEM 545, FRAME 6805.

"Venus," 19: 245–246.
REEL 11, ITEM 545, FRAME 6808.

"Verner, Karl Adolph," 19: 272.
REEL 11, ITEM 545, FRAME 6810.

"Vico, Giovanni Battista," 19: 301–302.
REEL 11, ITEM 545, FRAME 6812.

"Walton, Izaak," 19: 460.
REEL 11, ITEM 545, FRAME 6814.

"Webb, Beatrice," 19: 590.
REEL 11, ITEM 545, FRAME 6816.

"Webb, Sidney James, 1st Baron Passfield," 19: 591.
REEL 11, ITEM 545, FRAME 6818.

"Weber, Max," 19: 592–593.
REEL 11, ITEM 545, FRAME 6820.

"Webster, Daniel," 19: 593–596.
REEL 11, ITEM 545, FRAME 6823.

"Weizsäcker, Freiherr Viktor von," 19: 613–614.
REEL 11, ITEM 545, FRAME 6826.

"Wesley, John," 19: 633–635.
REEL 11, ITEM 545, FRAME 6828.

"Whitehead, Alfred North," 19: 703–705.
REEL 11, ITEM 545, FRAME 6831.

"Whitman, Walt," 19: 712–716.
REEL 11, ITEM 545, FRAME 6834.

"Wieland, Christopher Martin," 19: 724.
REEL 11, ITEM 545, FRAME 6838.

"William Ockham," 19: 746–748.
REEL 11, ITEM 545, FRAME 6840.

"William of Champeaux," 19: 748.
REEL 11, ITEM 545, FRAME 6843.

"Winckelmann, Johann Joachim," 19: 771–772.
REEL 11, ITEM 545, FRAME 6845.

"Wittgenstein, Ludwig Joseph Johann," 19: 809–810. {Unsigned. Francis Squibb, co-author.}
REEL 11, ITEM 545, FRAME 6847.

"Wittig, Joseph," 19: 810–811.
REEL 11, ITEM 545, FRAME 6849.

"Wolf, Friedrich August," 19: 812–813.
REEL 11, ITEM 545, FRAME 6852.

"Wolfram von Eschenbach," 19: 816.
REEL 11, ITEM 545, FRAME 6855.

"Wundt, Wilhelm Max," 19: 934–935.
REEL 11, ITEM 545, FRAME 6857.

"Wycliffe, John," 19: 938–939.
REEL 11, ITEM 545, FRAME 6860.

"X," 19: 955.
REEL 11, ITEM 545, FRAME 6863.

"Xenophon," 19: 957–958.
REEL 11, ITEM 545, FRAME 6865.

"Y," 19: 967.
REEL 11, ITEM 545, FRAME 6867.

"Z," 19: 1029.
REEL 11, ITEM 545, FRAME 6869.

"Zarathustra," 19: 1038–1039.
REEL 11, ITEM 545, FRAME 6871.

"Zen," 19: 1042–1043.
REEL 11, ITEM 545, FRAME 6874.

"Zeno of Citium," 19: 1044–1045.
REEL 11, ITEM 545, FRAME 6877.

"Zeno of Elea," 19: 1045–1046.
REEL 11, ITEM 545, FRAME 6880.

"Zeus," 19: 1048–1050.
REEL 11, ITEM 545, FRAME 6882.

"Zoroastrianism," 19: 1079–1082.
REEL 11, ITEM 545, FRAME 6885.

"Zweig, Stefan," 19: 1086–1087. {Unsigned.}
REEL 11, ITEM 545, FRAME 6888.

"Zwingli, Huldreich," 19: 1087–1088.
REEL 11, ITEM 545, FRAME 6891.

Dominic, Saint, de Guzman 24.6.1170 – 6.8.1221. Intended for *The American People's Encyclopedia* but not published. 1962 (ca.). 3 pp. Four Wells. Unpublished.
REEL 11, ITEM 547.

Die Erschaffung aus dem Nichts? 1962 (ca.). 46 pp. Four Wells and Archiv der Eugen Rosenstock-Huessy Gesellschaft. {Fourth version of the article, "Das Versiegen der Wissenschaft und Der Ursprung der Sprache," *Die Sprache des Menschengeschlechts,* Bd. 1 (1963), pp. 655–683. Pp. 1–2, new beginning; pp. 44–46, new ending.} Unpublished.
REEL 11, ITEM 548.

Grammatical Method – 1962, The Eugen Rosenstock-Huessy Lectures, Vol. 24; Barnard College, New York, Spring 1962 (Jericho, Vt.: Argo Books, 1994), 51 pp. in transcription, 3 lectures on audio cassettes. College course title (Prof. Harold Stahmer): "Religion and Contemporary Culture." {= Unpublished item, In Defence of the Grammatical Method (1962).}
REEL 18, ITEM 649. SEE ALSO REEL 14, ITEM 614.

In Defence of the Grammatical Method. Three Lectures at Barnard College, Columbia University, New York, in Harold M. Stahmer's course, "Religion and Contemporary Culture." 1962. 87 pp. Four Wells.{= *Grammatical Method – 1962.*} Unpublished.
SEE REEL 18, ITEM 649.

"Interview, Radio Bremen (Irmgard Bach, 1958)," *Bremer Beiträge.* Auszug des Geistes (Bremen: Verlag B. C. Heye & Co., 1962): 106–126. {Also in *Ja und Nein* (1968), pp. 127–147; *I Am an Impure Thinker* (1970), pp. 166–181 ("Immigration of the Spirit").}
SEE (1968) JA UND NEIN OR (1970) I AM AN IMPURE THINKER.

Der Inventar Einleitung zu *Die Frucht der Lippen - Die Strategie der Sprache* (= Erstmaliger Titel der *Sprache des Menschengeschlechts*). Anfang Band II. 1962 (ca.). 5 pp. Four Wells. {Abgedruckt in: Dr. Eckart Wilkens, "Die Schrift" und "Gemeinde," zwei Adventsandachten Eugen Rosenstock-Huessys aus dem Felde 1916. Köln 23.10.1981 S. 3–7 Dazu 5 S. Inhaltsübersichte.} Unpublished.
REEL 11, ITEM 549.

"Karfreitag, Karsamstag, Ostersonntag," Südwestfunk (1962). {= *Die Sprache des Menschengeschlechts*, Bd. 2 (1964), pp. 428–448.} Tape.

Die misshandelte Zeit. Drei Rundfunkvorträge [1. Der illegitime Mensch; 2. Die entschwundene Gegenwart; 3. Die dreieinige Zeit.] Radio Basel, April 2, 9, and 16, 1962. 30 pp. Four Wells and Archiv der Eugen Rosenstock-Huessy Gesellschaft. {Also in *Friedensbedingungen* (1988), pp. 41–70.} Unpublished.
REEL 11, ITEM 550.

Notfall. [Later incorporated in "'Im Notfall'," *Neue Sammlung* (1963): 527, 8th line from the bottom to p. 528, 8th line from the top.] 1962 (ca.). 2 pp. Four Wells. Unpublished.
NOT MICROFILMED.

St. Augustine – 1962, The Eugen Rosenstock-Huessy Lectures, Vol. X; Saint Augustine by-the-Sea, Santa Monica, California, June 1962 (Jericho, Vt.: Argo Books, 1994): 149 pp. in transcription, 6 lectures on audio cassettes. Santa Monica Church Talks title: "The Bionomics of Language."
REEL 18, ITEM 650.

"Sermon on Philippians 3:21," Congregational Church, Norwich, Vt., May 13, 1962. 4 pp. Four Wells. Unpublished.
REEL 11, ITEM 547A.

Die Sprache des Menschengeschlechts. Eine leibhaftige Grammatik in vier Teilen. Broschüre zur Ankündigung der 2 Bänden von 1963 und 1964 (Heidelberg: Lambert Schneider Verlag, 1962), 12 pp. {Table of contents of the first volume: Der Autor. Das Werk. Die Vorrede. = *Die Sprache des Menschengeschlechts*, Bd. 1 (1963), pp. 17–22.}
REEL 11, ITEM 544.

"Der technische Fortschritt erweitert den Raum, verkürzt die Zeit, zerschlägt menschliche Gruppen. Protokolle der Tagung 2. – 4. März 1962 der leitenden Mitarbeiter der Firma Daimler-Benz in der Evangelischen Akademie Bad Boll (Walter Hähnle)," *Materialdienst* 4, Pressestelle Bad Boll (1962), 14 pp. {Also in Friedensbedingungen (1988), pp. 107–117 and in *Daimler Werkzeitung* 1919/20 (1991) pp. XLV–L.}
SEE (1988) FRIEDENSBEDINGUNGEN.

"Über die Verlegung der Fürstenschulen nach Westdeutschland," *Alma Mater Joachimica* 12, Zeitschrift der Vereinigung alter Joachimsthaler e.V. (August 1962): 150–151.
REEL 11, ITEM 552.

The Wailers. 1962 (?). 9 pp. Four Wells. Unpublished.
REEL 11, ITEM 551.

Witchcraft. A first draft. Intended for *The American People's Encyclopedia* but not completed and not published. 1962 (ca.). 20 pp. handwritten; typescript by L. van der Molen, 4 pp. Archiv der Eugen Rosenstock-Huessy Gesellschaft. Unpublished.
REEL 11, ITEM 546.

1963

Abstammen und Zustammen. In Eugen Rosenstock-Huessy's handwriting: Zum Abschluss von "Frucht der Lippen," not incorporated in the German text. 1963 (ca.), 8 pp. pp. 84–91. Four Wells. Unpublished.
REEL 11, ITEM 553.

"Europas Amerika und Amerikas Europa," *Offene Welt* 79, Zeitschrift für Wirtschaft, Politik und Gesellschaft (Köln and Opladen: Westdeutscher Verlag, 1963): 108–113. {Also in *Die Sprache des Menschengeschlechts*, Bd. 2 (1964), pp. 310–319.}
REEL 11, ITEM 555.

"Der Glaube der Ökonomen," *Hersg. Süddeutscher Rundfunk, Hauptabteilung Erziehung und religiöses Wort* (Ostersonntag, April 14, 1963), 11 pp. {Also in *Friedensbedingungen* (1988), pp. 217–226.}
SEE (1988) FRIEDENSBEDINGUNGEN.

"Der Glaube der Ökonomen," Süddeutscher Rundfunk (Ostersonntag, April 14, 1963). {= "Der Glaube der Ökonomen," *Süddeutscher Rundfunk* (1963). Also in: *Friedensbedingungen* (1988), pp. 217–226.} Tape.
SEE (1988) FRIEDENSBEDINGUNGEN.

"'Im Notfall' oder die 'Zeitlichkeit des Geistes.' Für Margarete Susman zum 80. Geburtstag," *Neue Sammlung* 3, Heft 6, Göttinger Blätter für Kultur und Erziehung (November–December 1963): 518–530. {Reprint, Göttingen: Van Den Hoeck & Ruprecht, 1963. See unpublished item, Notfall (1962).}
REEL 11, ITEM 556.

"'Der Konzil in Permanenz.' Zur Frage der Universität," *Süddeutscher Rundfunk* interview with Dr. H. W. Krautkrämer (September 19, 1963), 22:40–23:00 hours in the series, "Aus dem Hochschulleben, Kommentare und Berichte." Tape.

Logik auf Probe (title should be: **Logik vor Gericht**). 1963 (?). Pp. 50–90. Archiv der Eugen Rosenstock-Huessy Gesellschaft. {First-draft translation of *The Origin of Speech* (1981), Ch. 6 ("Logic on Trial"). Omitted, beginning p. 510, in *Die Sprache des Menschengeschlechts*, Bd. 2 (1964), pp. 451–594 ("Im Prägstock eines Menschenschlags oder Der tägliche Ursprung der Sprache.").} Unpublished.
NOT MICROFILMED.

"Mensch und Technik," *Die Herausforderung, Darmstädter Gespräche*, ed. Heinz Winfried Sabris (Paul List Verlag, 1963): 110–112. {= "Das Gesetz der Technik," *Darmstädter Gespräch, Mensch und Technik* (first part, 1952). Also in *Friedensbedingungen* (1988), pp. 97–99.}
SEE (1952) "DAS GESETZ," OR (1988) FRIEDENSBEDINGUNGEN.

"Mündig, unbefangen, unentbehrlich," *Deutsches Pfarrerblatt* 63, Nr. 23 (1963): 570–572. {Also in *Die Sprache des Menschengeschlechts*, Bd. 1 (1963), pp. 110–118.}
SEE (1963) DIE SPRACHE DES MENSCHENGESCHLECHTS.

Notizen über Missverständnisse im Wissenschaftlichen Vokabular—Zur Ägyptologie. Zugeschickt an Prof. Dr. Siegfried Schott in Göttingen. 1962/1963. 4 pp. Four Wells. Unpublished.
REEL 11, ITEM 557.

"Die Ökonomie des Glaubens," *Hersg. Süddeutscher Rundfunk, Hauptabteilung Erziehung und religiöses Wort* (Ostermontag, April 15, 1963), 13 pp. {Also in *Friedensbedingungen* (1988), pp. 226–236.}
SEE (1988) FRIEDENSBEDINGUNGEN.

"Die Ökonomie des Glaubens," Süddeutscher Rundfunk (Ostermontag, April 15, 1963). {= "Die Ökonomie des Glaubens," *Süddeutscher Rundfunk* (1963). Also in: *Friedensbedingungen* (1988), pp. 226–236.} Tape.
SEE (1988) FRIEDENSBEDINGUNGEN.

On the Wings of the Dove Invocation. For the Marriage of Peter Drowne and Elizabeth (Libby) Thayer (June 22, 1963). 4 pp. Four Wells. Unpublished.
REEL 11, ITEM 558.

Die Sprache des Menschengeschlechts. Eine leibhaftige Grammatik in vier Teilen, Bd. 1, Erster und Zweiter Teil. (Heidelberg: Verlag Lambert Schneider, 1963), 810 pp.
REEL 11, ITEM 554.

Der Ton der fehlt. 1963. *Süddeutscher Rundfunk.* 15 pp. Four Wells. {Transcript of the tape "Weltfriedensdienst statt Weltbürgerkrieg" (1963).} Unpublished.
NOT MICROFILMED.

"Vorträge in der Sarepta-Schule," Bielefeld, Germany (May 5 and 6, 1963). Tape.

"Weltfriedensdienst statt Weltbürgerkrieg," *Süddeutscher Rundfunk* (December 1, 8, 15, and 22, 1963). {Revised in *Dienst auf dem Planeten* (1965).} Tape.
SEE REEL 12, ITEM 563.

1964

Für Lehrer. Eine Fussnote zur *Sprache des Menschengeschlechts.* 1964. 8 pp. Archiv der Eugen Rosenstock-Huessy Gesellschaft. Unpublished.
REEL 12, ITEM 565.

"Das Gehirn kann nicht bereuen," *Radio Bremen* interview with Hans Fischer Barnicol (October 10, 1964). {= "Das Gehirn kann nicht bereuen," *Mitteilungsblatt der Eugen Rosenstock-Huessy Gesellschaft* (1984): 2–9.} Tape.

Die Interims des Rechts, Für Franz Beyerle zum 80. Geburtstag (refers to the Dutch half-revolution). Four Wells. Private printing. 10 pp. November 1964. {Also in *Stimmstein* 3 (1990): 14–24.}
REEL 11, ITEM 559.

"Protestantismus und Seelenführung," *Deutsches Pfarrerblatt* 64, Nr. 17 (1964): 460–461. {= "Protestantismus und Seelenführung," *Protestantismus als Kritik und Gestaltung* (1929): 224–228, 248–253 (excerpts).}
SEE REEL 4, ITEM 225.

"Revolution als Dienst," *Radio Stuttgart* interview with Hans Fischer Barnicol. 1964. 9 pp. Four Wells. {= "Das Gehirn kann nicht bereuen" (1964), and "Das Gehirn kann nicht bereuen," *Mitteilungsblatt der Eugen Rosenstock-Huessy Gesellschaft* (1984).} Unpublished.
REEL 12, ITEM 562.

"Revolutionen oder Revolutionäre?" *Alma Mater Joachimica* Neue Folge, Heft 19, Zeitschrift der Vereinigung Alter Joachimstaler (May 25, 1964): 270–275. {= "Die Fortschritte der Gesellschaft?" *Frankfurter Hefte* (1959); = "Revolution, Soziologie und Universität," *Werbeheft* (1960), pp. 6–11.}
SEE REEL 10, ITEM 518.

***Die Sprache des Menschengeschlechts. Eine leibhaftige Grammatik in vier Teilen,* Bd. 2** {with an index of 26 pp. separately printed and included in a few copies of this edition}. Dritter und Vierter Teil (Heidelberg: Verlag Lambert Schneider, 1964), 904 pp.
REEL 12, ITEM 560.

"Talk by Rosenstock-Huessy," General Meeting of the Eugen Rosenstock-Huessy Gesellschaft (May 7, 1964). Tape.

"Time and Historicity of Man," *Philosophical Interrogations*, ed. Sydney and Beatrice Rome (Holt, Rinehart and Winston, 1964): 31–33.
REEL 12, ITEM 561.

1965

Autobiographic statement (August 12–13, 1965): pp. a–z, transcribed by George Allen Morgan, 11 pp. {= new version of *Ja und Nein* (1968), pp. 59ff. Harold M. Stahmer, private collection.} Unpublished.
NOT MICROFILMED.

Der Beruf aus neuer ökumenischer Sicht," Heidelberg (1965), tape. {= Unpublished item, "Der Beruf in neuer ökumenischer Sicht" (1986). Also in *Friedensbedingungen* (1985): 255–282.}
SEE (1988) FRIEDENSBEDINGUNGEN.

"Beruf und Job," Heidelberg (1965). Tape.

"Die Biologie der modernen Fabrik," *Norddeutscher Rundfunk*, a talk with industrialists and politicians in Hamburg (1965). Tape.

The Cross of Reality – 1965, The Eugen Rosenstock-Huessy Lectures, Vol. 28; Woods Hole, Mass., July 16, 1965 (Jericho, Vt.: Argo Books, 1994), 10 pp. in transcription, 1 lecture on audio cassette. {= *I Am an Impure Thinker* (1970), pp. 65–68 ("The Quadrilateral of Human Logic").}
REEL 18, ITEM 653.

Dienst auf dem Planeten—Kurzweil und Langeweile im dritten Jahrtausend (Stuttgart, Berlin, Köln, Mainz: W. Kohlhammer Verlag, GmbH, 1965), 140 pp. {Abridged English edition: *Planetary Service* (1978). Dutch translation: *Dienen op de planeet* (1988).}
REEL 12, ITEM 563.

Economy of Times – 1965, The Eugen Rosenstock-Huessy Lectures, Vol. 26; University of California at Santa Barbara, November 16 – December 14, 1965 (Jericho, Vt.: Argo Books, 1994): 79 pp. in transcription, 4 lectures on audio cassettes. College course title: "From the Economy of Times to the Economy of Markets."
REEL 18, ITEM 651.

Mihi est propositum. Ein autobiographischer Zusatz zur *Sprache des Menschengeschlechts* (August 15, 1965), 3 pp. Archiv der Eugen Rosenstock-Huessy Gesellschaft. {= *Ja und Nein* (1968), pp. 17–19.} Unpublished.
REEL 12, ITEM 566.

"The Quadrilateral of Human Thought," a paper prepared for a Symposium on the Thought of Eugen Rosenstock-Huessy, held at the Center for the Study of Religion and Social Issues, Miramar, Woods Hole, Mass. (July 19 – 21, 1965). 4 pp. Four Wells and Archiv der Eugen Rosenstock-Huessy Gesellschaft. {= *I Am an Impure Thinker* (1970), pp. 65–68 ("The Quadrilateral of Human Logic"). Cf. *Cross of Reality – 1965*.} Unpublished.
REEL 12, ITEM 567.

"Rückblick auf die *Kreatur*," *Rechenschaft 1925–1965*. Ein Almanach (Verlag Lambert Schneider, 1965): 95–105. {= "Rückblick auf die *Kreatur*," *Deutsche Beiträge zur Geistigen Überlieferung* (1947). Also in *Ja und Nein* (1965), pp. 107–118.}
SEE (1965) JA UND NEIN.

***Talk with Franciscans* – *1965*,** The Eugen Rosenstock-Huessy Lectures, Vol. 27; location and dates uncertain (Jericho, Vt.: Argo Books, 1994): 36 pp. in transcription, 2 lectures on audio cassettes.
REEL 18, ITEM 652.

"Das Volk Gottes in Gegenwart, Vergangenheit und Zukunft," *Freiburger Rundbrief* 16, Nr. 11, Beiträge zur Förderung der Freundschaft zwischen dem Alten und dem Neuen Gottesvolk im Geiste beider Testamente, 61/64 (July 1965): 69–76. {= "Das Volk Gottes," *Juden, Christen, Deutsche* (1961).}
REEL 12, ITEM 564.

1966

"Buch und Funk," *Hundert Jahre Kohlhammer 1866–1966* (W. Kohlhammer Verlag, 1966): 252–259.
REEL 12, ITEM 569.

Instructors' note on "The Speech of Humankind" (*Die Sprache des Menschengeschlechts*, 2 volumes, Heidelberg 1963 and 1964.) 1966 (ca.). 4 pp. Archiv der Eugen Rosenstock–Huessy Gesellschaft. Unpublished.
REEL 12, ITEM 574.

The Jewish and the Christian Trinity. An expanded translation, with some revisions, of the second part of "Das Volk Gottes in Vergangenheit, Gegenwart und Zukunft (1962): 198–220. [II. Die Dreieinigkeit in den beiden Israel.] Intended to be included in *Judaism Despite Christianity* (1969), but not accepted.) 1966 (ca.). 13 pp. Four Wells. Unpublished.
REEL 12, ITEM 583.

"Job Corps Interview, by Dick Broderson." WMTW, Poland Spring, Maine (October 18, 1966) 30 minutes, Argo video cassette.

***Lingo of Linguistics* – *1966*,** The Eugen Rosenstock-Huessy Lectures, Vol. 29; Western Washington State College, Bellingham, Washington, April 4 – 6, 1966 (Jericho, Vt.: Argo Books, 1994): 63 pp. in transcription, 3 lectures on audio cassettes.
REEL 18, ITEM 654.

"Die 'Objektiven Unwahrheiten des Bischofs Dr. Otto Dibelius'," *Darmstädter Blätter* 9 (1966): 46.
REEL 12, ITEM 570.

De onbetaalbare mens, trans. H. J. de Koster, with introduction by P. Smits (Rotterdam: Lemniscaat, 1966), 195 pp. {Translation of *Der unbezahlbare Mensch* (1955).}
REEL 12, ITEM 568.

Peace Corps – 1966, The Eugen Rosenstock-Huessy Lectures, Vol. 30; Vershire, Vt., July 13 – 15, 1966 (Jericho, Vt.: Argo Books, 1994): 40 pp. in transcription, 3 lectures on audio cassettes.
REEL 18, ITEM 655.

"Pfingsten hat schlechte Zeiten," Rundfunkvortrag (1966). Tape.

Tenses, Times and Trinity, or The Abuse of Education. (Originally intended to be included in *Judaism Despite Christianity* (1969). 1966 (ca.). 26 pp. Four Wells. Typescript by L. van der Molen, 13 pp. Unpublished.
REEL 12, ITEM 573.

Whom Money Cannot Buy, Ecodynamics of a Mechanized World and The Fractions of Man in Industry, a Three Phases Monograph. With a new preface by the author (1966), and the preface to the 1936 Beachhead Foreword. {= *The Multiformity of Man* (1948) with the translation of the second part of *Der unbezahlbare Mensch* (1955, 1957).} This second part has 66 pp.October 1966. Four Wells. Unpublished.
REEL 12, ITEM 571.

1967

Cruciform Character of History – 1967, The Eugen Rosenstock-Huessy Lectures, Vol. 31; University of the Pacific, Stockton, Calif., March 1967 (Jericho, Vt.: Argo Books, 1994): 65 pp. in transcription, 5 lectures on audio cassette. Tippet Lecture Series title: "The Cruciform Character of Mankind's History."
REEL 18, ITEM 656.

Geschichte muss erzählt werden. 1967. 28 pp. Archiv der Eugen Rosenstock-Huessy Gesellschaft. {First-draft partial translation of *History Must Be Told* (1954).} Unpublished.
NOT MICROFILMED.

The Ides of March—A Peroration. 1967. 3 pp. Four Wells. Unpublished.
REEL 12, ITEM 576.

Magna Carta Latina. The Privilege of Singing, Articulating and Reading a Language and of Keeping It Alive, with Ford Lewis Battles (Private printing, 1967), xxii + 296 pp. {= *Magna Carta Latina* (1975).}
SEE REEL 12, ITEM 575.

Universal History – 1967, The Eugen Rosenstock-Huessy Lectures, Vol. 32; University of California at Santa Cruz, Calif., 1967 (Jericho, Vt.: Argo Books, 1994): 396 pp. in transcription, 20 lectures on audio cassettes.
REEL 18, ITEM 657.

1968

"Die Akademie der Arbeit 1920. (a) Grundsätze über eine Bildungsstätte für erwachsene Arbeiter (p. 85). (b) Die Stellung der Akademie unter den anderen Schulen (p. 90)," *Zur Geschichte der Arbeiterbildung*, ed. Hildegard Feidel-Merz (Verlag Julius Klinkhardt, 1968): 85–92. {= *Im Kampf* (1926), pp. 92–98, 115–118; "Grundsätze über eine Bildungsstätte," *Die Akademie der Arbeit* (abridged, 1931); "Die Stellung der Akademie," *Die Akademie der Arbeit* (abridged, 1931).}
SEE (1926) IM KAMPF.

Correspondence and Existence. An early preface to *Judaism Despite Christianity* (1969), (Incomplete.) 3 pp. with a handwritten table of contents of 1 p. Four Wells. Unpublished.
NOT MICROFILMED.

"Das Ende der Dialektik Ketzer-Papst, oder: Das Jahrtausend des Samariters," *Die Wahrheit der Ketzer*, ed. Hans Jürgen Schultz (1968): 206–213. {= "Das Jahrtausend des Samariters," *Orientierung* (1968). See "Heretic and Pope," *Christianity and Freedom* (1968).}
REEL 12, ITEM 579.

"Exil. Translation of *Hugo von St. Victor. 12. Jh.,"*
vergangen-erlebt-überwunden, Schicksale der Familie Bonhoeffer, ed. Sabine Leibholz-Bonhoeffer (Wuppertal-Barmen: Johannes Kiefel Verlag, 1968): 119.
NOT MICROFILMED.

Fashions of Atheism – 1968, The Eugen Rosenstock Huessy Lectures, Vol. 32; University of Connecticut, Storrs, March 1968 (Jericho, Vt.: Argo Books, 1994): 20 pp. in transcription, 1 lecture on audio cassette. A lecture for Bob Luyster.
REEL 18, ITEM 658.

"Gedanken von Eugen Rosenstock-Huessy. Tageslosungen für den Monat November. Sprüche aus *Des Christen Zukunft* zusammengestellt von Pfarrer Rolf Sigg," *Von des Christen Freude und Freiheit,* Protestantische Monatschrift (Zürich, November 1968): 8–11. {*Des Christen Zukunft* in title refers to *Des Christen Zukunft* (1955).}
NOT MICROFILMED.

"Heretic and Pope," *Christianity and Freedom* 7, trans. James Burtness (Minneapolis, Minn.: Augsburg College, Spring 1968): 127–131. {See "Das Ende der Dialektik Ketzer-Papst," *Die Wahrheit der Ketzer* (1968); "Das Jahrtausend des Samariters," *Orientierung* (1968).}
REEL 12, ITEM 580.

Interview, "Rosenstock-Huessy back at Santa Cruz," *Mariner* 1, no. 2 (University of California at Santa Cruz, Friday, February 23, 1968): 1, 3.
NOT MICROFILMED.

Ja und Nein, Autobiographische Fragmente aus Anlass des 80. Geburtstags des Autors im Auftrag der seinen Namen tragenden Gesellschaft, ed. Georg Müller (Heidelberg: Verlag Lambert Schneider, 1968), 184 pp.
REEL 12, ITEM 578.

"Das Jahrtausend des Samariters," *Orientierung* 32, Nr. 7, Katholische Blätter für weltanschauliche Information (April 15, 1968): 85–87. {Abridged version of "Das Ende der Dialektik Ketzer-Papst," *Die Wahrheit der Ketzer* (1968). Translation in "Heretic and Pope," *Christianity and Freedom* (1968).} Interview.
SEE REEL 12, ITEM 580.

"The Mission of the Jewish State." 1968 (ca.). Manuscript of 3 pp.; title and typescript by L. van der Molen. 1 p. Four Wells. Unpublished.
REEL 12, ITEM 577.

"Plezier in het schelden," *In de Waagschaal* 24, Nr. 3 (Amsterdam: November 9, 1968): 46–48; Nr. 4 (November 23, 1968): 64–66; and Nr. 5 (December 7, 1968): 87–89, ed. J. M. Hasselaar. {= Translation of *Die Sprache des Menschengeschlechts,* Bd. 1 (1963), pp. 205–220 ("Die Lust am Lästern.")}
REEL 12, ITEM 581A.

Schwäbisch Hall und England. Ein Grundton zu den Erinnerungen von Sabine Leibholz-Bonhoeffer. 1968. 8 pp.; typescript by L. van der Molen, 2 pp. Archiv der Eugen Rosenstock-Huessy Gesellschaft. {Intended to be a foreword to Sabine Leibholz-Bonhoeffer's book, *vergangen-erlebt-überwunden.* Cf. "Exil" (1968).} Unpublished.
REEL 12, ITEM 582.

"Tribute from a 'Post-Goethian'," *Mitteilungen der Eugen Rosenstock-Huessy-Gesellschaft* 8 (June 1968): 3. {Originally in a Dartmouth College paper (1949).}
REEL 12, ITEM 581.

Die Umwandlung, Die Umwandlung des Wortes Gottes in die Sprache des Menschengeschlechts (Heidelberg: Verlag Lambert Schneider, 1968), 144 pp. {= *Soziologie* Bd. 2 (1958), pp. 759–760f; *Die Sprache des Menschengeschlechts,* Bd. 1 (1963), pp. 119–142 (and *Das Alter der Kirche* 1: 111–140); *Die Sprache des Menschengeschlechts,* Bd. 2 (1964), pp. 759–903.}
SEE (1958) SOZIOLOGIE, BD. 2;(1963) DIE SPRACHE DES MENSCHENGESCHLECHTS, BD. 1 AND 2.

The University – 1968, The Eugen Rosenstock-Huessy Lectures, Vol. 34; University of California at Santa Cruz, February 15, 1968 (Jericho, Vt.: Argo Books, 1994): 8 pp. in transcription, 1 lecture on audio cassette.
REEL 18, ITEM 659.

"Die Wahrheit der Ketzer," *Süddeutscher Rundfunk* (January 7, 1968), tape. {= "Das Ende der Dialektik Ketzer-Papst," *Die Wahrheit der Ketzer* (1968); "Das Jahrtausend des Samariters," *Orientierung* (1968), "Heretic and Pope," *Christianity and Freedom* (1968).}
SEE REEL 12, ITEM 580.

1969

"Anfänge meines Friedensdienstes," *Mitteilungen der Eugen Rosenstock-Huessy Gesellschaft* 11 (December 1969): 2.
REEL 13, ITEM 585.

Judaism Despite Christianity, The letters on Christianity and Judaism between Rosenstock-Huessy and Franz Rosenzweig, with an introduction by Harold Stahmer and essays "About the Correspondence" by Alexander Altmann and Dorothy Emmet, ed. Eugen Rosenstock-Huessy (University, Ala.: University of Alabama Press, 1969), 198 pp. {Paperback reprint, New York: Schocken Books, 1971 (without Ch. 5: "Hitler and Israel, or On Prayer").} {Translation by Dorothy Emmet of the correspondence between Eugen Rosenstock and Franz Rosenzweig 1916, as edited by Eugen Rosenstock: "Franz Rosenzweig und Eugen Rosenstock: Judentum und Christentum," the final portion of Franz Rosenzweig, *Briefe*, Berlin 1935. This translation contains annotations by Rosenstock-Huessy.}
REEL 12, ITEM 584.

"Letters to Dr. Georg Müller, Parts of," *Mitteilungen der Eugen Rosenstock-Huessy Gesellschaft* 11 (December 1969): p. 8 from letter of January 1965 (on the name *Sprachdenker*); p. 1 from letter of September 25, 1969 (on the unity of humankind); pp. 1–3 from letter of November 10, 1969 (on the experiments with voluntary service.)
NOT MICROFILMED.

"Nachträgliche Erwägungen Eugen Rosenstock-Huessys zu *Angewandten Seelenkunde* aus dem Erscheinungsjahr 1924." [1. 'Zusätze zum psychosozialen Programm.' *Rhein-Mainische Volkszeitung* 188 (August 12, 1924). 2. 'Brief an Joachim Sindermann vom Dezember 1924,'" *Mitteilungen der Eugen Rosenstock-Huessy-Gesellschaft* 10 (June 1969): 7–11.]
REEL 13, ITEM 586.

"Prolog (und Epilog) zu den Briefen Eugen Rosenstocks und Franz Rosenzweigs—fünfzig Jahre später übersetzt aus *Judaism Despite Christianity*," *Mitteilungen der Eugen Rosenstock-Huessy Gesellschaft* 11 (December 1969): 9–12. {= Translation of *Judaism Despite Christianity* (1969), pp. 71–76.}
REEL 13, ITEM 587.

1970

***I Am an Impure Thinker*,** with a foreword by W. H. Auden (Norwich, Vt.: Argo Books, 1970), 206 pp.
REEL 13, ITEM 588.

"Invocatio vom 28.6.1970," *Mitteilungen der Eugen Rosenstock-Huessy Gesellschaft* 13, (November 1970): 1–2 {Translation of unpublished item, Invocation (1970).}
REEL 13, ITEM 590A.

Invocation. At the 200th Anniversary of The First Church of Christ in Norwich, Vt., June 28, 1970. 4 pp. {= Invocatio vom 28.6.1970 (1970), a German translation. Four Wells.} Unpublished.
REEL 13, ITEM 590.

Letter to a theologian on the Trinity, Part of a, *Mitteilungen der Eugen Rosenstock-Huessy Gesellschaft* 12 (June 1970): 10.
NOT MICROFILMED.

***Speech and Reality*,** with an introduction by Clinton C. Gardner (Norwich, Vt.: Argo Books, 1970), 201 pp.
REEL 13, ITEM 589.

Der Volksname Deutsch, Wege der Forschung, Bd. 151, ed. Hans Eggers (Darmstadt: Wissenschaftliche Buchgesellschaft, 1970), pp. 32–102. {= *Unser Volksname Deutsch* (1928).}
NOT MICROFILMED.

"Zukunftsglaube. Ein Brevier für Futurologen, compiled by Dr. Georg Müller from Rosenstock-Huessy's writings," *Deutsches Pfarrerblatt* 70, Nr. 6 (1970), 12 pp.
NOT MICROFILMED.

1971

Letter to Wim Leenman at the founding of the Rosenstock-Huessy-Huis in Haarlem, 1970, Part of a, *Mitteilungen der Eugen Rosenstock-Huessy Gesellschaft* 15 (July 1971): 12.
NOT MICROFILMED.

1972

An interview with Eugen Rosenstock-Huessy by Kendig Brubaker Cully in *The Review of Books and Religion* 1, no. 6 (Belmont, Vt., Februrary 15, 1972): 2.
NOT MICROFILMED.

Letter to Ulrich Jung or Hans Peter Veraguth, June 6, 1964, First part of a, *Mitteilungen der Eugen Rosenstock-Huessy Gesellschaft* 17 (February 1972): 11–12.
NOT MICROFILMED.

1973

"Briefe," *Briefwechsel aus sieben Jahrzehnten* 2, Nr. 172, ed. Martin Buber (Verlag Lambert Schneider): 213–215; and 3, Nr. 242: 298ff.
NOT MICROFILMED.

"Eugen Rosenstock-Huessy über die Akzente seiner geschichtlichen Erfahrung," a selection of parts of letters to Georg Müller. The letters are used in the following order: December 1951, April 1955, November 1955, April 1960, February 1958, October 1958, July 1959, August 1959, March 1960. [1. Im Wirkbereich der Revolutionen; 2. Im Glauben an des Christen Zukunft; 3. Im Kreuz der Wirklichkeit und der Vollzahl der Zeiten], *Mitteilungen der Eugen Rosenstock-Huessy Gesellschaft* 18 (May 1973): 3–10. {= "Eugen Rosenstock-Huessy über die Akzente," *Alma Mater Joachimica* (1974).}
NOT MICROFILMED.

Multiformity of Man, without the foreword. (Norwich, Vt.: Argo Books, 1973). {See *The Multiformity of Man* (1949).}
SEE REEL 8, ITEM 423.

1974

"Eugen Rosenstock-Huessy über die Akzente seiner geschichtlichen Erfahrung" (from letters to Georg Müller). *Alma Mater Joachimica* 37, Zeitschrift der Vereinigung alter Joachimsthaler e.V. (March 1974): 721–728. {= *Mitteilungen der Eugen Rosenstock-Huessy Gesellschaft* 19 and 20 (Spring 1974): 25 and 27f.}
NOT MICROFILMED.

Letters to Adele Rosenzweig and to Else Freund, Parts of, *Mitteilungen der Eugen Rosenstock-Huessy Gesellschaft* 19 and 20 (Spring 1974): 25 and p. 27f. [To the mother of Franz from June 1921 and December 1922, on Franz's illness. To Else Freund from February 17, 1937, on her book on Rosenzweig.]
NOT MICROFILMED.

1975

"Briefe Eugen Rosenstock-Huessys aus der Frühzeit unserer Arbeitsgemeinschaft," *Mitteilungen der Eugen Rosensotck-Huessy Gesellschaft* 22 (November 1975): 4–13. A selection by Georg Müller of excerpts from letters on the origin and growth of the friendship between him and Rosenstock-Huessy. Letters of December 16, 1948; December 27, 1948; May 4, 1949; July 3, 1949; September 17, 1951; December 16, 1951; June 20, 1952; August 9, 1952; December 30, 1952; February 22, 1953; July 8, 1953.
NOT MICROFILMED.

"Eugen Rosenstock-Huessy über Universalgeschichte" (aus Briefen an Ernst Michel: 1. 1946, 17 September; 2. 1967, 12 May) *Mitteilungen der Eugen Rosenstock-Huessy Gesellschaft* 21 (January 1975): 15.
NOT MICROFILMED.

The Law of Liberty. A Fourth of July Sermon, ed. William James Association (Santa Cruz: William James Press, 1975), 8 pp. {="The Law of Liberty" (1944).}
SEE REEL 7, ITEM 381.

Magna Carta Latina. The Privilege of Singing, Articulating and Reading a Language and of Keeping it Alive, with Ford Lewis Battles (Pittsburgh, Pa.: The Pickwick Press, 1975), 296 pp. {= *Magna Carta Latina* (1967).}
REEL 12, ITEM 575.

Metanoia: To Think Anew, ed. William James Association (Santa Cruz: William James Press, 1975), 11 pp. {= *I Am an Impure Thinker* (1970), pp. 182–190, and p. 193ff.}
NOT MICROFILMED.

"Die Weggelaufene Eschatologie," *Mitteilungen der Eugen Rosenstock-Huessy Gesellschaft* 22 (November 1975): 1–2. {= *Friedensbedingungen* (1988), pp. 327–329; unpublished item, Die Weggelaufene Eschatalogie (1957).}
SEE (1988) FRIEDENSBEDINGUNGEN.

1976

"Briefliche Äusserungen zu zeitgenössischen Gedankengängen," *Mitteilungen der Eugen Rosenstock-Huessy Gesellschaft* 23 (April 1976): 6–14. On the progress of Rosenstock-Huessy's friendship with Georg Müller and the re-introduction of Rosenstock-Huessy's work in Germany after the Second World War. On Philosophy and Theology: Heidegger, Hegel, Teilhard de Chardin, Bloch, Moltmann, Karl Löwith. Parts of letters from December 31, 1953; March 13, 1954; July 16, 1955; March 11, 1957; August 3, 1954; January 22, 1955; July 3, 1962; September 25, 1965; October 10, 1965; October 21, 1965; December 12, 1965; November 2, 1966; May 9, 1967; December 15, 1969; December 7, 1969; April 19, 1970; May 13, 1968; July 13, 1968; August 6, 1968; October 14, 1968.
NOT MICROFILMED.

"Die Liturgie von Jerusalem," Briefkommentar zu Eugen Rosenstock-Huessys Schrift, *Die Umwandlung* (1968), *Mitteilungen der Eugen Rosenstock-Huessy Gesellschaft* 24 (October 1976): 4–11. [1. Vernehmendes Denken und Gelehrtenstreit; 2. Der Vorrang des Matthäus-Evangelium; 3. Vom Tod des Johannes.] Excerpts from letters to Georg Müller on a new understanding of the New Testament from the grammatical understanding of history: January 22, 1955; October 18, 1955; December 9, 1954; April 25, 1955; November 2, 1955; January 19, 1960; September 16, 1961; August 30, 1962; June 4, 1964; July 7, 1964; January 11, 1965; July 20, 1966; July 19, 1967; December 2, 1967; February 5, 1962; Easter 1962; May 26, 1962; May 17, 1965; May 27, 1965.
NOT MICROFILMED.

"Zwei Briefe an Martin Buber aus den Jahren 1924 und 1951," *Mitteilungen der Eugen Rosenstock-Huessy Gesellschaft* 24 (October 1976): 11–13. {From Martin Buber, *Briefwechsel aus sieben Jahrzehnten* Bd. 2 (1973): 213–215; and Bd. 3 (1973): 298f.}
NOT MICROFILMED.

"Zur Problematik des religiösen Sozialismus. Über Tillichs *Masse und Geist*," *Mitteilungen der Eugen Rosenstock-Huessy Gesellschaft* 23 (April 1976): 1–6.
REEL 13, ITEM 591.

1977

"Briefliche Äusserungen über Ursprung und Eigenart des sprachsoziologischen Denkens," *Mitteilungen der Eugen Rosenstock-Huessy Gesellschaft* 25 (April 1977): 6–16. Excerpts from letters to 1. Ernst Michel (June 17 and July 13, 1947); 2. Fritz Vilmar (November 22, 1958); 3. Klaus Thraede (Good Friday, 1959); 4. Franz Vonessen (November 28, 1959); 5. Helmut Schelsky (December 26, 1959); 6. Karl Heinz Ebert (January 10, 1960); 7. N. Köhnlein (July 6, 1964); 8. Ernst Jansen (May 26, 1967).
NOT MICROFILMED.

"Einladung zur Zeitbuchreihe 'Epoche'," *Mitteilungen der Eugen Rosenstock-Huessy Gesellschaft* 25 (April 1977): 4–6.
REEL 13, ITEM 593.

"Letters to Georg Müller on *Soziologie II*," *Mitteilungen der Eugen Rosenstock-Huessy Gesellschaft* 26 (October 1977): 5–11. Excerpts from letters in 1957: September 19 and 26; in 1958: February 19 and October 20; in 1959: April 23, May 7, May 20, June 11, June 23, July 14, July 27, August 3, October 15, November 20, December 28; in 1960: July 14, October 7, October 20, October 24, and November 22.
NOT MICROFILMED.

"Die Mitschöpfer, eine Einführung in die Universalgeschichte," *Mitteilungen der Eugen Rosenstock-Huessy-Gesellschaft* 25 (April 1977): 1–4. {A faulty translation of "The Co-Creators," a draft of the preface to both volumes of *Soziologie* (1956 and 1958). The four-page manuscript is in the Archiv der Eugen Rosenstock-Huessy Gesellschaft.}
REEL 13, ITEM 592.

"Zwei oder Drei in meinem Namen," *Mitteilungen der Eugen Rosenstock-Huessy-Gesellschaft* 26 (October 1977), 1–3. {Thoughts of Rosenstock-Huessy, selected by Franz Utt. = "Zwei oder Drei in meinem Namen," *Christ in der Gegenwart* (1977).}
NOT MICROFILMED.

"Zwei oder Drei in meinem Namen. Thoughts of Eugen Rosenstock-Huessy, selected by Franz Utt from *Der Atem des Geistes, Soziologie II*, and *Das Geheimnis der Universität*," *Christ in der Gegenwart* 25, Katholische Wochenschrift (Freiburg: July 19, 1977): 205–206. {= "Zwei oder Drei in meinem Namen," *Mitteilungen der Eugen Rosenstock-Huessy Gesellschaft* (1977).}
NOT MICROFILMED.

1978

The Fruit of Lips, or, Why Four Gospels? ed. Marion Davis Battles (Pittsburgh, Pa.: The Pickwick Press, 1978), 144 pp. {= English version of *Die Sprache des Menschengeschlechts*, Bd. 2 (1964), pp. 797–903; *Die Umwandlung* (1968), pp. 32–138.}
REEL 13, ITEM 594.

"Letters: 1. To W. W. Alexander, Nov. 6, 1940, pp. 68f. (in part); 2. To Frank Davidson, Dec. 28, 1940, pp. 111f.; 3. To Harold Lasswell, probably Feb. 1941, p. 149 (in part); 4. To Miss Katherine Taylor, 1942, pp. 209–12; 5. To Daniel Goldsmith, March 4, 1945, pp. 221–28," Jack J. Preiss, ed., *Camp William James* (Norwich, Vt.: Argo Books, 1978). {The letter to Dan Goldsmith appeared in: *Stimmstein* 2 (1988): 47–54.}
NOT MICROFILMED.

"On Natural Law," *Mitteilungsblatt der Eugen Rosenstock-Huessy Gesellschaft* (1978): 20–23. Letters to Hans Thieme, October 9, 1950; October 1950; November 25, 1950.
NOT MICROFILMED.

Planetary Service. A Way into the Third Millennium, trans. Mark Huessy and Freya von Moltke (Norwich, Vt.: Argo Books, 1978), 126 pp. {Abridged translation of *Dienst auf dem Planeten* (1965).}
REEL 13, ITEM 595.

Spraak en Werkelijkheid, trans. Elias Voet (Haarlem: Vereniging Rosenstock-Huessy-Huis, 1978), viii + 155 pp. {Translation of *Speech and Reality* (1970).}
REEL 13, ITEM 596.

1980

Militia Academica (1933). Herausgabe der Eugen Rosenstock-Huessy Gesellschaft (1980), 13 pp. {= Militia Academica (1933).}
SEE REEL 6, ITEM 296.

Ökonomen—Vortrag in der Aula der Heidelberger Universität 1. July 1960. Zum Thema: Der Glaube der Ökonomen und die Ökonomie des Glaubens. Herausgabe der Eugen Rosenstock-Huessy Gesellschaft (1980), 18 pp. {= "Ökonomen" (1960). Also in *Friedensbedingungen* (1988), pp. 237–254.}
SEE (1988) FRIEDENSBEDINGUNGEN.

William Stanleys—des sechsten Grafen von Derby—Sonette für Elisabeth de Vere 1591–1598. Übersetzt von Eckart Wilkens. September 1980. 45 pp. Archiv der Eugen Rosenstock-Huessy Gesellschaft. {Translation of unpublished item, "William Stanley, The Sixth Earl of Derby's Sonnets for Elizabeth de Vere 1591–1598" (1954).} Unpublished.
NOT MICROFILMED.

Zeitgeist, Mythos, Krieg. September 15, 1956. Herausgabe der Eugen Rosenstock-Huessy Gesellschaft (1980), 16 pp. {= Zeitgeist, Mythos, Krieg (1956).}
SEE REEL 10, ITEM 500.

1981

"Akademik oder Argonautik," *Mitteilungsblatt der Eugen Rosenstock-Huessy Gesellschaft* (1981): 5–10. {= Expanded verson of "Salamis und die Thermopylen," *Deutsche Universitätszeitung* (1950).}
REEL 13, ITEM 599.

The Origin of Speech, with introduction by Harold M. Stahmer and an editor's postscript by Hans R. Huessy (Norwich, Vt.: Argo Books, 1981), 141 pp. {= Original version of *Die Sprache des Menschengeschlechts,* Bd. 2 (1964), pp. 451–594 ("Im Prägstock eines Menschenschlags oder der tägliche Ursprung de Sprache"). Ch. 6, "Logic on Trial," is left out.}
REEL 13, ITEM 597.

Rosenstock-Huessy Papers, Vol. 1 (Norwich, Vt.: Argo Books, 1981), 229 pp.
NOT MICROFILMED.

De Vrucht der Lippen—Waarom vier evangelien, trans. Elias Voet and Sam Hartman; introduction by J. M. Hasselaar (Baarn: Ten Have, 1981), 126 pp. {Translation of *Fruit of Lips* (1978).}
REEL 13, ITEM 598.

1982

"Aphorismen über den Aphorismus," *Mitteilungsblatt der Eugen Rosenstock-Huessy Gesellschaft* (1982): 17–20. {= "Aphorismus und Kurztitel," *Eckart* (1929).}
SEE REEL 4, ITEM 220A.

Die Gesetze der christlichen Zeitrechnung. Vorlesungen an der Theologischen Fakultät der Universität in Münster. 1958, summer season. 457 pp. Four Wells and Archiv der Eugen Rosenstock-Huessy Gesellschaft. {From a tape transcribed by Jochen Lübbers 1979–1982.} Unpublished.
REEL 18, ITEM 660.

Toegepaste Zielkunde, trans. Sam Hartman (Haarlem: Vereniging Rosenstock-Huessy-Huis, 1982), 47 pp. {Translation of *Angewandte Seelenkunde* (1924); = *Die Sprache des Menschengeschlechts,* Bd. 1 (1963), pp. 735–810.}
REEL 13, ITEM 600.

1983

"Eugen Rosenstock an Paul Tillich," *Briefwechsel und Streitschriften,* Theologische, philosophische und politische Stellungnahmen und Gespräche, ed. Paul Tillich (Frankfurt: 1983): 256–299. Rosenstock-Huessy letters: (February 5, 1935); (February 7, 1935); (November 4, 1935). {Also in *Mitteilungsblätter der Eugen Rosenstock-Huessy Gesellschaft* 1. Halbjahr (1993): 30–57.}
NOT MICROFILMED.

"Künftige Widersacher der Kirche," *Mitteilungsblatt der Eugen Rosenstock-Huessy Gesellschaft* (1983): 2–10. {= "Europa ist nicht mehr die nette Mitte der Welt," *Die Welt* (1957). Also in *Friedensbedingungen* (1988), pp. 181–189.}
SEE (1988) FRIEDENSBEDINGUNGEN.

"Orientierung im dritten Jahrtausend, Heft 1," *Das Versiegen der Sprache,* ed. Eugen Rosenstock-Huessy Gesellschaft, Peter Ohnesorg, and Jochen Lübbers (Bielefeld: October 1983), 37 + 2 pp. {= *Der Atem des Geistes* (1951), Ch. 1, pp. 17–37.}
SEE (1951) DER ATEM DES GEISTES.

1984

Applied Science of the Soul, trans. James W. Kidd, with an introduction by Dr. Sandra Wawrytko (San Francisco: Golden Phoenix Press, 1984), xiv + 20 pp. {Translation of *Die Sprache des Menschengeschlechts,* Bd. 1 (1963), pp. 742–747, 751–752, 752–760, 764–768, 769–770, and 770–772.}
NOT MICROFILMED.

"Das Gehirn kann nicht bereuen," *Mitteilungsblatt der Eugen Rosenstock-Huessy Gesellschaft* (1984): 2–9. {Excerpts from an interview with Hans Fischer Barnicol in Heidelberg, used in a radio broadcast on October 10, 1964.}
REEL 13, ITEM 601.

"Orientierung des dritten Jahrtausends, Heft 2," *Namen und Gedanken,* ed. Eugen Rosenstock-Huessy Gesellschaft, Peter Ohnesorg, and Jochen Lübbers (Bielefeld: April 1984): 39–62. {= *Der Atem des Geistes* (1951), Ch. 2, pp. 39–62.}
SEE (1951) DER ATEM DES GEISTES.

"Verrückt gewordene Ökonomie oder mehrsprachiger Friede," trans. Eckart Wilkens (Köln: December 20, 1984), 36 pp. {= Translation of "Mad Economics or Polyglot Peace" (1944.) Also in *Stimmstein* 4 (1993): 69–116.} Unpublished.
SEE REEL 7, ITEM 384.

1985

Des Christen Zukunft oder Wir überholen die Moderne, with a foreword by Friso Melzer (Moers: Brendow Verlag, 1985), 288 pp. {Reprint.}
SEE REEL 9, ITEM 475.

"Das Gespräch vor Zeugen," *Mitteilungsblatt der Eugen Rosenstock-Huessy Gesellschaft* (1985): 5–9. {= "Das Gespräch vor Zeugen" (1919).}
SEE REEL 1, ITEM 61.

"Orientierung des dritten Jahrtausends, Heft 3" *Philologie oder Liturgik?* ed. Eugen Rosenstock-Huessy Gesellschaft, Peter Ohnesorg, and Jochen Lübbers (Bielefeld: July 1985): 63–82. {= *Der Atem des Geistes* (1951), chap. 3, pp. 63–82.}
SEE (1951) DER ATEM DES GEISTES.

"Was kostet die Geschichte?" *Mitteilungsblatt der Eugen Rosenstock-Huessy Gesellschaft* (1985): 2–5. {= *Die Sprache des Menschengeschlechts,* Bd. 1 (1963), pp. 348–353 ("Das Auf beim Hören und das Los beim Sagen"); Was kostet die Geschichte? (1955).}
SEE (1963) DIE SPRACHE DES MENSCHENGESCHLECHTS.

1986

Der Beruf in neuer ökumenischer Sicht. 27 pp. Archiv der Eugen Rosenstock-Huessy Gesellschaft. Unpublished. {Transcribed by Rudolf Hermeier, from tape, 1986. = Der Beruf aus neuer ökumenischer Sicht (tape, 1965). Also *Friedensbedingungen einer Weltwirtschaft* (1988), pp. 255–282.}
SEE REEL 13, ITEM 602.

Iedereen moet onderwijzen. Augustinus de eerste metanoom, trans. Sam Hartman and Hermien Vriezen-Rozemond (Haarlem: Vereniging Rosenstock-Huessy-Huis, 1986), 36 + iv pp. {Translation of "Jeder muss lehren: Augustin, der erste Metanomiker" (1940); = *Die Sprache des Menschengeschlechts,* Bd. 2 (1964), pp. 368–427; = *Der Atem des Geistes* (1951), pp. 95–165 (difference in title and beginning and end). See *Rosenstock-Huessy Papers, Vol. 1* (1981), Ch. 3 (forerunner).}
SEE REEL 12, ITEM 560.

In Verteidigung der grammatischen Methode. Überarbeitete Übersetzung von *Speech and Reality* (1970), pp. 9–44 von Rudolf Hermeier. 1986. 38 pp. Archiv der Eugen Rosenstock-Huessy Gesellschaft. Unpublished. {= translation of *Speech and Reality* (1970), pp. 9–44; improved translation of unpublished item, Lebende Gegenwart II (1960). Also in: *Friedensbedingungen* (1988), pp. 287–325.}
SEE (1970) SPEECH AND REALITY; (1988) FRIEDENSBEDINGUNGEN.

"Orientierung des dritten Jahrtausends, Heft 4/5," Jenseits der Geschlechter, ed. the Eugen Rosenstock-Huessy Gesellschaft, Peter Ohnesorg, and Jochen Lübbers (Bielefeld: 1986), 78 pp. {= "An die Russen?" *Frankfurter Hefte* (1959); *Die Hochzeit des Krieges* (1920), pp. 270–288, 289–302; = *Die Sprache des Menschengeschlechts,* Bd. 1 (1963), pp. 238–250, *Soziologie,* Bd. 2 (1958), pp. 734–738, 728–733, and 739–756; "Revolution, Soziologie und Universität," *Werbeheft* (1960), pp. 3–6.}
SEE (1959), ÄND DIE RUSSEN?"; (1920) DIE HOCHZEIT DES KRIEGES; (1963) DIE SPRACHE DES MENSCHENGESCHLECHTS; (1958) SOZIOLOGIE BD. 2; (1960) "REVOLUTION, SOZIOLOGIE UND UNIVERSITÄT."

"Theorien von gestern—Praktiken von wann?" *Mitteilungsblatt der Eugen Rosenstock-Huessy Gesellschaft* (1986): 13–18. {= "Theorien von gestern?" *Junge Wirtschaft* (1958). Also in *Friedensbedingungen* (1988), pp. 211–215.}
SEE (1958) "THEORIEN VON GESTERN?" OR (1988) FRIEDENSBEDINGUNGEN.

1987

"Brief an Rudolf Ehrenberg, 26 March 1947," *Jenseits all unseres Wissens wohnt Gott,* Hans Ehrenberg und Rudolf Ehrenberg zur Erinnerung, ed. Rudolf Hermeier (Moers: Brendow Verlag, 1987): 105–106.
NOT MICROFILMED.

Die Europäischen Revolutionen und der Charakter der Nationen, with a foreword by Karl Deutsch and a biographical note at the end by Rudolph Hermeier (Moers: Brendow Verlag, 1987), XXIII + 584 + 8 pp. {Reprint of the 1961 edition.}
SEE (1961) DIE EUROPÄISCHEN REVOLUTIONEN.

"Eva und die Folgen der Arbeitsteilung," *Stimmstein* 1, Jahrbuch der Eugen Rosenstock-Huessy Gesellschaft (Moers: Brendow Verlag. 1987): 51–58. {From *Der unbezahlbare Mensch* (1955), pp. 141–152; = *Der unbezahlbare Mensch* (1964), pp. 123–132.}
SEE (1955 OR 1964) DER UNBEZAHLBARE MENSCH.

"Hitler und Israel oder Vom Gebet," *Jenseits all unseres Wissens wohnt Gott,* Hans Ehrenberg und Rudolf Ehrenberg zur Erinnerung, ed. Rudolf Hermeier (Moers: Brendow Verlag, 1987): 147–159. {= revised translation by Rosenstock-Huessy of "Hitler and Israel, or, On Prayer," *Journal of Religion* (1945); *Judaism despite Christianity* (1969), pp. 178–194. Also in *Beiheft Stimmstein* (1992), pp. 83–100.}
SEE (1969) JUDAISM DESPITE CHRISTIANITY.

"Ich bin ein unreiner Denker (Vom Töchterlich-Werden des Denkens)," *Stimmstein* 1, Jahrbuch der Eugen Rosenstock-Huessy Gesellschaft (Moers: Brendow Verlag, 1987): 27–44. {= *Das Geheimnis der Universität* (1958), pp. 97–112, 168. Translation of *Out of Revolution* (1938), pp. 740–750; *I Am an Impure Thinker* (1970), pp. 1–19.}
SEE (1958) DAS GEHEIMNIS DER UNIVERSITÄT.

"Des Menschen Geist ist der heilige Geist" and "The Spirit of Man is the Holy Spirit," in *Franz Rosenzweig. Zum 25 Dezember 1926 Glückswünsche zum 40. Geburtstag — Congratulations to Franz Rosenzweig on his 40th birthday 25 December 1926,* ed. Martin Goldner (Millwood, N.Y.: Kraus Reprint, 1987): 44–45. Transcriptions and translations, with an introduction by Goldner, published on the centenary of Franz Rosenzweig's birth by the Leo Baeck Institute. {= Unpublished item, "Der Geist des Menschen ist der heilige Geist" (1926).}
SEE REEL 3, ITEM 180.

"Reflexionen über das Thema Quatember," *Stimmstein* 1, Jahrbuch der Eugen Rosenstock-Huessy Gesellschaft (Moers: Brendow Verlag, 1987): 45–50. {= *Das Geheimnis der Universität* (1958), pp. 129–133. = "Reflexionen über das Thema Quatember," *Quatember* (1953).}
SEE (1958) DAS GEHEIMNIS DER UNIVERSITÄT; (1953) "REFLEXIONEN ÜBER DAS THEMA QUATEMBER."

1988

Dienen op de planeet. Korte en lange adem in het derde millennium, trans. Elias Voet en Dé Mulder, with a foreword by Bas de Gaay Fortman (Haarlem: Vereiniging Rosenstock-Huessy-Huis, 1988), 130 pp. {Translation of *Dienst auf dem Planeten* (1965).}
NOT MICROFILMED.

Friedensbedingungen einer Weltwirtschaft. Zur Ökonomie der Zeit, ed. Rudolf Hermeier (Frankfurt am Main: Haag + Herchen Verlag, 1988), 339 pp., Arnoldshainer Schriften zur Interdisziplinären Ökonomie, Bd. 14.
REEL 13, ITEM 602.

Life Lines: Quotations from the Work of Eugen Rosenstock-Huessy, ed. Clinton C. Gardner (Norwich, Vt.: Argo Books, 1988), 83 pp.
REEL 13, ITEM 603.

Practical Knowledge of the Soul, trans. Mark Huessy and Freya von Moltke (Norwich, Vt.: Argo Books, 1988), 66 pp. {Translation of *Angewandte Seelenkunde* (1924) and *Die Sprache des Menschengeschlechts*, Bd. 1 (1963), pp. 735–810.}
REEL 13, ITEM 604.

"Saint Simon—der erste Soziologe," *Stimmstein* 2, Jahrbuch der Eugen Rosenstock-Huessy Gesellschaft (Moers: Brendow Verlag, 1988): 179–186 {= "Saint Simon," *Quatember* 3 (1958); also in *Soziologie,* Bd. 1 (1956).}
SEE (1958) "SAINT SIMON"; (1956) SOZIOLOGIE, BD. 1.

Die Tochter—Das Buch Rut, Eugen Rosenstock-Huessy und Martin Bubers Verdeutschung, ed. Bas Leenman, with commentary (Mössingen-Talheim: Talheimer Verlag, 1988), 46 pp. {Pp. 29–44 = *Die Hochzeit des Krieges* (1920), pp. 270–288. Also in "Orientierung des dritten Jahrtausends 4/5" (1986): 45–63.}
REEL 13, ITEM 605.}

1990

"God is Free," *Stimmstein* 3, Jahrbuch der Eugen Rosenstock-Huessy Gesellschaft (Mössingen-Talheim: Talheimer Verlag, 1990): 60–62 {From "God is Free," *Advance* (1945).}
SEE REEL 8, ITEM 389.

"Die Interims des Rechts," *Stimmstein* 3, Jahrbuch der Eugen Rosenstock-Huessy Gesellschaft (Mössingen-Talheim: Talheimer Verlag, 1990): 14–24. {= Private printing, *Die Interims des Rechts* (1964).}
SEE REEL 11, ITEM 559.

1991

Der Atem des Geistes, with a Zum Geleit and an index by Bas Leenman (Moers: Brendow Verlag, and Vienna: Amandus Verlag, no publication date, but known to be 1991), 294 pp. {= *Der Atem des Geistes* (1951).}
SEE REEL 8, ITEM 439.

Daimler Werkzeitung 1919/20, ed. Daimler Benz AG (Moers: Joh. Brendow & Sohn Verlag, 1991), 292 + 126 + LI pp. {A collection in book form of *Daimler Werkzeitung* issues.}
NOT MICROFILMED.

***Heilkraft und Wahrheit,* Konkordanz der politischen und der kosmischen Zeit,** with a Zum Geleit and an index by Bas Leenman (Moers: Brendow Verlag, and Vienna: Amandus Verlag, no publication date, but known to be 1991), 215 pp. {= *Heilkraft und Wahrheit* (1952).}
SEE REEL 9, ITEM 445.

1992

"Hitler und Israel oder Vom Gebet"—"Hitler and Israel, or On Prayer"—"Hitler en Israel of Over het gebed"—"Hitler i Izrael albo O modlitwie," *Beiheft Stimmstein,* ed. the Eugen Rosenstock-Huessy Gesellschaft, with introductions by Cynthia Harris; Jochen Lübbers; Bas Leenman; Adam Zak, S.J.(1992), 100 pp. {= "Hitler and Israel, or On Prayer," *Journal of Religion* (1945) and translation (1987). The other translations are new.}
NOT MICROFILMED.

1993

"Eugen Rosenstock an Paul Tillich," *Mitteilungsblätter der Eugen Rosenstock-Huessy Gesellschaft* 1. Halbjahr (1993): 38–57, with annotations by Michael Gormann-Thelen. {= "Eugen Rosenstock an Paul Tillich," *Briefwechsel und Streitschriften*, Bd. VI (1983).}
NOT MICROFILMED.

"Mad Economics or Polyglot Peace," *Stimmstein* 4, Jahrbuch der Eugen Rosenstock-Huessy Gesellschaft (Mössingen-Talheim: Talheimer Verlag, 1993): 24–68. {= Unpublished item, Mad Economics or Polyglot Peace (1944).}
SEE REEL 7, ITEM 384.

Obozy Integracyjne Naślązku w latach dwudziestych i trzydziestych, Pod redakcją Eugena Rosenstocka i Carla Dietricha von Trothy, trans. Gisela Nowicka and Jacek Rumiński (Wrocław: 1993), 120 pp. {Translation of *Das Arbeitslager* (1931).}
NOT MICROFILMED.

Out of Revolution: Autobiography of Western Man, with an introduction by Harold J. Berman (Providence and Oxford: Berg Publishers, Inc., 1993), xxii pp. + 797 pp. {New edition of *Out of Revolution* (1938).}
NOT MICROFILMED.

Toekomst Het Christelijk Levensgeheim, trans. Ko Vos, with a Ten Geleide, postscript, and short bibliography (Aalsmeer: Dabar/boekmakerij Luyten, 1993), 286 pp. {Translation of *Des Christen Zukunft* (1956) and *The Christian Future* (1946). For the sake of clarity to Dutch readers, the original English text has been followed in part and some additions in the German text have been left out (p. 10).}
REEL 13, ITEM 606.

"Die unsichtbare Welt," *Stimmstein* 4, Jahrbuch der Eugen Rosenstock-Huessy Gesellschaft (1993): p. 13. {Poem for Margrit, December 25, 1918.}
NOT MICROFILMED.

"Verrückt gewordene Ökonomie oder vielsprachiger Friede," *Stimmstein* 4, Jahrbuch der Eugen Rosenstock-Huessy Gesellschaft, trans. Eckart Wilkens (Mössingen-Talheim: Talheimer Verlag, 1993): 69–116. {Translation of "Mad Economics or Polyglot Peace" (1984). = unpublished item, "Verrückt gewordene Ökonomie" (1984).}
NOT MICROFILMED.

1994

"Laodizee. Wie rechtfertigt sich ein Volk?" *Mitteilungsblätter der Eugen Rosenstock-Huessy Gesellschaft* 1. Halbjahr (1994): 10–20. {Reprint of "Laodizee," *Frankfurter Allgemeine Zeitung* (1954). Cf. "Die Geschichtsnot und die Gefahr der Barbarei," *Gartenlaube* (1932).}
NOT MICROFILMED.

"Selbstgespräch des Verfassers," (Ein Nachwort zur englischen Ausgabe von *Des Christen Zukunft*, 1947), trans. Michael Gormann-Thelen, *Mitteilungsblätter der Eugen Rosenstock-Huessy Gesellschaft* 2. Halbjahr (1994): 25–33. {A German translation of the Soliloquy in *The Christian Future* (1947).}
NOT MICROFILMED.

"Sieger und Besiegte. Deutschland zwischen französischer und russischer Revolution," *Mitteilungsblätter der Eugen Rosenstock-Huessy Gesellschaft* 2. Halbjahr (1994): 28–49. {Publication of two versions of Sieger und Besiegte (1933).}
SEE (1933) SIEGER UND BESIEGTE.

1995

"Brief an *, Magdeburg 18.2.20 (über Karl Barths Römerbrief),"** *Tumult* 20 (Eugen Moritz Friedrich Rosenstock-Huessy, 1888–1973), eds. Frank Böckelmann, Dietmar Kamper, Walter Seitter (Vienna: Turia + Kant, 1995): 9–15.
NOT MICROFILMED.

"Das Dritte Reich und die Sturmvögel des Nationalsozialismus," *Tumult* 20 (Eugen Moritz Friedrich Rosenstock-Huessy, 1888–1973), eds. Frank Böckelmann, Dietmar Kamper, Walter Seitter (Vienna: Turia + Kant, 1995), pp. 16–36. {= "Das Dritte Reich," *Hochland* (1931).}
SEE (1931) "DAS DRITTE REICH."

"Die Geschichtsnot und die Gefahr der Barbarei," *Beiheft Stimmstein* 2, Jahrbuch der Eugen Rosenstock-Huessy Gesellschaft (February 1995): 118–126. {Reprint of "Die Geschichtsnot," *Gartenlaube* (1932).}
NOT MICROFILMED.

"Judas Ischariot und die preussischen Konservativen zum Auftreten der politischen Diabolik," *Tumult* 20 (Eugen Moritz Friedrich Rosenstock-Huessy, 1888–1973), eds. Frank Böckelmann, Dietmar Kamper, Walter Seitter (Vienna: Turia + Kant, 1995): 37–54. {= "Judas Ischariot," *Hochland* (1932).}
SEE (1932) "JUDAS ISCHARIOT."

"Kriegsheer und Rechtsgemeinschaft," *Tumult* 20 (Eugen Moritz Friedrich Rosenstock-Huessy, 1888–1973), eds. Frank Böckelmann, Dietmar Kamper, Walter Seitter (Vienna: Turia + Kant, 1995): 55–77. {= *Kriegsheer und Rechtsgemeinschaft* (1932).}
SEE (1932) KRIEGSHEER UND RECHTSGEMEINSCHAFT.

"Die Seele von William James," *Beiheft Stimmstein* 2, Jahrbuch der Eugen Rosenstock-Huessy Gesellschaft (February 1995):14–29. {Translation of The Soul of William James (1942).}
NOT MICROFILMED.

Vortrag von Professor Rosenstock: Über "Volk." Ein Beitrag zur Vertiefung des Begriffs "Volk" in leiblichem und geistigem Sinne. Convivium Viadrinum am 20–21. II. 1993. *Mitteilungsblätter der Eugen Rosenstock-Huessy Gesellschaft* (Jahrgang 1995): 55–60. {= Volk (1933).}
SEE (1933) VOLK.

1996

"Science, Superstition, Education and the Three Storeys of a University," *Stimmstein* 5, Jahrbuch der Eugen Rosenstock-Huessy Gesellschaft (1996). {= Science, Superstition, Education (1938).}
SEE (1938) SCIENCE, SUPERSTITION, EDUCATION.

"Wissenschaft, Aberglaube, Erziehung und Die Drei Stockwerke einer Universität," *Stimmstein* 5, Jahrbuch der Eugen Rosenstock-Huessy Gesellschaft, trans. Andreas Möckel and Lise van der Molen (1996). {Translation of Science, Superstition, Education (1938).}
NOT MICROFILMED.

1997

Au risque du langage, trans. Jean Greisch [*Zurück indas Wagnis der Sprache* (1957)] with a foreword by Michael Gormann-Thelen (Paris: Les éditions du Cerf, 1997).
NOT MICROFILMED.

Undated Works

Autobiographical Statement for Harold Stahmer. 4 pp. Harold M. Stahmer, private collection. Unpublished
NOT MICROFILMED.

Episcopatus regni Siciliae tempore Suevico. About 400 pp. of notes.
NOT MICROFILMED.

Humanity and Mankind. 14 pp. {= Rosenstock's translation of "Menschheit und Menschengeschlecht," Die Hochzeit des Kriegs (1920), pp. 289–303; = *Die Sprache des Menschengeschlechts,* Bd. 1 (1963), pp. 238–250. Also in "Orientierung des dritten Jahrtausends" (1986), pp 64–76.}
SEE (1963) DIE SPRACHE DES MENSCHENGESCHLECHTS.

Nicolaus von Cues. 12 pp. Archiv der Eugen Rosenstock-Huessy Gesellschaft. Unpublished.
REEL 13, ITEM 608.

Part III

Inventory of the Works on Microfilm

Part III

Inventory of the Works on Microfilm

The text that follows is a list of the contents of each reel in the microfilm edition of Rosenstock-Huessy's works. When the filming began, Lise van der Molen's bibliography was not yet complete. Hence, the reader should be aware that some items were not photographed in the order in which they appear in the Chronological Bibliography. Moreover, some items were photographed that were later deleted from the bibliography or were never included. These exceptions and other miscellaneous points are all noted with the entry.

The typographic style of the entries conforms to that of the bibliography: books are listed in italic; articles, chapters, and titles created by Lise van der Molen for untitled, unpublished works are framed in quotation marks; unpublished items are left in plain roman with no distinguishing marks.

The first fourteen reels cover the written works. The final four reels contain the transcriptions of the recorded English-language lectures as well as the transcription of one lecture in German presented in Münster, Germany.

Reel 1 (1903 – 1919)

Item

1. Notker Teutonicus (Labeo) von Sankt Gallen **1903**
2. Das Sechste Buch von Homers Odyssee **1903**
3. Deutsche Aufsätze (Unter Prima) **1904**
4. Deutsche Aufsätze (Ober Prima) **1905**
5. P. Clodius Pulcher **1906**
6. Das Angebliche Danteepigramm in Leipzig **1908**
7. Festspiel anlässlich Karls Physikum und Clairs Geburtstag und Burschung **1908**
8. *Landfriedensgerichte und Provinzialversammlungen vom neunten bis zwölften Jahrhundert* **1910**
9. *Herzogsgewalt und Friedensschutz* **1910**
10. *Briefe, B. G. und Amalie Niebuhrs an Dore Hensler und an Karsten Niebuhr* **1911**
11. Zur Germanisierung der Kirche aus dem Mittelalterlichen Festkalender **1911**
12. *Ostfalens Rechtsliteratur unter Friedrich II.* **1912**

13. *Rathaus und Roland im deutschen Stadtrecht zwischen 1186 und 1280* **1912**
14. "Zur Ausbildung des mittelalterlichen Festkalenders" **1912**
15. Das Herzogtum in der ersten Hälfte des deutschen Mittelalters **1912**
16. "Bruchstücke eines verkürzten Sachsenspiegels" **1913**
17. "Neue Literatur über die deutschen Königswahlen" **1913**
18. "Synodalis" **1913**
19. "Würzburg, das erste geistliche Herzogtum in Deutschland" **1913**
20. "Die Zuverlässigkeit der 'Lebensnachrichten über B. G. Niebuhr'" **1913**
21. Volksrecht und Hausherrschaft **1913**
22. *Königshaus und Stämme in Deutschland zwischen 911 und 1250* **1914**
23. "Principium Doctoris" **1914**
24. Review: Edwin Mayer-Hombergs *Die fränkischen Volksrechte im Mittelalter*, Die fränkischen Volksrechte und das Reichsrecht **1914**
25. Denkschrift des 30. Juli. Vorschlag an Prof. Dr. Richard Schmidt zur Staatenbildung unter den slavischen Nationalitäten nach dem Krieg **1914**
26. Vorlesungen Staatstheorien der Gegenwart, 2nd and 3rd series **1914**
27. An eine hohe Juristen-fakultät zu Leipzig **1914**
28. "Heiliges Römisches Reich Deutscher Nation" **1915**
29. "Die Verfassung Giolitti" **1915**
30. "Die Planetarischen Gesetze in Stamm, Staat und Reich" **1915**
31. Ursprung des Rechts **1915**
32. "Die Verdeutschung des Sachsenspiegels" **1916**
33. Die Sankt Georgs Reden **1916**
34. "Der Grund der inneren Krise" **1917**
35. "Ich und die Stunde sind eins. Zur Bestattung von Reinhold Wurzmann" **1917**
36. "Ist der Bundesrat Rat oder Regierung?" **1917**
37. Denkschrift über die Möglichkeit der Abwendung einer Militärdiktatur **1917**
38. Die europäischen Parteien **1917**
39. Ebenbild **1917**
40. Elsass-Lothringen und der Militarismus **1917**
41. Entwurf Europäisches Völkerkonzert **1917**

42. Freiheit der Meere **1917**
43. Das Gewissen der europäischen Parteien **1917**
44. Goethe und Bismarck **1917**
45. Luther und die Paulskirche **1917**
46. Das neue Bewusstsein Europas **1917**
47. Der Rechtsbestand des preussischen Wahlrechts **1917**
48. Reichskanzler und Premier **1917**
49. Schwarzrotgoldene Pflichten der Presse **1917**
50. Staat und Grenze **1917**
51. Der Verfassungsausgleich Europas **1917**
52. Vorurteile **1917**
53. Die Weltteile **1917**
54. Wer kann heut das Deutsche Reich regieren? **1918**
55. Die Wiedergeburt des Reichstags **1917**
56. "Der Kreuzzug des Sternenbanners" **1918**
57. "Volksstaat und Reich Gottes" **1918**
58. Die Bedingung des Friedens **1918**
59. Der preussische Staat **1918**
60. *Europa und die Christenheit* **1919**
61. Das Gespräch vor Zeugen **1919**
62. "Bolschewismus und Christentum" **1919**
63. "Der Bourgeois. Redeaktioneller Kommentar zu der Anzeige von Dr. Bruno Altmanns 'W. Sombart: *Der Bourgois*'" **1919**
64. "Etwas vom Innenleben fürs Innenleben" **1919**
65. "Der ewige Prozess des Rechts gegen den Staat" **1919**
66. "Der Gang des Arbeitstages" **1919**
67. "Gedanken über das Weltgeschehen" **1919**

67A. Geist und Zeitgeist **1919**

68. "Italien und Deutschland" **1919**
69. "Leonardo da Vinci" **1919**
70. "Der Wiederaufbau des Einzelnen" **1919**
71. Die Auferstehung der Wahrheit **1919**
72. Denkschrift: Über die geistige Sanierung des Daimlerwerks Krankheitsdiagnose **1919**
73. Frankfurt in der Staufferzeit 1152–1250 **1919**
74. Gedanken eines Kriegers **1919**
75. Die Institution in Recht und Staat **1919**
76. Die Krise der Universität **1919**
77. Der Mensch in Recht und Staat **1919**
78. Die Neubauverlage **1919**
79. Scio cui credidi **1919**

80. Strafrecht **1919**
81. Unter der Kanzel **1919**
82. Vorschlag zur Gründung von Kämpferbünden **1919**

Reel 2 (1920 – 1924)

Item

83. *Die Hochzeit des Krieges und der Revolution* **1920**
84. "Arbeitsgemeinschaft" **1920**
85. "Die Arbeitsgemeinschaft der Astronomen" and "Persönliches von Einstein" **1920**
86. "Einleitung zu: Adolf Wagenmann, *Wie schnell bewegen sich die Himmelskörper?*" **1920**
87. "Einleitung zu 'Die Heimkehr' von Hans Heinrich Ehrler" **1920**
88. "Das Ereignis der Relativitätstheorie" **1920**
89. "Fehlerquellen der praktischen Prüfung" **1920**
90. "Gesunde oder zweckmässige Arbeitshaltung" **1920**
91. "Jeder sein eigener Astronom" **1920**
92. "Des Kaufmanns Sorgen" **1920**
93. "Ein Kulturbild aus Norddeutschland" **1920**
94. "Die Leistung der Psychotechnik" **1920**
95. "Der Neubau der deutschen Rechtsgeschichte" **1920**
96. "Neu-Deutschland. Geschichte einer Siedlung" **1920**
97. "Psychotechnik" **1920**
98. "Sohn und Vater bei der Berufswahl" **1920**
99. "Der Stein der Weisen. Ein altes Gespräch" **1920**
100. "Die tiefste Quelle der Arbeit" **1920**
101. "Volksbildungstag in Braunnau am Inn" **1920**
102. "Wer hat Recht?" **1920**
103. Adolf Wagenmann **1920**
104. Deutschland in der öffentlichen Meinung des Auslandes **1920**
105. Politik der Weltalter **1920**
106. Reaktionär (J. F. Böhmer) und Revolutionär (Bakunin) **1920**
107. Volk, Persönlichkeit, Arbeit **1920**
108. "Ostblock oder Siberien?" **1921**

108A. "Laienbildung oder Volksbildung?" **1921**

109. Review: Alfred Freunds *Technik, Ihre Grundlagen für Alle* **1921**
110. Review: Dipl.-Ing. Dr. E. W. Seyferts *Der Arbeiternachwuchs in der deutschen Maschinenindustrie* **1921**
111. "Zwölf Bücher" **1921**
112. Ansprache an Gäste aus England in der Akademie der Arbeit **1921**

113. Aufbau und Verwaltung der Justiz **1921**
114. Ferien 1921 **1921**
115. Karlsruhe Seminar: Die Sprache der Werkstatt **1921**
116. "Paragraph 218 des Reichsstrafgesetzbuchs" **1921**
117. Das Recht! **1921**
118. *Werkstattaussiedlung* **1922**
119. "Die Akademie der Arbeit in der Universität Frankfurt a.M." **1922**
120. "An die Mitarbeiter der Akademie der Arbeit" **1922**
121. "Kastengeist und Mandarinentum" **1922**
122. "Die philosophischen Grundlagen des Arbeitsrechts" **1922**
123. Die Politik als Lehre vom Staat **1922**
124. *Zerfall und Ordnung des Industrievolks* **1923**
125. *Theophrast von Hohenheim* **1923**
126. "Angewandte Seelenkunde" **1923**
127. "Deutschlands Kommunisten und Faschisten" **1923**
128. "Eine Fahrt ins 'Neuwerk'" **1923**
129. "Was soll man denn sonst tun?" **1923**
130. "Darmstädter Vorträge Wissen und Reden von Staat und Gesellschaft **1923**
131. Die Erschütterung der Wissenschaft **1923**
132. Eugen Friedrich Moritz Rosenstock **1923**
133. Leben, Lehre und Wirken **1923**
134. Perioden der Geschichte **1923**
135. *Die Volksordnung* **1923**
136. Zur Quellenfrage des Sachsenspiegels **1923**
137. Die Zweischneidigkeit des geistigen Lebens **1923**
138. *Abbau der politischen Lüge* **1924**
139. *Industrievolk* **1924**
140. "Arbeiterbildung" **1924**
141. "Betriebsverfassung des Hochkapitalismus" **1924**
142. "Hegel und unser Geschlecht" **1924**
143. "Des Kaufmanns Dienst am Volke" **1924**
144. "Die nackte Arbeit" **1924**

Reel 3 (1924 – 1927)

Item

145. "Not und Wende in der Arbeiterbewegung" **1924**
146. Review, Ferdinand Ossendowskis *Tiere, Menschen und Götter* **1924**
147. Review, Otto Selzes *Die Gesetze der produktiven und reproduktiven Geistestätigkeiten* **1924**

148. "Schulreform und Hochschule" **1924**
149. "Staatsfamilie oder öffentliches Leben?" **1924**
150. Die Gesetze unserer Zeitrechnung **1924**
151. Die Gestalten unserer Zeitrechnung **1924**
151A. Die Wahrhaftigkeit des Hochschullebens **1924**
152. *Protestantismus und Volksbildung* **1925**
153. *Soziologie I. Die Kräfte der Gemeinschaft* **1925**
154. "Freizeiten her!" **1925**
155. Review: H. Hellers *Freie Volksbildung* **1925**
156. "Die seelischen Wirkungen der modernen Arbeitsordnung" **1925**
157. "Sozialpolitik und Arbeitsrecht" **1925**
158. Review: Leo Weismantels *Schule der Volkschaft* **1925**
159. "Werkstatthygiene" **1925**
160. "Werkstattkommandite" **1925**
161. Bericht über die beiden Referate am 9. und 10. Dezember 1925 **1925**
162. Englandreise Tagebuch **1925**
163. Für Ursprung der Sprache **1925**
164. Gesetz oder Sakrament? **1925**
165. Karl der Grosse und das Schicksal der Kirche **1925**
166. Der Lebensweg Fritz Mauthners **1925**
167. Versuchslehrgang des Instituts der Arbeit **1925**
168. Vom anderen Ende **1929**
169. Die Zeitliche Ordnung. Arbeitszeit **1925**
170. *Im Kampf um die Erwachsenenbildung* **1926**
171. *Lebensarbeit in der Industrie und Aufgaben einer europäischen Arbeitsfront* **1926**
172. Plan einer Deutschen Schule für Volksbildung und Volksforschung **1926**
173. *Vom Industrierecht* **1926**
174. "Die geistigen Bewegungen der Gegenwart" **1926**
175. "Macht und Schranken der Industrialisierung des Reichs" **1926**
176. "Protestantismus und Volksbildung" **1926**
177. "Robert von Erdberg" **1926**
178. Dr. Rosenstock's report on his visit to England **1926**
179. Die europäische Krise in England **1926**
180. "Der Geist des Menschen ist der heilige Geist" **1926**
181. Macht und Schranken der Industrialisierung **1926**
182. Schiffahrtrecht **1926**
183. *The Tribes of the Spirit* **1926**
184. Wirkungen der europäischen Krise auf England **1926**
185. "Alphons Maria Ratisbonne" **1927**

186. "Die geistige Struktur des deutschen Ostens" **1927**
187. "Gesetz oder Sakrament? Zur Ehediskussion" **1927**
188. "Hochschule und Arbeitslager" **1927**
189. "Hochschule und Arbeitslager" **1927**
190. "Notiz über sich selbst" **1927**
191. Review: Nikolaus Berdjajews *Das neue Mittelalter* **1927**
192. "Universität und Technische Hochschule" **1927**
193. "Die Verarmung des Typs" **1927**
194. "Deutscher Stamm, deutsches Volk, deutsches Reich, deutsche Nation" **1927**
195. Komburghefte **1927**
196. Der Weg Europas nach dem Krieg **1927**
197. Vom Neuland zwischen Pädagogik und Demagogik **1926**

Reel 4 (1928 – 1929)

Item

198. *Das Alter der Kirche. Kapitel und Akten* **1928**
199. "Ansprache bei der Beerdigung des Vaters Theodor Rosenstock" **1928**
200. "Das Arbeitslager für Jungarbeiter, Jungbauern und Jungakademiker in Löwenberg" **1928**
201. "Hochschule und Arbeitslager" **1928** (two entries)
202. "Idealistisches und namentliches Denken" **1928**
203. "The Impoverishment of the Type" **1928**
204. "Kirche und Arbeit—Eine Rede" **1928**
205. "Leben und Arbeit" **1928** (two entries)
206. "Die Namen Deutsch und Völkisch" **1928**
207. "Volksbildung in der Universität" **1929**
208. "Ein Wort von Augustin und eins von Goethe" **1928**
209. Arbeitsdienstpflicht in Bulgarien **1928**
210. *Arbeitsrecht* **1928**
211. Arbeitswissenschaft **1928**
212. Review: M. Värtings *Die Macht der Massen* **1928**
213. Das europäische Sechstagewerk **1928**
214. Die Lebensalter der Wirtschaft **1928**
215. Volkskirche und Volkssiedlung **1928**
216. Was geht die Industrie die Erwachsenenbildungen an? **1928**
217. Pfarrer und Laie in der Kirchenpolitik **1928**
218. Deutsche Schule für Volksforschung und Erwachsenenbildung sucht zehn Ingenieure **1927**

219. *Politische Reden* **1929**
219A. *Die ungeschriebene Verfassung* **1929**
220. A magánjog néhány új alapfogalmáról **1929**
220A. "Aphorismus und Kurztitel" **1929**
221. "Dienstpflicht?" **1929**
222. "Erwachsenenbildung und schlesisches Arbeitslager" **1929**
223. "Die Freizeit des Akademikers" and Interview, on *Werkstattaussiedlung* **1929**
223A. Jugend und Alter and Jugend und Alter in der modernen Gesellschaft **1929** (two entries)
224. "Kirche und Beruf" **1929**
225. "Protestantismus und Seelenführung" **1929**
226. Review: Karl Heldmanns *Das Kaisertum Karls des Grossen* **1929**

Reel 5 (1929 – 1931)

Item
227. "Die Schranke des Sozialpolitikers" **1929**
228. "Der Sozialismus als Antithese" **1929**
229. "Symbol und Sitte als Lebenmächte" **1929**
230. "Unser Volksname Deutsch und die Aufhebung des Herzogtums Bayern" **1929**
231. "Vom Staat zum Stamm" **1929**
232. Der beschränkte Untertanenverstand **1929**
233. Das englisches Budget **1929**
234. Enttäuschte Wirtschaft **1929**
235. Erwachsenenbildung und Betriebspolitik **1929**
236. Die Grenzen des Sozialpolitkers **1929**
237. "Die Presse als Träger und Erzieher der öffentlichen Meinung" (unpublished) **1929**
238. Recht und Wirtschaft **1929**
239. Soziologie (course lecture notes) and Soziologie 1. und 4. Stunde **1929**
240. *Die Arbeitslager innerhalb der Erwachsenenbildung* **1930**
240A. "Deutsche Nation und deutsche Universität" **1930**
241. "Dringe ein Dringe ein Zion dringe ein in Gott" **1930**
242. "Erwachsenenbildung und Betriebspolitik" **1930**
243. "Die Kirche am Ende der Welt" **1930**
244. "Die Kirche und die Völker. Abriss und Überblick" **1930**
245. "Menschenmacht und Massenmacht" **1930**

246. "Opvoeding der volwassenen in de Duitsche Gewesten" **1930**
247. "Reverendissime!" **1930**
248. "The Social Function of Adult Education" **1930**
249. "Über 'Reich,' 'Staat' und 'Stadt' in Deutschland von 1230–1235" **1930**
250. Bericht über das dritte schlesische Arbeitslager für Arbeiter, Bauern und Studenten **1930**
251. Erwachsenenbildung in den deutschen Landen **1930**
252. Die Heimkehr der Europäer **1930**
253. Das Recht und die rechtswissenschaftlichen Methoden **1930**
254. *Soziologie* (unpublished) **1930**
255. Und dreimal: Die Nation **1930**
256. Wandlungen im Recht **1930**
257. *Das Arbeitslager* **1931**
258. *Die Europäischen Revolutionen. Volkscharaktere und Staatenbildung* **1931**
259. *Revolution als politischer Begriff in der Neuzeit* **1931**
260. "Arbeitslager als Sonntag" **1931**
261. "Das Dritte Reich und die Sturmvögel des Nationalsozialismus" **1931**
262. "Weil der Geist weht, wo er will...Zur Frage Tillichs: Gibt es noch Universität?" **1931**
263. Bemerkungen zu Emil Brunner **1931**
264. Erwiderung. Zu Dr. Adolf Scheffbuch über die Preissenkung in: *Volksdienst* **1931**
265. Der Kampf zwischen Stadt und Land im 17. Jahrhundert **1931**
266. Stadt und Land **1931**
267. Die Umkehr in der Ausbildung **1931**
268. Unser Weg **1931**
269. Urwelt. Zum Ende der grossen europäischen Revolutionen **1931**
270. Der Zauber des Menschen **1931**

Reel 6 (1932 – 1939)

Item

271. *Arbeitsdienst—Heeresdienst?* **1932**
272. *Kriegsheer und Rechtsgemeinschaft* **1932**
273. "'Abschlag,' 'Abschlagen,' 'abschlägig,' abschläglich,' 'Abschlagung'" **1932**
274. "Der Arbeitsdienst als Erzieher" **1932**
274A. "Aus der Geschichte des Arbeitsdienstes **1932**
275. "Die Geschichtsnot und die Gefahr der Barbarei" **1932**

276. "Henrich Steffens" **1932**
277. "Judas Ischariot und die preussischen Konservativen" **1932**
278. "Les Étudiants et l'université au service de la société" and "Die Judenemanzipation" **1932**
279. "Mannwerdung" **1932**
280. "Sklaverei oder Regeneration?" **1932**
280A. Die Funktion des Apostel Paulus und die Sendung der Deutschen **1932**
281. "Weshalb heissen wir Deutsche?" **1932**
282. "Zur Strategie des Arbietsdienstes" **1932**
283. "Arbeitslosenversicherung" **1932**
284. "Die Arbeitslosenversicherung vermehrt das Übel der Arbeitslosigkeit" **1932**
285. Denkschrift zur Schliessung der Akademie für Kunst und Kunstgewerbe zu Breslau **1932**
286. Führer und Funktionär oder die radikale Wendung der Soziologie **1932**
287. Der heilige Karl und der eiserne Karl **1932**
288. Politische Geschichte als Heilsgeschichte **1932**
289. Rede des Herrn Prof. Rosenstock-Huessy gehalten in der Protestversammlung gegen die Schliessung der Akademie **1932**
290. Sozialaristokratie und Arbeitslosigkeit **1932**
291. Theodizee oder Laodizee? **1932**
292. "Arbeitslager" **1933**
293. Das Amt der Jugend **1933**
294. Apologia pro vita mea **1933**
295. "Arbeitskraft ohne gestern und morgen" **1933**
296. Militia Academica **1933**
296A. Sieger und Besiegte **1933**
297. Volk **1933**
298. "The Army Enlisted Against Nature" **1934**
299. Address delivered before Parent Teacher Association of Shady Hill School **1934**
300. The Rhythm of Society **1934**
301. Model of Emperors and The Role of the Apostle Paul in the Papal Revolution of the 11th Century **1934**
302. "Franz Rosenzweig und Eugen Rosenstock" **1935**
303. "The Predicament of History" **1935**
304. The Inheritors of Industry **1935**
305. Syllabus, Kuno Francke Lectures **1935**
306. The University of Logic, Language and Literature **1935**

307. "The Role of Language" **1935**
308. *The Multiformity of Man: Economics of a Mechanized World* **1936**
309. Ends and Beginnings of Philosophy **1936**
310. "The Singular and the Plural in the Sciences" **1937**
311. Dr. Johnson's Cat and the Assimilation of Reality **1936**
312. *A Classic and a Founder* **1937**
312A. Articulated Speech **1937**
313. The One and the Many **1937**
314. *Out of Revolution* **1938**
315. Eugen Rosenstock-Huessy (on *Out of Revoution*) **1938**
316. The Future of Natural Law **1938**
317. Mythical Grammar **1938**
318. On the *De Magistro* of St. Augustine **1938**
318A. *Our Means of Resistance* **1938**
319. The Patience for Liberty **1938**
320. Privilege and Future Opportunity of the University **1938**
321. Revolution as a political concept **1938**
322. *The Science of Bodies and The Appeal to Somebody* **1939**
323. Science, Supersition, Education and The Three Storeys of a University **1938**
324. "Review: Crane Brinton's *The Anatomy of Revolution* and Roger Bigelow Merriman's *Six Contemporaneous Revolutions* **1939**
325. Christmas 1939 **1939**
326. Education in the Third Phase of the Industrial Era **1939**
327. The Happy Guilt **1939**
327A. Language, Logic, Literature **1939**
328. The Pacification of the New Nationalism **1939**
329. The Penetration of the Cross **1939**
330. Perpetual Features of Education **1939**
331. The Rise and Fall of Nationalism and Internationalism **1939**
332. The Spirit of Recognition **1939**

Reel 7 (1940 – 1944)

Item

333. *The Artist and His Community* **1940**
334. "Correction on Paying the Price" **1940**
335. "Rendering Accounts" (three versions, listed as 335A, 335B, and 335C) **1940**
336. "A Peace Within" **1940**
337. "What They Should Make Us Think" and "What We Should Make Them Do" **1940**

338. The Battle against Segregation **1940**
339. The Meaning of Morale **1940**
340. Purpose of Camp William James **1940**
341. Minutes of CCC Meeting **1940**
342. "Youth and Authority" **1940**
343. The Antidote to Teaching **1940**
344. The Atlantic Revolution **1940**
345. Attack on My Generation **1940**
346. A Draft of a Petition to His Excellency The President of the United States **1940**
347. Forerunner of *The Christian Future* **1940**
348. The German Plan of War for 1940 **1940**
349. God in America or Survival Values for Americans **1940**
350. Man Must Teach (pamphlet) **1940**
351. Peace in Deed **1941**
352. The Question of the Empty Grave **1940**
353. The Credentials of Teaching; Faculty Seminar with Dr. Rosenstock-Huessy; Time and Space in Education; and *A Township College* **1940**
354. "A Balance Sheet. Confidential Report on Camp William James" **1941**
355. Draft preface to *The Cross of Reality* **1941**
356. The End of the World or When Theology Slept **1941**
357. Faculty Address on The Future of Christianity **1941**
358. Faculty Address on "The Potential Christians of the Future" **1941**
359. History makes sense **1941**
360. Hölderlin and Nietzsche **1941**
361. Rules for the Second World War **1941**
362. The Three Sciences **1941**
363. "Charge to Rev. Roy Chamberlain" **1942**
364. "The Domestic Parallel to War" **1942**
365. "Population Trends and Economic Changes" **1942**
366. Comments on the Document by Emil Brunner, "The Ethical Reality and Function of the Church" **1942**
367. For Prof. John U. Nef (on the method of sociology) **1942**
368. Friedrich Nietzsche's Function in the Church and the Crisis of Theology and Philosophy and Nietzsche's Masks **1942**
369. Nietzscheana **1942**
370. "Nietzsche's Untimeliness" **1942**
371. The Future Way of Life **1942**
372. How Leadership May be Taught without Doing More Harm than Good **1942**

373. Philosophy and The Social Sciences **1942**
374. Sex and Sequence **1942**
375. Soldiers of the Impossible **1942**
376. The Soul of William James **1942**
377. Supertime, or The Correspondences of Society **1942**
378. First Cycle of Letters to Cynthia (Harris) **1943**
379. The "quarters" of speech **1943**
380. Two Reflections on the Role of Egypt **1954**
381. "The Law of Liberty" **1944**
382. Demons of Peace or The Soul at War **1944**
383. The Listener's Tract **1944**
384. Mad Economics or Polyglot Peace **1944**
385. The Next Homer **1944**

Reel 8 (1944 – 1951)

Item

386. Surrender to Whom? **1944**
387. There are no Synonyms **1944**
388. "War-Election-Genius" **1944**
389. "God is Free" **1945**
390. "Hitler and Israel, or, On Prayer" **1945**
391. Establishing Relations **1945**
392. The New Re-production Economy after the World Wars **1945**
393. Grammar as Dogma or as Social Science? **1945**
394. How Is New Speech Created? **1945**
395. In answer to a request of Sgt. Albert (Joe) de Vivo **1945**
396. The Individual's Right to Speak and Some Final Terms of Grammar **1945**
397. The Life of Life **1945**
398. The New Nature of Christianity **1945**
399. "Our Raft in Time" and "World History, Church History, History of Society" **1945**

399A. The Renaissance of Mind and Body **1945**

400. The Wooer's Fate **1945**
401. *The Christian Future* **1946**
402. *Planetary Man* and "Planetary Man" **1946** (two entries)
403. The United States and Communism **1946**
404. "Biology and the Life of Life" **1946**
405. Jungfrauengeburt **1946**
406. Our Faith in Science **1946**

407. Untragic America **1946**
408. Vitamine **1946**
409. "Ascent of Taurus" **1947**
410. Review, Ernst Michels *Renovatio* **1948**
411. Epilogue to The Spirit of the Alphabet and "The Spirit of the Alphabet" **1947**
412. Antwort oder Anruf an den Verfasser der Rede **1947**
413. Autobiography by Eugen Rosenstock-Huessy **1947**
414. Christ Moses Pharao **1947**
415. The Metabolism of Science **1947**
416. Revolution **1947**
417. Staat **1947**
418. William James der Philosoph des modernen Amerikanischen Lebens **1947**
419. Die Wollust, Die Syphilis, Die Eifersucht **1947**
420. "Outside the Church" **1948**
421. "Symblysma oder Überschwang der Jesuiten" **1948**
422. Our Urban Goggles **1948**
423. *The Multiformity of Man* **1949**
424. "Liturgical Thinking" **1949**
425. "Was bedeutet die Stadt für das christliche Leben?" **1949**
426. Prolegomena for Ursula and Walter Seemann **1949**
427. The Secret of the University (translation). (This item is not in the bibliography) **1950**
428. "Das Geheimnis der Universität" **1950**
429. "Salamis und die Thermopylen" **1950**
430. "William James. Der Philosoph des amerikanischen Lebens" **1950**
431. Indivisibillimus **1950**
432. *Das Kreuz der Wirklichkeit* **1950**
433. Biology and the Life of Life **1946**
434. Sun and Horizon **1950**
435. V. Der Vollständige und der Selbstständige Mensch **1950**
436. Die Ordnung unseres geistigen Lebens (two entries) **1950**
437. Saturnalien **1950**
438. What is new about sociology? **1950**
439. *Der Atem des Geistes* **1951**
440. *Die Europäischen Revolutionen und der Charakter der Nationen* **1951**

Reel 9 (1951 – 1956)

Item

441. "Armistice Day" **1951**
442. "Die jüdischen Antisemiten oder die akademische Form der Judenfrage" **1951**

442A. Translation of "Die jüdischen Antisemiten" **1951**

443. "Vivit Deus" **1951**
444. Memorandum on Books and Manuscripts **1951**
445. *Heilkraft und Wahrheit* **1952**
446. Funeral Prayer **1952**
447. "Das Gesetz der Technik" **1952**
448. "Original Grace" **1952**
449. Creed **1952**
450. Death by Abstractions **1952**
451. Die "Hundert Tage" **1952**
452. *Liturgical Thinking versus Theology* **1952**
453. U. S. Specialist Report **1952**
454. "Der Gast" **1953**
455. "Ich bin ein unreiner Denker" **1953**
456. "Jakob Grimm und unser Erlebnis der deutschen Sprache" **1953**
457. "Partner und Stämme der Industrie" **1953**
458. "Reflexionen über das Thema Quatember" **1953**
459. "Was ist der Mensch? Eine Laienabwehr" **1953**
460. "The Crusade of the Star-spangled Banner" **1953**
461. "Dich und Ich" **1954**
462. "Dich und mich. Lehre oder Mode?" **1954**
463. "Glückhafte Schuld" **1954**
464. "Die Heimkehr der Gesellschaft" and "The Homecoming of Society" **1954**
465. "Laodizee—Wie rechtfertigt sich ein Volk?" **1954**
466. "Pentecost and Mission" **1954**
467. "Before and After Karl Marx. Prophesies Fulfilled and Unfulfilled" (This item is not in the bibliography, but see Reel 16, Item 635) **1954**
468. The Co-creators **1954**
469. Die Deutschen im Gespräch **1954**
470. History Must be Told (record jacket) **1955**
471. Letter to Mr. Herberg **1954**
472. Time Bettering Days **1954**
473. William Stanley's, The Sixth Earl of Derby, Sonnets for Elizabeth de Vere **1954**

474. *Der unbezahlbare Mensch* **1955**
475. *Des Christen Zukunft* **1955**
476. "Drei Gaben des Heiligen Geistes" **1955**
477. "Ehe auf Vertrag" **1955**
478. "Glaube und Hoffnung" **1955**
479. "Raumzeit oder Zeitraum? **1955**
480. "Die Sprache des Westens" **1955**
481. "Why do good people suffer?" **1955**
482. Bible Study, Peter-Paul-John **1955**
483. "Hitler und Israel oder Vom Gebet" **1955**
484. Lecture on "The Driving Power of Western Civilization" **1955**
485. Myth, Saga, Legend and Necessity **1955**
486. Primus Sermo Secundus Sermo Tertius Sermo **1955**
487. (6) Die ältesten amtlichen Berichte über die Evangelien **1955**
488. The Terms of the Creed **1955**
489. 360 + 5 and The Year as Period **1955**
490. Was kostet die Geschichte? **1955**
491. *Soziologie,* Bd. 1 **1956**
492. "Das Christentum inkognito" **1956**
493. "Herakleitos von Ephesos schreibt an Parmenides von Elea" and "Heraklit and Parmenides" **1956**
494. "Praise Him Above, Ye Heavenly Hosts" **1956**
495. "Soziologie. Auszüge" **1956**
496. "Der Verrat im 20. Jahrhundert" **1956**
497. Epochenteilung–Epochenbildung **1956**
497A. Evozieren und Revozieren **1956**
498. Holy Holy Holy **1956**
499. There is more time than you think **1956**

Reel 10 (1956 – 1958)

Item

500. Zeitgeist, Mythos, Krieg **1956 and 1980**
501. *Frankreich-Deutschland* **1957**
502. Two letters: "An Bürkle" and "An Achim" **1957**
503. *Zurück in das Wagnis der Sprache* **1957**
504. "Eine Generation allein ist nicht geschichtsmächtig" **1957**
505. Review, Henri Pirenne, "Mohammed and Charlemagne" **1957**
506. "Sermon on Philippians 3:20, 21, 4:4, 5c" **1957**
507. "Vorwort" **1957**
508. Arbeitstagung mit Prof. Eugen Rosenstock-Huessy in der Evangelischen Akademie Arnoldshain **1957**

509. "Die Europäische Wandlung" **1957**
510. Frage und Antwort and Die Kunst der Frage **1957**
511. "Gast und Geist oder Stammeszunge und Geisteszunge" **1957**
512. Der Verlust der Kontinuität und Integration in der modernen Gesellschaft **1957**
513. Die Weggelaufene Eschatologie **1957**
514. Zur Verteidigung der grammatischen Methode **1957**
515. *Das Geheimnis der Universität* **1958**
516. *Soziologie,* Bd. 2 **1958**
517. "Bestimmung der Wirtschaft in einer revolutionierten Welt" **1958**
518. Revolution, Soziologie und Universität **1960**
519. "Saint-Simon—der erste Soziologe" **1958**
520. "Theorien von gestern—Praktiken von wann?" **1958**

Reel 11 (1958 – 1964)

Item

521. Postscript einer gewesenen Rechtshistorikers (This item is not in the bibliography) **1958**
522. Talk by Eugen Rosenstock-Huessy at Four Wells **1958**
523. Theologians and Nihilists (This item is not in the bibliography) **1958**
524. *Bibliography – Biography* **1959**
525. "Die Bemannung der Hochschule" **1959**
526. "Epilog zu: Furor Teutonicus oder Furor Classicus?" **1959**
527. "Friedensbedingungen einer Weltwirtschaft" **1959**
528. "Funeral Service for Margrit Rosenstock-Huessy **1959**
529. "Die Götter des Landes und der Götze Raum" **1959**
530. "Tribalism" (transcription) **1959**
531. "Zeitbessernde Tage?" **1959**
532. "Abseitige" Gedanken zur Soziologie nach Schleskys "Ortsbestimmung der Soziologie" **1959**
533. Afterglow **1959**
534. Ökonomen **1960**
535. Der Ton der fehlt **1960**
536. Die Wiedergeburt der Wissenschaft aus der Vollmacht der Sprache **1960**
537. "The Generations of the Faith" **1961**
538. "Stalins Einebnung und die Chronologie der Weltkriegsrevolution" **1961**
539. "Das Volk Gottes in Vergangenheit, Gegenwart, Zukunft" **1961**
540. Francis L. Lieber **1961**

541. Stomatology **1961**

542. Die Weigerung des Quintaners **1961**

543. Die zwölf Töne des Geistes **1961**

544. Die Sprache des Menschengeschlechts (Broschüre) **1962**

545. Contributions to *The American People's Encyclopedia* (Items in curved brackets were microfilmed but were later removed from the Chronological Bibliography when it was determined that their authorship could not be confirmed):

Abélard, Pierre; {Animism; Aristotle; Augustine, Saint; Bacon, Roger}; Conceptualism; Concordance; Confessions of Saint Augustine; {Cross}; Dante Alighieri; David; Descartes, René; Dialectic; Dialogue; Dionysius the Areopagite; Divine Comedy, The; Duns Scotus; Edwards, Jonathan; Emerson, Ralph Waldo; Existentialism; Faraday, Michael; {Grimm's Law}; Homer; Name; Newman, John Henry Cardinal; Nietzsche, Friedrich Wilhelm; Nominalism; Paracelsus; Plato; Republic (as form of government and work by Plato; two entries); Research; Revolution; Saint-Simon, Claude Henri de; Social Sciences; Socrates (Plato, Socrates, and Athens); Sudhoff, Karl; Swedenborg, Emmanuel; Timaeus; {University}; Vahlen, Johannes; Vaihinger, Hans; Valentinius; Vampire; Ventris, Michael George Francis; Venus; Verner, Karl Adolph; Vico, Giovanni Battista; Walton, Izaak; Webb, Beatrice; Webb, Sidney James; Weber, Max; Webster, Daniel; Weizsäcker, Freiherr Viktor von; Wesley, John; Whitehead, Alfred North; Whitman, Walt; Wieland, Christopher Martin; William Ockham; William of Champeaux; Winckelmann, Johann Joachim; Wittgenstein, Ludwig Joseph Johann; Wittig, Joseph; Wolf, Friedrich August; Wolfram von Eschenbach; Wundt, Wilhelm Max; Wycliffe, John; X; Xenophon; Y; Z; Zarathustra; Zen; Zeno of Citium; Zeno of Elea; Zeus; Zoroastrianism; Zweig, Stefan; Zwingli, Huldreich.

546. "Witchcraft" **1962**

547. Dominic, Saint, de Guzman **1962**

547A. "Sermon on Philippians 3:21" **1962**

548. Die Erschaffung aus dem Nichts? **1962**

549. Der Inventar. Einleitung zu *Die Frucht Der Lippen* **1962**

550. Die misshandelte Zeit **1962**

551. The Wailers **1962**

552. "Über die Verlegung der Fürstenschulen nach Westdeutschland" **1962**

553. Abstammen und Zustammen **1963**

554. *Die Sprache des Menschengeschlechts*, Bd. 1 **1963**
554A. Translation of "Ein Komma" (This item is not in the bibliography) **1963**
555. "Europas Amerika und Amerikas Europa" **1963**
556. "'Im Notfall' oder die 'Zeitlichkeit des Geistes'" **1963**
557. Notizen über Missverständnisse im Wissenschaftlichen Vokabular—Zur Ägyptologie **1963**
558. On the Wings of the Dove Invocation **1963**
559. *Die Interims des Rechts* **1964**

Reel 12 (1964 – 1969)

Item

560. *Die Sprache des Menschengeschlechts*, Bd. 2 **1964**
560A. Translation of "Die Zahlensprache der Physik," Part IV, Ch. 2 (This item is not in the bibliography) **1964**
561. "Time and Historicity of Man" **1964**
562. "Revolution als Dienst" **1964**
563. *Dienst auf dem Planeten* **1965**
564. "Das Volk Gottes in Gegenwart, Vergangenheit und Zukunft" **1965**
565. Für Lehrer. Eine Fussnote zur *Sprache des Menschengeschlechts* **1964**
566. Mihi est propositum **1965**
567. "The Quadrilateral of Human Thought" **1965**
568. *De onbetaalbare mens* **1966**
569. "Buch und Funk" **1966**
570. "Die 'Objektiven Unwahrheiten des Bischofs Dr. Otto Dibelius'" **1966**
571. *Whom Money Cannot Buy* **1966**
572. Aphorisms as printed in *The Viking Book of Aphorisms*, selected by W. H. Auden and Louis Kronenberger (This item is not in the bibliography) **1966**
573. Tenses, Times and Trinity **1966**
574. Instructors' note on *The Speech of Humankind* **1966**
575. *Magna Carta Latina* **1975**
576. The Ides of March **1967**
577. Israel: Jews, Christians, Muslims or "The Mission of the Jewish State" **1968**
578. *Ja und Nein* **1968**
579. "Das Ende Der Dialektik Ketzer-Papst" **1968**
580. "Heretic and Pope" **1968**
581. "Tribute from a 'Post-Goethian'" **1968**
581A. Plezier in het schelden **1968**

582. Schwäbisch Hall und England **1968**
583. The Jewish and the Christian Trinity **1966**
584. *Judaism Despite Christianity* **1969**

Reel 13 (1969 – Undated Works)

Item

585. "Anfänge meines Friedensdienstes" **1969**
586. "Nachträgliche Erwägungen Eugen Rosenstock-Huessys zu *Angewandten Seelenkunde* aus dem Erscheinungsjahr 1924" **1969**
587. "Prolog (und Epilog) zu den Briefen Eugen Rosenstocks und Franz Rosenzweigs" **1969**
588. *I Am an Impure Thinker* **1970**
589. *Speech and Reality* **1970**
590. Invocation **1970**
590A. "Invocatio vom 28.6.1970" **1970**
591. "Zur Problematik des religiösen Sozialismus" **1976**
592. "Die Mitschöpfer, eine Einführung in die Universalgeschichte" **1977**
593. "Einladung zur Zeitbuchreihe 'Epoche'" **1977**
594. *The Fruit of Lips, or, Why Four Gospels?* **1978**
595. *Planetary Service* **1978**
596. *Spraak en Werkelijkheid* **1978**
597. *The Origin of Speech* **1981**
598. *De Vrucht der Lippen* **1981**
599. "Akademik oder Argonautik" **1981**
600. *Toegepaste Zielkunde* **1982**
601. "Das Gehirn kann nicht bereuen" **1984**
602. *Friedensbedingungen einer Weltwirtschaft* **1988**
603. *Life Lines: Quotations from the Work of Eugen Rosenstock-Huessy* **1988**
604. *Practical Knowledge of the Soul* **1988**
605. *Die Tochter—Das Buch Rut* **1988**
606. *Toekomst Het Christelijk Levensgeheim* **1993**
607. Von einer Grammatik der benannten Menschen **1955**
608. Nicolaus von Cues **Undated**
609. Die Akademische Muse (This item is not in the bibliography) **Undated**
610. 4 Equations in Time (This item is not in the bibliography) **Undated**

Reel 14 (Miscellaneous Dates and Classifications)

Item

611. The Ego (This item is not in the bibliography) **Undated**
612. *Liturgical Thinking versus Theology* **1952**
613. The Egyptian Ka and Mythical Man **1947**
614. In Behalf of the Grammatical Method **1962**
615. On Baptism (This item not in the bibliography) **Undated**
616. Neue Tendenzen Demokratischen Denkens (This item is not in the bibliography) **Undated**
617. Der Zauber des Menschen **1931**
618. Conditions for Peace (This item is not in the bibliography) **Undated**
619. Religionsphilosophie der Gesellschaft **1927**
620. Über einige neue Grundbegriffe des Privatrechts **1929**
621. Eastern and Western Christendom **1941**
622. Tutilo of St. Gallen and the Origin of Drama **1957**
623. What Future the Professions? (transcription) **1960**
624. Das Kreuz der Wirklichkeit **1950**
625. Entwurf Vorwort zu einer 2. Auflage der *Vollzahl der Zeiten* **1958**

Reel 15 (1949 – 1954)

The Eugen Rosenstock-Huessy Lectures, Vols. 1 – 8

Item

626. *Circulation of Thought* – Vol. 1 **1949**
627. *Universal History* – Vol. 2 **1949**
628. *Universal History* – Vol. 3 **1951**
629. *Potential Teachers* – Vol. 4 **1952**
630. *Cross of Reality* – Vol. 5 **1953**
631. *Hinge of Generations* – Vol. 6 **1953**
632. *Make Bold To Be Ashamed* – Vol. 7 **1953**
633. *Comparative Religion* – Vol. 8 **1954**

Reel 16 (1954 – 1956)

The Eugen Rosenstock-Huessy Lectures, Vols. 9 – 16

Item

634. *Circulation of Thought* – Vol. 9 **1954**
635. *Four Disangelists* – Vol. 10 **1954**
636. *History Must Be Told* – Vol. 11 **1954**

637. *Universal History* – Vol. 12 **1954**
638. *History Must Be Told* – Vol. 13, LP record **1955**
639. *Universal History* – Vol. 14 **1955**
640. *Circulation of Thought* – Vol. 15 **1956**
641. *Greek Philosophy* – Vol. 16 **1956**

Reel 17 (1956 – 1959)

The Eugen Rosenstock-Huessy Lectures, Vols. 17 – 20

Item

642. *Universal History* – Vol. 17 **1956**
643. *Universal History* – Vol. 18 **1957**
644. *American Social History* – Vol. 19 **1959**
645. *Historiography* – Vol. 20 **1959**

Reel 18 (1959 – 1968)

The Eugen Rosenstock-Huessy Lectures, Vols. 21 – 34

Item

Lecture in Münster, **1958**

646. *Man Must Teach* – Vol. 21 **1959**
647. *Liberal Arts College* – Vol. 22 **1960**
648. *What Future for the Professions?* – Vol. 23 **1960**
649. *Grammatical Method* – Vol. 24 **1962**
650. *St. Augustine* – Vol. 25 **1962**
651. *Economy of Times* – Vol. 26 **1965**
652. *Talk with Franciscans* – Vol. 27 **1965**
653. *Cross of Reality* – Vol. 28 **1965**
654. *Lingo of Linguistics* – Vol. 29 **1966**
655. *Peace Corps* – Vol. 30 **1966**
656. *Cruciform Character of History* – Vol. 31 **1967**
657. *Universal History* – Vol. 32 **1967**
658. *Fashions of Atheism* – Vol. 33 **1968**
659. *The University* – Vol. 34 **1968**
660. "Die Gesetze der christlichen Zeitrechnung" **1982**

Eugen Rosenstock-Huessy (1888–1973): A Biographical Note

Eugen Rosenstock was born in Berlin on July 6, 1888, the son of Theodor and Paula Rosenstock. Theodor was a banker who had been compelled to enter that profession to support his widowed stepmother and his stepsister; if he had been able to choose, he would have sought a scholarly education. In due course, however, Theodor became a member of the prestigious Berlin Stock Exchange. Paula Rosenstock was the daughter of the head of a well-known Jewish school in Wolfenbüttel. Eugen was the fourth child among six sisters.

After his first years in a school for wealthy families, Eugen Rosenstock transferred to the Joachimsthaler Gymnasium, a school known for its rigorous academic standards, particularly in the classics. Following his father's wish, Eugen went on from there to study law at the universities of Zürich, Heidelberg, and Berlin. At age seventeen he joined the Protestant Church, which did not seem much of a conversion to him because Christian habits had already become a part of family life. Gradually, however, his faith became central to his work. In 1909, at the age of twenty-one, he received a doctorate in law from the University of Heidelberg. Aside from law, the study of history and philology were his abiding passions from early on. In 1912, he began to teach constitutional law and the history of law at the University of Leipzig, the youngest Privatdozent at the time.

Early in 1914, Rosenstock went to Florence to conduct historical research with his brother-in-law, Ernst Michel, then editor of the German encyclopedia Brockhaus. There, he met a young Swiss woman, Margrit Huessy, who was studying the history of art in Florence. They married that same year, just before the outbreak of World War I. Drafted at once as a lieutenant in the mounted artillery, he was stationed at or near the Western front throughout the war, including eighteen months at Verdun. During this period he organized courses for the troops, replacing the limited instruction in patriotism with broader topics. In 1916, he and his friend, the Jewish philosopher Franz Rosenzweig, also on active duty, exchanged letters on Judaism and Christianity. That correspondence has since become well known, and much of it is now contained in *Judaism Despite Christianity* (1969).

Rosenstock was keenly aware that World War I was an historical watershed. At the end of the war, not wishing to return to teaching at the University of Leipzig, he sought new options better suited to a changed world. Together with a member of the board of Daimler-Benz, the German car maker, he started and edited the first factory newspaper in Germany, the

Daimler Werkzeitung. Also, together with Leo Weismantel, Werner Picht, Hans Ehrenberg, Karl Barth, and Viktor von Weizsäcker, he founded Patmos Verlag, which was devoted to publishing works focused on new religious, philosophical, and social perspectives. A journal, *Die Kreatur* (1926–30), followed, edited by Josef Wittig, a Roman Catholic; Martin Buber, a Jew; and von Weizsäcker, a Protestant.

Among the contributors were Nicholas Berdyaev, Lev Shestov, Franz Rosenzweig, Ernst Simon, Hugo Bergmann, Rudolf Hallo, and Florens Christian Rang. Each of these men had, between 1910 and 1932, in one way or another, offered an alternative to the idealism, positivism, and historicism that dominated German universities. Rosenstock himself published in 1920 *Die Hochzeit des Krieges und der Revolution* (The Marriage of War and Revolution), a collection of essays related to current events that were full of prophesies and warnings. Unfortunately, some of these were later to be fulfilled.

In 1921, Margrit and Eugen had a son, Hans. In 1925, they legally changed their name to Rosenstock-Huessy, but it was not until after Eugen's emigration to the United States that he used the hyphenated name professionally.

Although never a Marxist, Rosenstock was invited to found and direct Die Akademie der Arbeit (Academy of Labor) in Frankfurt/Main in 1921. This institution offered courses and seminars for blue-collar workers, but he resigned in 1923 over differences with trade union representatives. Nevertheless, he did not give up his involvement with adult education and his efforts to give industrial workers a voice of their own in society.

In 1924, Rosenstock published *Angewandte Seelenkunde* (Practical Knowledge of the Soul) wherein he outlined for the first time his radically new method for the social sciences based on language, the spoken word, and his "grammatical approach," which he later called "metanomics." This method remained at the heart of all his later works and was expanded upon in his two volume *Soziologie* (1956–1958): Volume I, On the Forces of Common Life (when space governs), and Volume II, On the Forces of History (when the times are obeyed). He further elaborated these ideas in another two-volume book, *Die Sprache des Menschengeschlechts: Eine Leibhaftige Grammatik in Vier Teilen* [The Speech of Humankind: A Personal Grammar in Four Parts] (1963–1964).

Rosenstock was awarded a second doctorate in philosophy from the University of Heidelberg in 1923 for his scholarly medieval study, *Königshaus und Stämme in Deutschland zwischen 911 und 1250* [The Royal House and the Tribes in Germany between 911 and 1250], which he had written in Leipzig and published in 1914. He then lectured at the Technical

University of Darmstadt in the faculty of social science and social history until he was offered a job at the University of Breslau as a full professor of German legal history, a position he held from 1923 until January 30, 1933.

In Breslau, apart from being an inspiring and admired teacher, Rosenstock-Huessy became active in many other ways. In response to and together with some of his students, he helped organize workcamps for students, farmers, and workers as part of an effort to deal with the atrocious life and labor conditions at the coal mines in Waldenburg, Silesia. When Rosenstock's friend, the Catholic priest Josef Wittig, was excommunicated and lost his right to teach church history at the University of Breslau, he stood by Wittig and together they published *Das Alter der Kirche* [The Age of the Church] (1927–1928). That work contained two volumes of essays on the life of the Church and a third volume devoted to a statement about Wittig's excommunication.

In 1931, Rosenstock wrote and published the first of his major works: *Die Europäischen Revolutionen—Volkscharaktere und Staatenbildung* [The European Revolutions and the Character of Nations], one thousand years of European history created in five different European national "revolutions" that collectively came to an end in World War I.

On January 30, 1933, Germany fell to National Socialism, and Rosenstock-Huessy left Breslau at once. By the end of that year and with the help of C. J. Friedrich, professor of government at Harvard University and the only person Rosenstock knew in the United States, he had been appointed Kuno Francke Lecturer in German Art and Culture at Harvard.

Rosenstock-Huessy frequently mentioned God in class. This grated on the secular beliefs of other Harvard faculty members. Profound differences of opinion ensued and led, in 1935, to his accepting an appointment as professor of social philosophy at Dartmouth College, Hanover, New Hampshire. He made his home in nearby Norwich, Vermont. He taught at Dartmouth until his retirement in 1957, inspiring generations of students.

Despite the "falling out" with Harvard, Rosenstock-Huessy had made important friendships there that helped him when he began to write again. His first effort was to rewrite in English his earlier book on revolutions, under the title *Out of Revolution: Autobiography of Western Man* (1938). The Nietzsche scholar, George Allen Morgan, assisted him in the preparation of *The Christian Future or the Modern Mind Outrun* (1946). Alfred North Whitehead, also at Harvard, was among Rosenstock-Huessy's admirers.

Rosenstock-Huessy continued his pioneering efforts on behalf of voluntary work service in the United States. At the urging of Eleanor Roosevelt, the journalist Dorothy Thompson, and other prominent figures, President Franklin D. Roosevelt tapped Rosenstock-Huessy to lead the creation of a special Civilian Conservation Corps camp in the woods of Vermont. Involving mainly students from Dartmouth, Radcliffe, and Harvard, its purpose was to train young leaders to expand the seven-year-old CCC from a program for unemployed youth into a work service that would accept volunteers from all walks of life. It was called Camp William James because of that philosopher's search for a "moral equivalent of war." It was disbanded when the United States entered World War II. Rosenstock-Huessy's writings about voluntary work service have often been cited as influential in the design and development of the Peace Corps twenty-five years later.

After the war and continuing through his retirement from Dartmouth, Rosenstock-Huessy was a frequent guest professor at many universities in Germany and the United States. He remained active in lecturing and writing until his final years. His output comprises more than 500 essays, articles, and monographs, including 40 books.

His connections to the local community were, and always remained, strong. In 1959, Margrit Rosenstock-Huessy died. In 1960, Freya von Moltke, widow of Helmuth James von Moltke, who opposed National Socialism and was executed by the Nazis, came to share Rosenstock-Huessy's life. Her husband had been a student of Rosenstock's in Breslau and a participant in the original Silesian workcamps. Rosenstock-Huessy died on February 24, 1973, but his extraordinary insights continue to touch and inspire the lives of many people from all walks of life.

A Guide to the Works of Eugen Rosenstock-Huessy was designed by Gilbert Design Associates in Providence, Rhode Island and printed by McNaughton & Gunn in Saline, Michigan.

The typeface is Aldus, designed for Linotype in 1952–53 by Hermann Zapf. It was named after the 15th-century Venetian printer Aldus Manutius.

The book was bound by Dekker Book Bindery.

500 casebound copies for Argo Books, Essex, Vermont

February 1998